JACQUES MARITAIN AND THE FRENCH CATHOLIC INTELLECTUALS

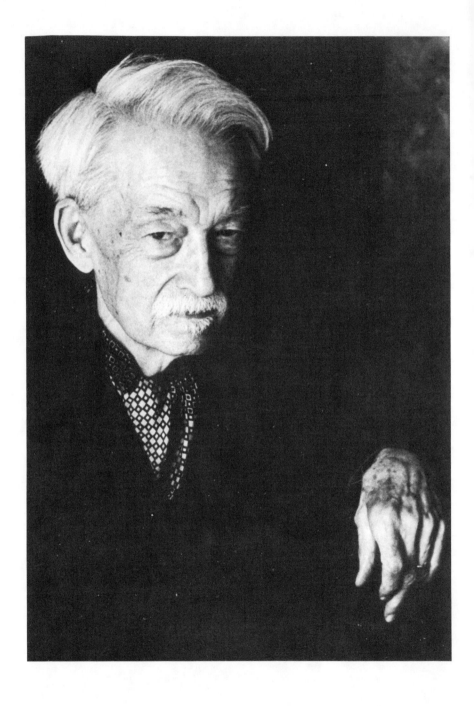

Jacques Maritain and the French Catholic Intellectuals

BERNARD E. DOERING

UNIVERSITY OF NOTRE DAME PRESS

Notre Dame – London

Library of Congress Cataloging in Publication Data

Doering, Bernard E.
    Jacques Maritain and the French Catholic intel-
lectuals.

    Includes index.
    1. Maritain, Jacques, 1882 – 1973. 2.
Philosophers — France — Biography. 3. Catholics —
France — History — 20th century. 4. France —
Intellectual life — 20th century.
I. Title.
B2430.M34D63   1983   194   82 – 40377
ISBN 0 – 268 – 01202 – 4

TO JANE

Contents

Acknowledgments

NO BOOK IS THE WORK of one individual. Like our lives, our books are influenced by so many persons that it is impossible for an author to recall all those who participated either directly or indirectly in the making of a book. It would be futile for me to try to express my gratitude to each one who, in the course of a conversation or a letter, by hints about avenues of research, by suggested corrections, or simply by gracious encouragement, has contributed to the writing of this book.

However, I would like to express my appreciation to a number of people in a very particular way. First to Wallace Fowlie, who suggested the topic of the book and has shown continued interest in my work. To the late Professor Joseph Evans, Director of the Maritain Center at the University of Notre Dame when I began working on this study, for generously making available whatever I needed from the Maritain Center for my research and for countless other acts of assistance. To the trustees of the Maritain Archives: the late Brother Heinz Schmitz, Professor Olivier Lacombe and Madame Antoinette Grunelius, for permitting me to consult certain documents prior to the date they were to be made public.

I am particularly grateful to Madame Grunelius for the long hours she spent searching out the documents I needed, and above all for the long hours of conversation and her generous and cordial hospitality which made my stay at the Centre d'Etudes Jacques et Raïssa Maritain so fruitful and so pleasant. I am most grateful, too, to Brother Jean-Marie Allion, a Little Brother from Toulouse, who was working at the Maritain Archives in Kolbsheim during the summer of 1981 and who acted as my personal "amanuensis," for giving so generously of his time reading letters to select those that would interest me, copying documents

I needed and typing legible copies of letters written in almost indecipherable script.

I am also most grateful to Henry Bars for our long and helpful conversations, and above all for his unselfishly putting at my total disposition unpublished manuscripts of his own on topics I was treating in my book. Finally, I express my appreciation to Anthony O. Simon for his countless acts of kindness and encouragement, and in particular for having given me complete access to the correspondence between his father, Yves R. Simon, and Jacques Maritain, which, with Deba P. Patnaik, he is presently preparing for publication. All quotations from the Maritain/Simon correspondence are from this collection. Copies of the Maritain/Simon letters can be found at the Maritain Center of the University of Notre Dame and at the Maritain Archives in Kolbsheim, France.

Unless otherwise indicated, the English translations of all French texts are my own.

Introduction

ONE OF THE MOST striking phenomena of twentieth-century French letters is the Catholic Literary Revival, which was the more remarkable for the fact that it began from almost nothing. Considering the situation in France in the early 1880s, one cannot avoid the impression that, in all its long history, the Church had scarcely ever found itself in such desperate straits.

Positivism reigned supreme, often under the form of an ambitious and complacent scientism which saw no need for the supernatural and which therefore felt called to undermine the structure of traditional metaphysics and, consequently, of Catholic theology. The only metaphysicians who enjoyed any acceptability were those who turned to a system of Kantian idealism which, to many minds, appeared sufficient to found a moral system without God and to make religion useless. For anything that resembled a religious climate, one had to turn to Renan, whose memories of seminary life and ecclesiastical vocabulary gave way with age to a skeptical laicism — or to an aging Victor Hugo, who in countless *alexandrins* constructed a jumbled metaphysical system in which the name of God appeared, to be sure, but certainly not the traditional Christian God of the Bible and even less, of Calvary.

In the literary world the spirit of positivism led, on one hand, in the tradition of *Parnasse*, to a kind of decorative paganism and voluptuous erudition which tended to describe with subtlety and perfection a beautiful object without ever looking for its soul. On the other hand, in the tradition of Medan, it led to an epic but vulgar naturalism.

In the political order, the adamant antirepublicanism of Popes Pius IX and Pius X allied the Church with the antidemocratic forces of reaction. The papal condemnation of Lammenais, Lacordaire, Montalembert, Lord Acton and the Catholic liberal

1

political movement Sillon stiffled any attempts to create a *rapprochement* between the Church and contemporary politics.

What few Catholic literary figures there were exercised little influence. Veuillot and Hello, though respected, were not read outside the Catholic circle. Few readers were convinced by the Baudelarean religious dandyism of Barbey d'Aurevilly and Villiers de L'Isle-Adam, and particularly not the Church. The numerous pious brochures and books of Sulpician spirituality or frantic apologetics circulated only in the ecclesiastical world and among the dwindling public of believers. They convinced few outside the fold, for they were read almost exclusively by those who were already convinced. After the Syllabus of Errors (1864) and the proclamations of the Immaculate Conception (1854) and Papal Infallibility (1870), the "intellectual world" expected little of relevance from the Catholic Church. The Church was in a state of siege, and within the Catholic ghetto a kind of intellectual and spiritual inbreeding was taking its toll.

It was into such a world that Jacques Maritain was born. The prestige of Christian letters was at perhaps its lowest point. But this was at the lowest point of a curve which was soon to turn up and rise steadily, until, toward the middle of the twentieth century, Catholic letters attained a summit of prestige unparalleled for several centuries.

Jacques Maritain was born in Paris on November 18, 1882, the son of Paul Maritain, a prosperous lawyer, and Geneviève Favre, the daughter of Jules Favre, one of the founding fathers of the Third French Republic. Maritain was reared by his mother in an atmosphere of liberal Protestantism and humanitarian rationalism. He received his early formal education at the Lycée Henri IV, where he became the close friend of Ernest Psichari, grandson of Ernest Renan. The two young men shared the same passion for the world of ideas and the same humanitarian ideals which had made the Renans and the Favres two of the most representative of the great intellectual and political families of liberal and republican France.

Maritain continued his studies as a student of natural science at the Sorbonne. After he received a *licence en philosophie* there, he met his future wife, Raïssa Oumansoff, a brilliant young science student of Russian-Jewish origin, with whom he shared his despair at being unable to find answers to questions about the meaning of life and the capacity of the human intellect to arrive at truth. After he met Péguy in 1901 he devoted considerable time to proofreading and other odd jobs at Péguy's socialist bookshop and office of the *Cahiers de la Quinzaine*. Disillusioned with the relativism and scientism of their masters at the Sorbonne, he and Raïssa, upon the invitation and urging of Péguy, attended the courses of Henri Bergson at the Collège de France. Bergson threw open the doors of their intellectual prison and liberated in them "the sense of the absolute."

The Maritains met Léon Bloy in 1905. Overwhelmed by the simplicity and purity of Bloy's faith, by his apocalyptic vision of the world and by his uncompromising fidelity to the vocation to sainthood, they began to study Catholicism and were received into the Church in 1906. After passing his *agrégation de philosophie* at the Sorbonne, Maritain became interested in biology. He and his wife spent 1907 and 1908 in Heidelberg, where he studied under Hans Driesch. Upon returning to France, he undertook the tedious work of editing the *Dictionnaire de la vie pratique* for the publisher Hachette because he needed money, and he felt he would have to sacrifice his intellectual independence if he accepted a position in one of the state schools.

Maritain began his teaching career at the Collège Stanislas in 1912 and was appointed professor of philosophy at the Institut Catholique just before the First World War. Encouraged by his spiritual director, Father Humbert Clérissac, Maritain began a tenuous but much publicized association with Action Française and collaboration with Henri Massis on *La Revue Universelle*, which lasted until the papal condemnation of Action Française in 1927.

Shortly after the war the Maritains moved to Meudon, where they held (in their home) the famous weekly reunions of the Cercle d'Etudes Thomistes (Thomistic Studies group), which were frequented not only by Catholic intellectuals from France but by intellectuals of many religious persuasions from all over the world. It was here that the defense of the papal condemnation of Action Française was organized, that a project was elaborated with Emmanuel Mounier which later became the magazine *Esprit*, that many of the manifestos for justice and peace were drawn up during the troubled thirties, that plans were made to aid the refugees of the Spanish Civil War.

Maritain had always been strongly inclined toward a very literal kind of evangelism and from his student days had manifested passionate love for the poor and the humble who thirst after justice. During these years at Meudon, Maritain continued his career as a speculative philosopher, but more and more he turned his pen to the problems posed by the world and the Church. His uncompromising application of the principles of the Gospels to questions of social and political justice gained him bitter enemies as well as enthusiastic followers.

At the outbreak of the Second World War, Maritain was on a lecture tour in the United States and Canada, where he had given courses annually since 1933. During the war he lived in Greenwich Village and his apartment became a meeting place for American intellectuals and artists and for those exiled from Europe. He played an important role in founding the Ecole Libre des Hautes Etudes, of which he later became president. Without prejudice to his numerous lectures at American universities, he devoted himself to the rescue and relief of victims of the Nazi racist persecutions, to weekly broadcasts to the Free French and to the defense of democratic institutions. These were probably the busiest years of Maritain's life.

After refusing General de Gaulle's offer, near the end of the war, of a position on the Comité National de la France Libre, he agreed, after the war, to serve as French ambassador to the Vatican from 1945 to 1948. In 1947, as head of the French delegation to the General Conference of UNESCO in Mexico City, Maritain was elected president of the conference and delivered the opening address. At the end of his term as ambassador to the Vatican, Maritain accepted the post of professor emeritus at Princeton University, where he taught moral philosophy according to the tradition of St. Thomas Aquinas. In 1951 he was offered a chair at the Collège de France, one of the greatest academic honors that can be received in France. However, he was reluctant to begin another career at the age of sixty-nine, and felt bound to continue his work in the United States.

Early in 1961 Maritain returned to France, after the death of his wife, where, except for his annual visits to the Grunelius family (in whose home his papers and documents were stored), he passed his last years in retirement and seclusion in the monastery of the Little Brothers of Jesus of Charles de Foucauld at Toulouse, publishing the journal of his wife Raïssa and those books he'd had no time to complete during his busy sojourn in America. In 1965 he came from his retirement to be signally honored at the close of the Second Vatican Council as the world's outstanding Catholic intellectual.

When Maritain began his literary career in 1914, the Catholic Renascence was already under way, and by the time Maritain's first book appeared, Barres and Bourget had set the traditional and nationalist tone of the early revival. Claudel had already established himself as a poet and a playwright. Péguy, with his first *Jeanne d'Arc* and the founding of *Cahiers de la Quinzaine*, and Bloy, with his apocalyptic fulminations, had already set the tone for another current in the revival, a current more open to contemporary political and social developments. But with the publication of *Art et scolastique* in 1920, Maritain became a central figure in the Catholic Literary Revival. His influence extended far beyond his professional field of philosophy. To the Cercle d'Etudes Thomistes held in his home in Meudon came philosophers, theologians (Catholic, Protestant, Orthodox and Jewish), specialists in Oriental studies, artists, novelists, playwrights, poets, musicians, journalists, politicians.

A study of his influence, which extended in many directions, must necessarily be limited in this book, whose object is to determine the extent of Maritain's political debt to certain French literary figures and his influence on the political and social thinking of others during the turbulent years from 1920 to 1970, and thus to assess his role in the Catholic Literary Renascence and in the renewal of the Catholic Church that culminated in the Second Vatican Council.

The *écrivain engagé* is a perennial phenomenon of French letters. Hugo, Lamartine and Vigny, for example, were as politically and socially involved in their period as any writer during World War II and after. French literary figures were immersed in the political and social turmoil during the difficult years between 1920 and 1970, the major years of Maritain's political and social *engagement*, but what has not been examined is Maritain's relation to other French literary figures over the political issues of these years. References concerning Maritain's influence in such matters abound in the journals, memoirs and political writings in the periodicals and newspapers of the day, but no one as yet has compiled and organized this material to evaluate Maritain's role in changing the political and social orientation of the Catholic Literary Renascence, which is the object of this study.

CHAPTER 1

Action Française:
Maurras, Massis, Maritain

THE "PEACE AND EQUILIBRIUM" which followed upon Jacques Maritain's conversion to the Catholic faith were shattered in 1926 by the crisis of Action Française. With the possible exception of his conversion, no event proved more important in determining the course of Maritain's life. Action Française, a traditionalist and monarchist movement, led by Charles Maurras and supported by many Catholics of conservative background, was condemned in December 1926 by Pius XI for its political positivism and its tendency to make religion subservient to politics. This crisis divided France almost as deeply as did the Dreyfus case at the turn of the century, and in many respects the same divisions were later renewed over the Spanish Civil War and the Vichy government.

Maritain's political activities after his conversion had been limited to intermittent expressions of sympathy for the victims of political and social injustice and to an occasional forceful insistence that evangelical renewal of the principles of Christianity was the *sine qua non* for the reestablishment of order and peace in society. His preoccupations were purely speculative and religious, and he seems to have had no intention of soiling his hands in sordid partisan politics. Through the crisis of 1926, however, he came to realize how impossible it is for a philosopher worthy of his calling to hold himself completely aloof from life in the lofty towers of speculation. Because political activity is directly dependent upon philosophical tenets, the philosopher has to become "engaged," at least to the extent of judging and interpreting political events and of suggesting guiding principles of action. So Maritain turned from the speculative world of absolutes and abstractions, in which he moved with grace and freedom, to the contingent world of human anguish, applying the abstract prin-

6

ciples of his thought to the practical solution of political and social problems.

Without the crisis of 1926, we would probably never have seen such outstanding contributions to political and social thought as *Primauté du spirituel, Humanisme intégral, Du régime temporel et de la liberté, Christianisme et démocratie, La Personne et le bien commun,* and *Man and the State.* His break with Action Française was to cost him dearly in loss of friends, bitter criticism and even violent abuse; but, charting his course in his *Lettre sur l'indépendance,* he made his way carefully between the pitfalls of the right and the left to a position of recognized prominence in both Europe and America.

It is difficult to explain, or even understand, how Maritain let himself be associated with Action Française. His family background would seem to have made him congenitally incompatible with the movement. He was the grandson of Jules Favre, one of the founders of the Third Republic; his mother was Geneviève Favre, *"la grande républicaine,"* a very close friend of Péguy, as was Maritain himself. He married a Russian Jewess, which must have rankled the anti-Semitic tendencies of Maurras and his followers — tendencies which must have given Maritain himself second thoughts about his connections with the group. He was the godson of Léon Bloy, a defender of the Jews, whom one can scarcely imagine relishing Maurras and his kind.

Maritain had been an ardent socialist in his youth,[1] and never, even during the days when he was erroneously considered the official "philosopher of Action Française," did he lose his profound sympathy for the laboring classes or his zeal for social justice. The names of writers, artists and musicians whose works he admired (Bloy, Cocteau, Rouault, Chagall, Severini, Satie and Lourié, for example) indicate how little appreciation he had for the neoclassicism of the Ecole Romane, the official literary and artistic school of Action Française. There seemed to be nothing in his background or his inclinations to justify such an association — for which, indeed, Maritain never ceased to reproach himself. And yet a combination of circumstances — "a blind little providence," says Raïssa Maritain — led him into an extended (approximately fifteen years) but very uneasy association with Maurras and his movement.

It was Father Clérissac who first urged Maritain to become a member of Action Française. Maritain never actually became a member, but he did let himself be persuaded (about 1911) to subscribe to Maurras' newspaper *Action Française*, the official organ of the movement, and read it with some regularity in deference to the wishes of Father Clérissac. The enthusiastic young neophyte had profound respect for this holy and learned Dominican and considered him a man of "perfect integrity of conscience." It was Father Clérissac who had instructed him in the Catholic faith, received him into the Church, introduced him to the writings of the Angelic Doctor and acted as his spiritual director.

The institution of spiritual direction has played an important part in the Church's traditional teaching on the life of sanctity. The writings of the great saints and mystics on this subject, compiled, organized and distilled into the science of "mystical theology," invariably advise those who aspire to sanctity and the higher states of mystical union with God to seek the guidance of a holy and learned man. The ordinary Christian has his confessor for a guide; but the man who aspires to sanctity needs more professional guidance in the practice of perfection. Having chosen a spiritual director of appropriate holiness and learning, the aspirant is advised to submit himself entirely to this man, even to the point of blind obedience, in all that is related to the spiritual life. Moreover, in the manuals of perfection it is quite common to find this blind obedience extended even to matters that have no direct connection with the spiritual life. Though these manuals, strictly speaking, express the opinions of their individual authors and do not carry the authority of the official teaching of the Church, they have traditionally been followed rather closely, especially in seminaries and religious houses.

One of the most popular manuals of Christian perfection in France in the 1920s was *The Spiritual Life* by Father Adolphe Tanquerey.[2] In article 2 of chapter 5 the author gives a brief history of the institution of spiritual direction from the writings of saints and doctors of the Church such as Cassian, John Climacus, Bernard of Clairvaux, Vincent Ferrer, John of the Cross, Francis de Sales, Alphonsus Ligouri, etc. Maritain was familiar with the writings of many of these men, in particular St. John of the Cross, and he was certainly familiar with this and other current manuals of the spiritual life. Here are a few quotations from Tanquerey pertaining to submission to one's spiritual director:

Aspirants to sanctity are urged "to open their heart to the elder charged with the direction of their life; to disclose to him without false shame their secret thoughts, and to submit themselves entirely to his decision as to what is good and evil" (p. 258).

"The director must be respected as the representative of God, clothed as he is with God's authority, in what regards our most intimate and most sacred relations with God. Hence, if he has shortcomings, let us not dwell on them, but simply regard his authority and his mission. A penitent will thus carefully avoid any criticism whereby the filial respect due his director is lost or lessened" (p. 267).

"Strictly speaking our director may be mistaken, but we make no mistake in obeying him, except, of course, were he to give counsel opposed to faith or morals" (p. 269).

Such teaching may be valid in some cases, but it is fraught with many dangers, and to these dangers Maritain let himself fall victim. In accepting baptism in the Catholic Church, he had taken an irrevocable step, so to speak, in total darkness. He had subordinated the light of reason to the light of faith. According to the teachings of the Church that he was entering, the act of faith is an act of the will which enables the intellect to accept a truth it cannot explain by reason, but solely on the authority of God, who reveals the truth. Reason can be used to show that the truths of faith are not irrational — that is, contrary to reason — but, beyond this, reason is tongue-tied before such mysteries as the Trinity, the Incarnation, or the Real Presence in the Eucharist.

The idea of committing the whole purpose and direction of one's life irrevocably (an aspirant is not admitted to baptism in the Church unless he considers his commitment irrevocable) to a set of truths for which he was, by definition, incapable of finding a rational explanation or understanding was for Maritain, whose whole training had been scientific and positivist, certainly a commitment made in "total darkness," from a purely natural and rationalist point of view. In speaking of Ernest Psichari's conversion in *Antimoderne* (pp. 234ff.), Maritain has a long digression on the light of faith contrasted with the light of reason. He is evidently speaking from personal experience in his remarks about the intellectual darkness of the act of faith. About two months before Maritain's baptism, Léon Bloy wrote to Pierre Termier, a friend of the Maritains: "They still want to enter the Church, but the final step, the one which is irrevocable, terrifies them."[3]

The immediate cause of Maritain's conversion was not the adroit arguments of the apologists but the rationally inexplicable phenomenon of Léon Bloy, who became his godfather. In entering the Church, Maritain determined to go all the way. Totally committed to the proposition of his godfather, that the only misfortune in life is not to be a saint, Maritain submitted completely, and blindly, to the direction of Father Clérissac, even to letting his spiritual director form his political conscience. Maritain, who took the idea of conversion quite literally, once described himself to Cocteau as a man whom God had turned inside out like a glove, and one aspect of his conversion consisted in turning his back on the political and social ideas he had formed in his early days, when "Humanity" had held for him the place of God.[4] Father Clérissac offered him another political orientation, which he accepted uncritically as an essential part of becoming a Catholic. If Maritain did not do actual violence to his critical sense in accepting the political illusions of Father Clérissac, he at least had ignored the warnings of his reason and refused to make the necessary distinctions he was wont to make in his philosophical writings.[5] Because his political opinions were in strict accord with those of Pius X, Father Clérissac saw in democracy and the republican form of government a diabolical incarnation of the errors condemned in the Syllabus of Errors.[6] He could not envisage a democracy untainted by Modernism and the anticlericalism characteristic of the Third Republic. Moreover, it is very likely that Clérissac included Pius X's anti-Modernist profession of faith as part of the ceremony of Maritain's baptism.[7]

In his book *Maurras et notre temps*, Henri Massis reports a conversation between himself and Maritain at the home of the latter's mother, Madame Favre, long after the crisis had passed. Maritain and Massis had drifted apart in the years that followed the crisis. In 1932 Massis began preparing his book *Evocations*, and moved by the memories of their early friendship and of their comradeship with Ernest Psichari, he had come to seek out his friend of former days. Massis reconstructs from memory (as is his wont) an extended conversation that took place on this occasion in Maritain's study. Whether the words attributed to Maritain were actually spoken by him is subject to doubt; however, they seem to give a rather accurate account — judging from what Maritain and his wife say in their writings — of Father Clérissac's political views and his influence on the young philosopher. Maritain began by confessing his remorse for having seconded Father Clérissac's efforts to bring Massis into Action Française:

> Ah! said Maritain, his head bent toward me, I have often reproached myself for that, among my many other failures of foresight! . . . This responsibility weighs heavily on me and still torments me. . . . I can't forget that it was Father Clérissac and I who encouraged you to turn toward Action Française.

Supposedly, Maritain went on to explain the reasons for Father Clérissac's attitude and for his own submission to his director's recommendations:

> Before Father Clérissac became my director, I had no connection with Action Française; in fact, I knew nothing about it! All my research was in the field of metaphysics and I had no interest whatever in politics. What I had seen of it in my youth was enough to disgust me; in my opinion it was nothing more than the most horrible of the idols of this world! It is enough to say that I was a disciple of Léon Bloy. . . . I had not read even a single book by Maurras, and I hadn't the least desire to do so. I subscribed to the newspaper in 1911 and I read it without ever having opened one of his books. If I read Maurras' daily column, it was because Father Clérissac had persuaded me that I should be associated with Action Française! I had accepted this, as I had all the rest, with complete docility, out of obedience, out of submission to my director; and I convinced myself that this decision was an integral part of all I had to accept in entering the Church. . . .
>
> But what could Father Clérissac have been thinking . . . ? Here is how I explain it to myself: the restoration of the monarchy seemed to Father Clérissac indispensable to the restoration of the Church in our society; in his eyes, the monarchy alone was able to re-establish the Church in the fullness of its rights. He noted with horror all that the Church had been forced to abandon in fact or to leave in escheatage since the Revolution. . . . He recognized the source of the blows struck against the notions of hierarchy and order, which are essential to the life of the Church, and he placed the Church above all else; hence he detested democracy as an evil . . . he knew the dangers which at that particular time "Modernism" posed to the dogmatic teaching of the Faith. The fact that Action Française, from outside the Church, opposed these errors, the fact that it denounced relentlessly the influence of Bergson, and the anti-intellectualism of Blondel or Laberthonnière, all this made the movement all the more dear to him. . . . Father Clérissac thus convinced me that Action Française alone was able to prepare, in the political order, the conditions necessary for the re-establishment of an integral order.[8]

These somewhat too fertile reconstructions of conversations in Massis' book picture with relative fidelity the essential elements of the situation, but they must be approached with caution for they often seem colored in certain details by the author's prejudices. A case in point is the last sentence in the conversation quoted above. It is true that Father Clérissac may have convinced Maritain that Action Française was one of the many means, in the political realm, to prepare the conditions necessary for the reestablishment of order in society. It is very unlikely, however, that he convinced Maritain that it was the *only* means to such an end. During the twenty years between his conversion and the crisis, Maritain spoke often of the necessary conditions for renewal of the social order, and in every case *the* condition was a return to the spirit of Christianity and the practice of the evangelical virtues of justice and charity. Not once in this connection did Maritain mention Action Française, and he consistently refused to teach in the institute founded by Maurras. It is probable that Father Clérissac convinced Maritain that Action Française could *contribute* to the renewal of society; but one must not overlook the fact that as Maritain became more familiar with the movement, through reading Maurras' daily newspaper, his criticisms and reservations became, as we shall see, more frequent and more forceful.

In general, however, the words about Father Clérissac attributed to Maritain by Massis confirm the impression given by Raïssa in *Les Grandes Amitiés:*

> Father Clérissac passionately admired Maurras; and in his disgust for the modern world, in his pure enthusiasm for the metaphysical notion of order, he trusted a movement then developing under the aegis of violence in the service of order, the spiritual dangers of which he did not discern. Maurras' school had at that time a certain intellectual vitality, and had not yet hardened in its worst characteristics; this explains in part Father Clérissac's illusions.[9]

Henry Massis takes exception to the word "illusions" in this text. He claims that Raïssa Maritain had no right to speak of Father Clérissac's "illusions" since, even before 1910, it was public knowledge that Rome was investigating the spiritual integrity of both Maurras' movement of Nationalisme Intégral and the political and theological Modernism of Catholic liberals. All this theologico-political discussion resulted, he claims, in the condemnation of the liberals, while Action Française emerged with clean skirts:

From that time on, everything had been said on the substance of the question. . . . Father Clérissac therefore already
knew all that could be said about the "spiritual dangers" of
the Maurrassian school.[10]

Hence, Massis concludes, with baffling logic, Father Clérissac's recruiting for Action Française in 1911 and 1912 could not
have been done in ignorance: everything he needed to know was
clearly put down in the Vatican *dossier* on Maurras, "that dossier
which Pius X in 1911 had refused to take out of his drawer."[11] Is it
not possible that Father Clérissac could have had "illusions" about
the contents of a *dossier* that was not made public? And is it not
possible that Pius X's refusal to take the *dossier* from his drawer
might have fostered the "illusion" that the spiritual dangers it
mentioned were not serious enough to merit condemnation?

Massis is caught with his *non sequiturs* showing, but his confusion goes even deeper; he is mistaken about dates and events.
There certainly was an anti-Modernist campaign from 1907 to
1910, which culminated in the encyclical *Pascendi* and the Syllabus of Pius X, in the prohibition of the works of such Catholic
liberals as Loisy, Laberthonnière and Le Roy, in the persecution
of clerical scholars who sought to interpret Christian doctrine in
the light of modern social and scientific developments and,
finally, in the condemnation of Marc Sangnier's Catholic liberal
political movement Sillon. Professors who were suspected of
Modernist tendencies were removed from the faculties of Catholic
educational institutions and seminaries, their publications were
suppressed or prohibited and an anti-Modernist loyalty oath was
administered to the clergy and candidates for the clergy. The
partisans of Action Française were overjoyed. Contrary to what
Massis says, there was no official investigation of Maurras and
Action Française until 1913 — and this investigation appears to be
the one which, according to Massis, would have made it impossible for Father Clérissac to have harbored any "illusions" about
Action Française in 1911.

Previous to 1911, questions had been raised about the orthodoxy of Maurras' position on Christianity; reports had been
sent to Rome in increasing numbers and warnings were issued to
the laity by highly placed clerics. These complaints may well
have appeared to monarchist and conservative clergy like Father
Clérissac as the death spasms of Catholic liberals, who had been
dealt a mortal blow by Pius X's Syllabus of Errors. Nevertheless,

the complaints became so numerous and insistent that they prompted an investigation of Maurras in 1913. The result was that the Sacred Congregation of the Index found seven of Maurras' books extremely dangerous and placed them on the Index on January 16, 1914. It was the *dossier* of this investigation of 1913–14 (not 1911)[12] that Pius X refused to take out of his drawer, reserving to himself the right to choose the date for promulgation of the condemnation. Until such a date, the condemnation would not be official and binding on Catholic consciences.

It is true, as Massis says, that Father Clérissac could not have been ignorant of the objections to Maurras in certain ecclesiastical circles. These objections were common knowledge. This knowledge, however, did not come, as Massis insists, from decorous and dignified public discussion of the merits of Action Française, carried on with "an elevation of tone and with speculative gravity and decorum,"[13] but rather from the ecclesiastical grapevine, whose tendrils extended deep into the Vatican and into the heart of Maurras' movement. It is certainly not true that "everything had been said about the fundamental issues," as the violent debates of 1926–29 were later to show. Of course, in 1914 everyone in Action Française knew of the condemnation, but they took Pius X's politically expedient procrastination as a sign of approval.[14]

Father Clérissac died on November 16, 1914, but from the time of the unofficial condemnation (in January) there is no sign that he made the slightest effort to dissociate himself or his spiritual wards from the movement. Rome had not yet spoken, so the case was not yet closed. Father Clérissac, like so many other French clerics, was laboring under the illusion that promulgation of the Index listings could be held off indefinitely, that the possibility of another liberal Pope like Leo XIII was out of the question and that the future of the Church, as well as civilization, lay with the political parties of the far right. And it was to this man that Maritain had submitted himself with complete docility in matters of the spiritual life.

The new political orientation urged on him by his spiritual director must have appeared to Maritain to have been somehow connected with the spiritual life, since many of the tenets of the liberalism to which Action Française was opposed had been condemned by the Vatican as contrary to faith and morals. Maritain took seriously the old priest's "pitiless" mockery of his democratic leanings and socialistic tendencies, which Father Clérissac told him (according to Raïssa) were but "the remains of the old man which had to be put off."[15] He seems to have considered that a change in political allegiance was part of his entering completely into the life of the Church.

It was not the influence of Father Clérissac alone that tended to make Maritain ignore his misgivings about Action Française. The approbation, tacit or explicit, of such high-ranking ecclesiastical dignitaries and theologians as Pius X, Cardinal Billot and Dom Besse (who led Bernanos into Action Française) cannot be discounted. Dom Delatte, abbot of the famous Benedictine monastery of Solesmes, where Maritain often made retreats, was an ardent admirer of Maurras. Through the Cercle d'Etudes Thomistes, Maritain was in close contact with the clerical and lay leaders of the Thomist revival, who were almost to the man politically conservative. The opinions of such unworldly men and great scholars as Fathers Thomas Pègues and Réginald Garrigou-Lagrange, who saw only the single-minded opposition of Action Française to the worldly forces of Modernism, certainly weighed heavily with the young philosopher.[16] Eugen Weber says, in a precise description of Maritain's situation in the early 1900s:

> The influence of men like these was very great at a time when young people of the educated classes, ill at ease before the critical ideas of a rationalist Sorbonne, turned in droves toward the Church, hoping to find in it the principles of order and social discipline that might help to stave off the destruction of their world.[17]

It may not be without significance that at the very time when Father Clérissac was urging adherence to the monarchist and conservative political position as an essential part of his entering completely into the life of the Church, Maritain was going through a religious crisis, assailed by the first serious doubts about the faith he had embraced in 1907. In his *Carnet de notes* he says:

> Was it in 1911, or 1912? I was suddenly assailed by violent temptations against the faith. Up until that time the graces of baptism had been such that I seemed to *see* what I believed. Everything was so evident. Now I had to learn what was meant by the darkness of faith. I was no longer a babe in arms; I was brutally put down on the ground. I remember

the long hours of interior torture, on Orangerie Street, alone in my fourth floor room which I had made into a kind of refuge for my work. I kept from speaking about it, and eventually, by the grace of God, I came through this trial greatly strengthened; but I was no longer a child. I found consolation in telling myself that all this was necessary, if I were going to be of any service to others.[18]

An act of faith is an act of the will that leads the intelligence to give its assent to belief without the benefit of rational evidence. May not this acceptance, however misguided, of the suggestions of Father Clérissac have been part of the desperate efforts of a man to surrender himself completely to the precious faith he felt himself in danger of losing?

All these explanations are not meant as a justification for Maritain. They are simply an attempt to understand how he could have let himself be so misled, for he was mistaken, and seriously. With naive and imprudent docility, he failed to distinguish between what constituted, for a Catholic, the supreme teaching authority of the Church and what was merely the expression of personal opinion by individual clergymen. This mistake is a fact of history, and no one, least of all Maritain, has tried to explain it away. No one has been more severe in condemning this intellectual negligence than the Maritains themselves. Wherever one finds reference to this period in the writings of either Maritain or his wife, one also usually finds expressions of self-reproach for their "ignorance of the limits of spiritual direction," for their "untimely docility," their "undue obedience," their "unpardonable thoughtlessness," "inadvertence," "naiveté and lack of consideration," and for their uncritical readiness "to make obligatory for themselves what went against their very inclination."[19]

As his doubts and misgivings about Action Française grew, and he was to examine his political allegiance carefully, he recognized the foolishness of his "blind" obedience to Father Clérissac in political matters. Every subsequent position he took was based on painstaking consideration in the light of his philosophical principles and the voice of his conscience. At the outbreak of the Spanish Civil War, for example, he saw immediately — through critical, intelligent examination — what Bernanos refused to see until he was personally confronted with the brutal reality of Falangist atrocities. And Maritain held to his convictions, in spite of the "official" declaration of Pius XII in favor of

Franco and in the face of violent opposition from the majority of the Catholic clergy and laity — even to the extent of threats of condemnation by the Sacred Congregation of the Index. Maritain had learned his lesson painfully, but well.

When Maritain eventually broke with Action Française, it was not due to a sudden conversion brought about by slavish obedience to Rome's decision (an illusion engendered and fostered by his "friend" Henri Massis, who found it expedient for himself and for the movement to portray Maritain as a fuzzy intellectual and an unprincipled turncoat). As early as 1914 — the year Father Clérissac died and twelve years before the condemnation — Maritain had written to Maurras of his astonishment at the way in which Maurras made use of a historical allusion to give a false impression of the monarchist situation:

> Permit me to tell you that I was astonished to see you make such a rapid and summary allusion in your article. . . . You know that for me it is not a question of practical politics, but of the truth.

In 1918, eight years before the condemnation, Maurras wrote to Maritain: "I will not fail to read attentively Father Clérissac's book."[20] Maritain had sent him a copy of Father Clérissac's *Mystère de l'Eglise* (Maritain had written the preface), in which chapter 6 treats the relations between Church and State and their relative positions of authority over men. (We shall see other examples of his growing misgivings.)

Through the influence of Father Clérissac, then, Maritain became associated with Action Française. As will be seen, he tried to keep this association completely apolitical. He considered the association not so much membership in a political party as a kind of rallying of friends and kindred spirits to defend common philosophical causes and to attack common philosophical enemies. To this comradeship Maritain gave himself wholeheartedly. In spite of his desire to remain politically detached, he was closely associated with the movement in the mind of the general public, so that at one time he was known as the official philosopher of Action Française. This impression was fostered, in particular, by his participation in the early 1920s in the founding and editing of *La Revue Universelle*.

Before his death in the war in 1918, a young royalist, Pierre Villard, filled with the same disillusion and the same craving for religious and philosophical certitude that had troubled Maritain before his conversion, came to seek advice from the young Thomist, whose fame was increasing every day. Though Maritain saw little of Villard, the two exchanged a very active correspondence until the latter's death in the war. So impressed was Villard with Maritain and his work that he left a legacy of more than a million francs, to be divided equally between Maurras and Maritain. This legacy was a welcome surprise, for it enabled Maritain to free himself from the time-consuming tasks which kept him from devoting himself completely to the renewal of Christian philosophy. To supplement the scanty salary he received from the Institut Catholique, he had agreed to edit the *Dictionnaire de la vie pratique* and to prepare a *Lexique orthographique* for the publisher Hachette. Villard's bequest gave Maurras and Maritain complete liberty in the disposition of their inheritance, contenting himself with an expression of general intention. The purpose of the legacy, Villard said, was to contribute "to safeguarding what remains of the moral and intellectual patrimony of our country. . . . this patrimony cannot be saved without a return to the Christian method and without a reflowering of the Faith."[21]

Concerning the publicity to be given to Villard's legacy, Maritain wrote a letter to Maurras which shows his desire to be associated as little as possible with Action Française:

> At any rate, in whatever concerns me, after consulting my friends and authorized counselors, I definitely believe that it is preferable that my name not be mentioned for the moment and that no allusion whatever be made to the legacy I have received.
>
> Doubtless it will be painful for me not to publish the admirable words in which Pierre Villard speaks of his religious aspirations; but I believe that I will conform more faithfully to the intentions of our friend by sacrificing for the moment this exterior manifestation of his sentiments to the real and effective good that he proposed as his objective, and to the attaining of which, any publicity, at least in what concerns me, would create considerable obstacles.
>
> If you make public some part of the will and of Pierre Villard's letter, I ask you to limit the publication strictly to the part which concerns you and to say nothing of what touches me.[22]

In January 1920, Maurras suggested that they each contribute 50,000 francs from this legacy for founding a review which might serve as a sounding board for the ideas and principles of Action Française in political and social activity, on the one hand, and on the other hand for Christian and particularly Thomist thought in religion and philosophy.

Maurras was an astute man. He may have felt the need, in the face of the ever increasing animadversions sent to Rome and the clerical warnings about his movement, to associate himself closely with a Catholic thinker who was above ecclesiastical reproach. Besides, might not Maritain prove a formidable enemy if he were to drift into the liberal camp, for many of whose principles he showed a dangerous sympathy? Had not Maritain, shortly before this, attacked the modern capitalist economy as founded on "two principles contrary to nature: the fecundity of money and the finality of the useful"?[23] Had he not always preached the necessity of reestablishing social justice as prerequisite for any kind of order and peace in society?[24] Had he not questioned the morality of the economic principles that were used to justify interest-bearing loans? Had he not, in 1907, brought these doubts to Dom Delatte (who, of course, put them aside with the back of his hand), and did he not persist in these doubts even after the facile and confident assurance of the famous abbot?[25] Was he not known for his public association with Jews? Nevertheless, Maurras asked Maritain to take charge of the religious and philosophical pages of the review. Jacques Bainville, whose ideas about history Maritain was far from sharing,[26] was to be in charge of the historical, social and political sections while Massis (later to become editor in chief) was to work under Bainville as literary editor. The publication was to be called *La Revue Universelle*.

Massis, who had spoken to Maritain of the project in September 1919, minimized the role of Action Française, explaining that the review needed the movement's vast reading public to get under way. He was careful to make it clear (Did he detect in Maritain some suspicious diffidence regarding Action Française?) that the review would be an "independent organ," with no formal *liaison* with the movement.[27] Later, however, Massis was to write about his and Maritain's collaboration in terms that smacked of the subordination of religion to politics, a tendency for which the movement was soon to be condemned by Rome. Massis wrote:

> The name of Bainville was enough to define the dominant lines of the political, historical, social and literary thought of such a publication. My collaboration and that of my

friend Jacques Maritain added an element which gave the review the character of a Catholic publication.[28]

Maritain hesitated. Certain aspects of the movement and of Maurras' attitude troubled him. On July 11, 1919, Raïssa made an entry in her diary which seems to imply that the opinion she expressed was shared by her husband: "The political positivism of Maurras now leaves much to be desired." This sentence concludes an assertion that society could be saved only if truth and justice were pursued for their own sake,[29] which was one of her husband's favorite themes. Years later, in an entry in Maritain's diary concerning the period 1914 to 1926, he speaks of his misgivings about Action Française and of a reason for his association with the movement and his acceptance of Maurras' proposal about *La Revue Universelle:*

> At that time the partisans of Action Française still enjoyed, in my opinion, the prestige of their patriotism, and I presumptuously imagined that I would be able to help them separate this patriotism and the healthy ideas it contained from the positivist system of Maurras and his nationalist idolatry, of whose danger I was becoming more and more aware. . . . Maurras' profound atheism, the cult of violence and the intellectual tyranny which raged among his disciples, the way he conducted his polemic activity, which grew daily more odious (until the day when it became clear to me in all its lies, its cynical use of calumny during this ferocious campaign against Georges Valois), — I closed my eyes to all this in the absurd hope of bringing about doctrinal corrections and installing a Christian philosophy in the very heart of a school whose political principles I did not realize, having at that time only very superficial ideas in that domain, suffered from incurable errors.[30]

Influenced by the memory that Father Clérissac had strongly encouraged such a review and had often spoken to Maritain and Massis on the subject, and tempted by the immense reading public the review would open to the Catholic and Thomist revival,[31] Maritain decided to accept. From its very inception, *La Revue Universelle*, both because of the names of its backers, editors and contributors and because of the tenor of its articles, was considered by the public as the official intellectual organ of Action Française. And though his contributions were concerned entirely with theoretical philosophy, Maritain was soon considered the official philosopher of the movement.

> Thus, alas, there seemed to be accentuated that kind of *entente cordiale* between Action Française and me [wrote Maritain], founded on equivocation and due to my political naiveté of those days and to the influence of Father Clérissac.[32]

Maritain insists that his role as philosophical editor of *La Revue Universelle* was the absolute limit of his cooperation with Maurras. However, he proved most active in this enterprise, publishing no fewer than thirty-six articles and reviews from April 1920 until February 1927, when he severed all connection with the review and with Action Française. And his contributions, much to his subsequent embarrassment and regret, were not free from an occasional satirical aside at the expense of democratic institutions. Such remarks were the "last vestiges of the political influence of Léon Bloy and Father Clérissac," Raïssa explains,[33] but these remarks became less and less frequent and overt criticisms of many positions sacred to Action Française became more numerous.

His very first article for the review was an attack on positivism as destructive of intelligence; indeed his antagonism to this fundamental principle and Maurrasism was a persistent theme with Maritain during the early 1920s. In 1921 he published an article in defense of the Jews.[34] More than once he proposed that the Russian Revolution was the instrument of God's justice, to sweep away the corruption and tyranny of the established regime.[35]

Maritain was asserting the autonomy he had demanded as philosophical editor, and his frequent attacks on intellectual positivism may perhaps be explained as an effort to erase a serious intellectual *faux pas* he had made (probably due to his close friendship with Massis) at the turn of the century. Massis says that Maritain wrote these words to him at this time:

> God has made us two brothers to serve and fight together, but as a guide there is only one for both of us, and it is He. . . . When I think of the ten years that have passed since our meeting, how marvelous His Grace has been and how beautiful has been the path He has led us to follow! We have begun to bind our sheaves together.[36]

The friendship between Maritain and Massis began in 1913, when Psichari brought Massis to Maritain's home, and it grew deeper with the years. The moving dedication of his book *Jugements* to Maritain and the eloquent expression of his admiration for him in *L'Honneur de servir* testify to the profound feeling of Massis for his friend. (At the time that they were collaborating on *La Revue Universelle*, they were also associated in an offensive against André Gide.) Contrary to his practice, Frédéric Lefèvre, who published in *La Nouvelle Revue Française* his hour-long interviews with prominent literary figures from France and other countries of Western Europe, interviewed Massis and Maritain together.[37] In this series of interviews, the names of these two men are almost invariably linked together, whether for praise or for criticism, by numerous men of letters. "Massis-Maritain" seems to have been pronounced almost as one word.

It was probably in deference to this friendship that Maritain made the mistake of letting it be known that he approved the Parti de l'Intelligence, which Massis founded in 1919. Massis did not intend this party to be a political organization, but an intellectual federation of Europe for the defense of the humanistic, Christian West against intellectual bolshevism. This European federation would be formed under the aegis of France, the guardian of all civilization, and the manifesto that Massis wrote for the Parti de l'Intelligence was remarkably Maurrasian in tone. It is difficult to determine the reasons for Maritain's approbation. He did not sign the manifesto. It is hard to imagine Massis not approaching him, considering their closeness, their connection in the public eye, and Maritain's prestige.

On the other hand, Maritain seems to have made no effort to destroy the impression that he was a member of the party or to separate himself from the group. Jacques Rivière, the editor of *La Nouvelle Revue Française*, saw immediately what Maritain should have seen from the outset: the new party was subordinating intelligence to national interest — was making truth subservient to Caesar. In the September 1919 issue of his review, Rivière published a perceptive and scathing attack which accused the adherents of the party of wearing blinkers on their intelligence. In one line in particular, he found the essential error of the manifesto:

"In a word, we know what we want and what we do not want."
. . . The key word has been given out. These gentlemen "know what they want and what they do not want," and for

them the intelligence is the means to obtain the first and to obviate the second. It is there to "classify," to place in hierarchical order, to impose on what is real a form that has been chosen and decreed once and for all.[38]

When Massis commented on this article in 1959, in his book *De l'homme à Dieu*, he provided a perfect example of the kind of intellectual prostitution that Rivière had in mind. He dismissed the criticism that the Parti de l'Intelligence had failed to distinguish between truth and politics and had shackled the freedom of the intellect with a kind of *"empirisme organisateur,"* as if these were essentially irrelevant remarks that might be expected from the literary liberals. Then, lifting a quotation out of context from Rivière's attack, he used it as a testimonial of approbation for his Parti de l'Intelligence.[39]

How could Maritain have given his approbation, or how could he have let the equivocation continue, if he did not approve? Nothing should have been more opposed to his instincts as a philosopher. Probably nothing was ever to cause him more anguish, remorse or embarrassment than this culpable negligence. Raïssa wrote in 1945:

> What regrets he would feel later for not having separated himself immediately from this unfortunate anomalous group that Massis was to "launch" under the name of the "party of the intelligence," as if the two words could be joined and as if the first did not insult the second.[40]

Rivière's article must have awakened Maritain to his professional responsibility; for as we have seen, with his very first article in *La Revue Universelle*, a few months later, he began a series of persistent attacks on the intellectual attitude represented in Massis' manifesto. However, never once during the years from 1919 till his break with Action Française does he seem to have publicly criticized Massis by name, which permitted the equivocation about his approbation to persist.

Although Maritain's public defense of the 1926 papal condemnation of Action Française was to be the reef on which his friendship with Massis came to pieces, there were indications that the friendship was weakening long before that time. Their community of interests became more and more tenuous as Maritain, during the decade preceding the 1926 crisis, committed himself more and more to friends, ideas and organizations inimical to Action Française. Massis was present at the inauguration of the

Cercle d'Etudes Thomistes in 1914, and seems to have been an enthusiastic member of the group during the early meetings. After 1920, even at the height of his collaboration with Maritain on *La Revue Universelle*, his name becomes conspicuous by its absence from the attendance lists for the meetings and retreats of the Cercle. People began to attend regularly who were hardly congenial to Massis: Fumet, Cocteau, Sachs, Ramuz, Borne, Merleau-Ponty and Cattaui, for example. Massis wrote a letter to Maritain about this time, reprimanding him for spending so much valuable time on the *"enfants perdus"* who came knocking at his door (Cocteau, Maurice Sachs, Cattaui!) and urging him to devote more time, as was his duty, to "young Frenchmen who are authentic Christians of good racial stock."[41]

From 1924 on, Maritain was closely associated with Hindu and Chinese intellectuals[42] and with the Russian philosopher Nicolas Berdyaev, a kind of pre-Johannine Russian Orthodox ecumenicist.[43] In the late twenties and early thirties, specialists in Eastern studies, such as Louis Massignon and Olivier Lacombe, took a very active part in the meetings in Meudon. All this could hardly have been congenial for Massis, who during these years was zealously proclaiming his rather fanatical idealization of Western Christian culture and his supreme contempt for the "barbarities" of the East in a book he was preparing, *Défense de l'occident*. Before the book appeared, Massis sent the galley proofs for corrections and suggestions to Maritain, who read the manuscript with meticulous care, filling the margins with animadversions that, when put together, cover nine single-spaced typewritten pages. They show how far apart Maritain and Massis (and Maurras as well) had grown in their attitudes toward history, politics, culture and art. "This formula is too much like Maurras. . . . What good does it do to abuse them in such a manner? . . . After all, there are some nuances to be considered. . . . This goes far beyond the sense of the quotation. This isn't what he meant. . . . In all this it seems to me that one should show pity rather than indignation. . . . Impossible. . . . I think this is unjust. . . . Much too hard and absolute. . . . Such summary judgments can do enormous harm in such cases. . . . You cannot say that of all the East. . . . This note seems dangerous to me," etc., etc.[44] In a letter he sent back with the proofs, Maritain wrote:

> I would not be telling you the truth, my dear Henri, if I did not tell you the impression of sadness and pain that remains

with me. . . . What arouses these apprehensions in me . . . is the impression as a whole that your book leaves with me. . . . That impression is the following: a book animated by the spirit of combat; not by the spirit of justice. Justice alone is strong and efficacious.[45]

In 1925, two years before the publication of Massis' book, Maritain wrote him of the dangerous influence of Maurras that he found in Massis' thought:

I read in the *Revue catholique des idées et des faits* a message of Maurras to all Latinity, which appears to me far from satisfying. "Latinity," I have no idea what that can be, no more than "organity" or "germanity" or his other racial expressions. On the other hand we know very well what Christianity and Catholicity mean. I'm afraid that your position is being confused with that of Maurras, whose acknowledged authority is so strong that it would risk deforming in the minds of your readers the true meaning of your work. . . . If your defense of the Christian West is confused with the defense of Latinity in the nationalist or racist sense, in the strictly Maurrasian sense, the whole undertaking will be spoiled.[46]

When Maritain founded the series *Roseau d'Or* in 1925, to provide a forum for authors in sympathy with the ideas discussed at the meetings at Meudon, he asked Massis to be one of the editors, along with Fumet, Cocteau, Ramuz, Lefèvre (mentioned above) and Ghéon, but there was no real rapport between Massis and the other editors (with the possible exception of Ghéon). Maritain seems to have asked him in deference to their old friendship and in an effort to draw him away from Maurras and into the Cercle. It failed, however, for a fervent disciple of Maurras could hardly feel at home when such personalities as Jean de Menasce, Charles Du Bos, Yves Simon, René Schwob, Jacques Madaule, François Mauriac, Julian Green and Emmanuel Mounier were in regular attendance. It is little wonder, then, that Massis gradually dissociated himself in public from Maritain.

Although Massis frequently expressed regret over the loss of Maritain's friendship, it was he, not Maritain, who took the initiative in breaking it off.[47] For many years Maritain was indefatigable in his efforts to persuade Massis to submit to Rome. He felt a great responsibility for Massis since he himself had introduced him to Action Française.

Massis' claim that Maritain's change of heart about Action Française was quite sudden and took him by surprise is completely unfounded. Besides Maritain's numerous associations with persons and groups directly opposed to the spirit of Action Française, there is the evidence of his book *Une Opinion sur Charles Maurras et le devoir des Catholiques* (1926). As early as October 1925, more than a year before the official condemnation, Maritain was at work on this book, putting down his reactions to certain criticisms and accusations made by a group of Belgian Catholics against Maurras.

A Belgian priest, Abbé Van den Hout, had asked Maurras, Massis and Maritain for papers which would explain Maurras' movement and its principles and allay the fears of many Belgian Catholics, but Maritain was the only one who took the request seriously enough to write a paper in October of 1925. When he received no further word from Abbé Van den Hout, he put it aside in a drawer; but when, almost a year later, his friend Abbé Charles Journet, professor at the major seminary in Fribourg and editor of the Catholic review for French-speaking Switzerland, *Nova et Vetera*, asked him for a study of Maurras from a strictly Catholic point of view, for publication in his review, Maritain took his paper from the drawer. He sent a copy to Maurras for his criticism, remarking that the study was done "in an absolutely independent manner and from a completely theological point of view. This can endow with more authority what the article says in your favor, but it also exposes me to the risk of displeasing you at certain moments."[48] In gentle but no uncertain terms, Maritain made a number of reservations and distinctions about the movement and laid down the conditions which would have to be met to make Action Française acceptable to Catholics. It is important to note that these were the very stipulations to which Maurras and Daudet (the editor of *Action Française*) were to cry *"Non possumus!"* when they were demanded by Rome.

Maurras, writing of the "great emotion" with which he read the study, replied on September 25:

What misunderstandings you have dissipated. But will not others arise from what you have written? . . . How I would like to find the leisure some day to chat with you about political science, of that element — let us call it mechanical — which this science seems to me to contain; of how it is distinguished from morals, whose application begins, it seems to me, only at that point where there is an act of the will, that is to say *political action* — all of which puts aside certain grave questions of political structure.[49]

It is inconceivable that Maritain did not discuss these ideas with Massis too before their publication. As a matter of fact, in September 1926, shortly after Pius XI wrote a letter to Cardinal Andrieu of Bordeaux approving many of the latter's allegations about the dangers of Action Française, Maurras and Massis visited Maritain at Meudon to confer on a strategy of defense. It was decided that Maurras would publicly state his position with regard to the Catholic Church, Maritain would show on what conditions the doctrine and practices of Maurras could be reconciled to the Church, and Massis would recount the services Action Française had already rendered to Catholicism. One is led to believe that Maritain, alone of the three, took the imminent danger of condemnation very seriously, for he alone carried out his task.[50]

Maritain's *Opinion sur Charles Maurras* in many places reads like a gentle but firm warning to the leader of Action Française. Very early on, the author spoke of the "somber uneasiness" he habitually felt about Maurras. He expressed a certain admiration for Maurras, but could not understand his "deeply upsetting admiration for Anatole France." He explained that Maurras' *"politiques d'abord"* could be acceptable to a Catholic if "politics comes first" is understood not in the order of intention (i.e., in the order of ends, where politics is not an absolute end in itself, subservient to no other), but in the order of execution (i.e., "in the order of temporal realizations of human action").[51] It is explicitly stated that the science of politics must always be subordinate in the moral sphere to the science of theology — a hierarchy that Maurras was accused of reversing.

> From the viewpoint of political science, there is thus a danger of shutting oneself up in an empiricism as if within a self-sufficient doctrine and of refusing the higher syntheses which alone can lead to science in the true sense of the word. The error into which one risks falling is that of political "materialism."
>
> From the religious point of view, there is danger of considering the Church in the goods which it dispenses secondarily and in addition to its primary and essential good, i.e., inasmuch as the Church is the best protector of social good, more than in its essential end, function and dignity,

which is to dispense to men supernatural truth and the
means to eternal life and which confers on her the right to
intervene in temporal affairs.[52]

Though Maritain praised him for his insistence on order in
society, for the role he gave intelligence in directing human affairs, and for his opposition to liberalism, Maritain charged that
there was in Maurras, particularly in his early works, a dangerous
agnosticism that gave no consideration to the supernatural end of
man. He suggested that the Catholic members of Action Française
form study groups within the party, having as their object not
political action but religious formation, the study of Catholic doctrine, the teachings of the popes and dogmatic and moral theology, all directed by theologians and controlled by ecclesiastical
authority, "to complete and to correct the teachings, the opinions
and the examples received from certain of their political masters."[53] Could Maurras have failed to recognize himself here?
    The last section of the book was written after the letter of
Pius XI to Cardinal Andrieu, concurring in the latter's accusations
against Action Française. Maritain called for sincere and complete filial obedience to the wishes of the pope. He recalled that
the exhortations of the pope in the years following World War I,
asking the victorious nations to soften, in the interests of a dur-
able peace, the harsh conditions imposed on conquered Germany,
"were not followed . . . with any particularly noticeable zeal by
those for whom their anti-liberal principles should have nevertheless made obedience much easier."[54] He condemned that exaggerated "nationalism" which refused obedience to the Church in
those domains where the Church exercises the legitimate
authority conferred on it by Christ.[55] What Maritain called for on
the part of the Catholics in Action Française was "unfeigned
obedience" of the spirit.[56] One could easily have mistaken the
brochure for the papal allocution to which Maurras refused to
submit. Nor could Massis have missed these points.
    Another evidence that Massis could not have been surprised
by Maritain's decision to defend the papal position was that Maritain persuaded Maurras, before the public condemnation, to
write a letter to the pope expressing his willingness to make some
concessions in view of establishing a *modus vivendi*. It was Massis
who brought Maurras to Maritain's home for a meeting with
Father Garrigou-Lagrange, the eminent French Thomist theologian of right-wing sympathies, to prepare Maurras to write such a
letter. The meeting was a failure, as far as Maritain was con-

cerned, "because of Maurras' obstinacy."[57] The letter which Maurras wrote after this meeting evidently did not satisfy the pope, for he did not reply. Instead, he issued the consistorial allocution *Misericordias Domini*, forbidding Catholics to belong to Action Française. As soon as he read of the pope's allocution, which he had feared was to come, Maritain wrote to Maurras of being "cruelly disappointed that nothing had been done [by Maurras and Massis] about the matter discussed in September."[58]

The banner headline in the December 24, 1926, edition of Maurras' paper read *"Non possumus!"* When Maritain heard of this reply, he gave up all hope of saving the situation for his friends in the movement.[59] Five days later, on December 29, 1926, Pope Pius XI promulgated the 1914 decree placing seven of Maurras' books on the Index. To this list of 1914 the pope, on his own initiative, added Maurras' newspaper *Action Française*. The newspaper was crucial to the entire movement, and if Catholics had obeyed the prohibition, Action Française would have died. The fact that it did not die is evidence of the extent to which a great number of French Catholics had become Maurrassians, and they continued to subscribe to *Action Française* and to the opinions they read in it. This fact is also evidence, perhaps, of the inherent justice of the condemnation, from the Church's point of view.[60]

On January 11, Maritain wrote to Maurras protesting the vitriolic and abusive attacks on the pope in *Action Française* and announcing his complete and definitive separation from the movement:

> It is with an immense sadness that I write to you. . . . Why must it be that things so lofty still remain, let me speak frankly, so inferior to the situation, and are communicated through the practical position of the newspaper that is daily more disappointing? The affection in which I hold you, and which I protest once again here, itself forces me to explain myself clearly to you on this matter.
>
> Yesterday, in order to conform to the rule that binds us all, I was obliged to write to the director of the newspaper to cancel my subscription. After reading today's issue, I must tell you that I find it absolutely impossible to accept the manner in which the Pope is treated there. The allusions to the two Popes of the fifteenth century is not only odious, it is also completely invalid and beside the point, for in each of these two situations the Pope did not give an order to the

faithful in the name of his indirect power over the temporal, as is the case in the present circumstances.

I cannot understand how you yourself, after the declarations of persevering respect which you have made, . . . have been able to allow Pius XI to be insulted so cruelly. Nor do I understand how you can permit the particular judgments of men of the greatest authority to be opposed to the judgment of the Pope. You have always fought against the heresy of private judgment; you have always worked to give men's minds a proper feeling for authority, for hierarchy, for the *conservative order of being*. That you should be led to an attitude that is in practice strictly protestant and anarchic will be for many a horribly painful scandal.

As to the two documents you have published, I cannot imagine from what theologians they could have emanated — one can always find theologians to obfuscate with captious sophistry the rectitude of Christian judgment — in themselves they are worth nothing.

Theologically, the question can be presented in a very simple manner. . . .

And in a last attempt to convince Maurras, Maritain laid out, in seven clear and simple points, the argument he had explained in more detail in *Une Opinion sur Charles Maurras*. He concluded the seventh point, and the letter, in these words:

Man's providence can and ought to judge only by what it can know; but God's Providence judges according to secrets hidden within itself and according to the real state of human capabilities and of human hearts, which is inaccessible to us. . . . The Ruler of the Universe loves you. . . . I too love your soul and that is why I speak to you in this way.[61]

During the early months of 1927, Maritain began working on a study of the relationship between Church and State which was finished in May and published two months later under the title *Primauté du spirituel*. This book occasioned a series of violent attacks against Maritain in the pages of *La Revue Universelle,* and even an attempt to have his writings condemned by the Holy See. In December of that year, along with four theologians, Maritain published a defense of the papal condemnation called *Pourquoi Rome a parlé;* he supplied the chapter "Le sens de la condamnation de l'Action Française." This was followed, two years later, by another book written by the same authors, *Clairvoyance de Rome*.

Maritain suffered greatly to see so many of his longstanding friendships disintegrate because of the condemnation. He tried his best to save these friendships and seems to have done nothing to destroy them, beyond taking his position in favor of Rome and signing or publishing, as a matter of conscience, a number of political manifestos which opposed the positions taken by his former friends. In fact, as Massis himself admitted, the door at Meudon was always open. Maritain made little mention of Massis in his writings after 1927. He did, however, make repeated attempts, through his own efforts or indirectly through friends, to win Massis back to Rome.

On the other hand, Massis' frequent and sometimes maudlin protestations of absolute fidelity to Maritain ring hollow in the face of some of his actions. He participated actively in a cabal to discredit Maritain before Rome and to have him condemned as a heretic. In 1936, Massis encouraged one of his collaborators at *La Revue Universelle*, a former pupil of Maritain's, Joseph Desclausais, to present the case against Maritain to the traditionalist and conservative theologians of the Roman Curia.[62] This was not the first or the last of such attempts. Nor did Massis consider it inconsonant with his protestations of love and respect for Maritain to encourage, both publicly and through private correspondence, a campaign of vilification against his friend.

After the condemnation, as *La Revue Universelle* became more and more a mouthpiece of Action Française, Maritain became more and more uneasy in his role as philosophical editor. He was disturbed at being linked so closely to Massis after the publication of his *Défense de l'occident*. In an undated letter, written between June 27 and August 3, 1927, Maritain suggested that in the prospectus of the review, after the phrase "Each of its collaborators writes under his own personal responsibility," the following sentence be inserted: "*Primauté du spirituel* is no more representative today of the position of Henri Massis than yesterday the *Défense de l'occident* was representative of the position of Jacques Maritain."

Maritain had already spoken on several occasions to Massis of his possible resignation as philosophical editor, but now he wrote:

> Don't you think that in the present circumstances it would be better for all concerned if my collaboration on *La Revue Universelle* be considered at least as suspended until a new policy is established? I had already spoken to you in this

regard more than a year ago, before this whole business of
Action Française. I wrote to you again recently [Apr. 31 and
June 8, 1927] of this matter. Such a break seems to me very
necessary.[63]

Massis showed the letter to Maurras, who asked him to try
to persuade Maritain to remain as editor, and Massis wrote to his
friend:

> Would that I could persuade you, my dear Jacques, not to
> abandon an undertaking which once seemed so useful to you
> and which, for my part, I find more indispensable than ever.
>
> Doubtless there is the problem of the publication of
> your book. As far as I am concerned, I will do everything in
> my power to see that it does not become the object of con-
> troversy and dissension, for the only one to profit from this
> would be our common adversary. . . .
>
> You have in mind, as I do, the audience of young
> people who are to continue our work. However sublime and
> perfect the words you speak to them may be, how will they
> understand them? How will they apply your advice? These
> young writers of today, you know them well, are not very
> brave in the face of the present crises; by every means pos-
> sible they seek to escape, to flee . . . don't they despise [the
> intellect] in their own particular way by asking of it some
> *possibility of escape?* Halévy observed the other day: "Dos-
> toievsky, Proust, Brémond, Valéry, every book they put out
> is another itinerary of retreat; they have all been followed."
> Won't some of them in their ignorance, weakness and cow-
> ardice interpret this *"primauté du spirituel"* in just this way
> in such troubled times as you remind them of? I fear that for
> many of them "contemplation" . . . may be a way of forget-
> ting and losing themselves. . . . The pessimists, the worriers
> will discern in your statements a kind of "hidden catas-
> trophism" which corresponds to their personal feelings and
> will only strengthen them. I understand very well that you
> have no intention of giving such advice: but I have already
> observed the depression that the reading of your book has
> caused in many sincere minds; they have neither the intel-
> lectual culture, nor the spiritual formation to fortify them
> against the false suggestions of their defeatist mentality. . . .
> "There is nothing left but poetry," said one of them to me;
> "There is nothing left but the spiritual," another will say —

but I'm afraid that they will understand these expressions in a rather anarchic manner and that they are closer to a Benda than to you. For, as in the past on the subject of Bergson, where you two seemed to agree, this critic now defends the "transcendent" and rises up against the "religion of the temporal" (*NRF* of Aug. 1); he too attacks nationalism and politics and opposes the "real or practical mode of existence" to the "uninvolved metaphysical mode." Whether he is of the "left" or the "right," the young Frenchman of today hears Benda and Maritain; in his mind, filled with vague notions, don't the voices of the two risk being confused in one single expression of abandon, in which his selfishness will find its justification?[64]

I quote this letter at length for it is filled with expressions that Massis, once Maritain had severed his connection with Action Française and *La Revue Universelle*, again used, behind Maritain's back, in an organized campaign to denigrate and discredit the former "philosopher of Action Française." For example, several months later at a banquet Massis gave a speech that was filled with snide allusions to Maritain and, to expose his "friend" to the ridicule of Massis' audience, employed the identical expressions he had used in his letter to attempt to win Maritain back to *La Revue Universelle*. After reading an account of the speech, Maritain protested to Massis (in a letter), in the name of their friendship, such treatment at his hands:

I read the speech you gave at the Charles-Benoit banquet the day before yesterday. I cannot hide from you the fact that it caused me a great deal of pain. Before such an audience, whose baseness and whose trumped-up accusations against me you should have been able to appreciate, and who evidently understand in your words an allusion to my book *Primauté du spirituel*, it seems to me you could have abstained from such expressions as "itinerary of retreat," "under the pretext of metaphysics and transcendence," "under the pretext of contemplation." It does no good to speak of contemplation in such terms, especially before such a bunch of roisterers! Either these clichés mean nothing, or they mean that to choose in favor of God is to make oneself "inattentive to all reality," "to refuse to come to grips with current events," etc. Come now! you know very well that in *Primauté* I did no more than recall the law of the gospels. . . .

I would have preferred not to speak to you of these things. But I am forced to by what you have said. This banquet in itself was not a very clean affair. The *mud slinging* was manifest everywhere as well as the conniving to make people who in all other respects are obedient, at least exteriorly, to Rome, appear to be supporters of Action Française. Up till now, my dear Henri, you have been able to show a certain amount of reserve. Now they have succeeded in linking you publicly with them.[65]

A year later (Oct. 25, 1928), when Maritain complained (again in a letter) of lies circulated in an article by a certain Planhof and seconded by Pierre Tuc, and in which Massis seemed to be involved, Massis did not reply directly to Maritain's accusations and questions, but affected injured innocence:

Do you really feel that it is necessary to interrogate me on such a matter? . . . Is it not sad that I have to defend myself? I would have thought it unnecessary to assure you that there are certain things that I would not permit to be said about you in my presence. . . . And I am surprised that you should turn to me to establish the truth, as if I were an accomplice in the lies or the calumnies of which you so justly complain.

The only excuse I find for this is your sadness. Mine is no less.[66]

Maritain believed Massis, but it wasn't long before he felt obliged to complain again to Massis about what a young man named Maxence had written about him, again with the apparent complicity of Massis, who again played the role of injured innocence:

My dear Jacques,

If you believed that no one could turn me against you and if you thought, as I think, that our friendship is not at the mercy of what someone or other may say, you would have spared me such questions.

But why come to me? You should go to Maxence to get an explanation of his conduct in your regard. I gave him the assignment of furnishing you an explanation.[67]

Needless to say, in spite of the "assignment" Massis had given him, Maxence "carefully abstained from furnishing the slightest explanation."[68]

When Massis' manifesto for the "defense of the West" appeared in 1934, Maritain wrote to him that on the relation of the Christian faith to temporal affairs, their judgments were becoming more and more divergent. Two years later, Massis, now the editor in chief of *La Revue Universelle*, published a vicious and unjust attack on Maritain, filled with deliberate misrepresentations, by a certain Joseph Desclausais, whom (as we saw) Massis and his cohorts sent to Rome to seek Maritain's condemnation by the Holy Office. On June 18, 1936, Maritain protested this traitorous treatment:

> I cannot tell you what pain I felt, not because of what the author of the article has done, but because of what you have done. That you should criticize my position, or have it criticized, that is your right. But you know how to read texts, and you have doubtless read mine. To permit the thought of a friend to be disfigured, and in such a flagrant manner, and in the very review which you edit, is something I would not have expected of you. I suppose that after reflection you will perceive how unheard of this manner of acting with me really is.[69]

Massis' covert attacks and sniper tactics continued as late as 1953. Two months after the death of Maurras, he took charge of publishing — posthumously — *Le Bienheureux Pie X, sauveur de la France*, in which Maurras tried to establish the innocence of Action Française by showing that a former pope, whose cause for canonization had been begun and who had already been declared "Blessed," had given his approval to the very things for which the present pope had condemned the movement. Massis attached an appendix to the book which again accused Maritain of the "heresies" for which he had failed to have the philosopher condemned years before. Michel Mourre, in his book *Charles Maurras*, reproached Massis for the flagrant injustice of this inclusion:

> One is saddened to find at the end of this volume an appendix that is violently unjust to M. Jacques Maritain. To accuse him of Modernism only shows a complete ignorance of the thought and personality of the author of *Antimoderne* and of *Humanisme intégral* and that he is being judged according to a miserable caricature.[70]

In 1951, when Maritain, at the height of his prestige, was receiving signal honors and serving in positions of national and international responsibility,[71] Massis expressed his pity for this poor, deluded philosopher, who — according to Massis — had been checked by personal failure in his ambition to restore Christian philosophy; abandoned by his true disciples of the right, "who drink at other springs"; ridiculed by his pseudo disciples of the left, who "make fun of his 'retrograde scholasticism' "; and disregarded by the world, which found his ideas "out of touch and *passé.*" "In the twilight of his life," he said, "Maritain is alone."[72]

But Massis made the same statements about Duhamel, Bernanos, Mauriac, Drieu de la Rochelle, Montherlant and Malraux.[73] Whoever abandoned the friendship of Massis was a "miserable creature" who finished his days in solitude and regret. Everyone else was "alone" because they had wandered off to other friends and companions.

CHAPTER 2

Action Française: Bernanos, Massis, Maritain

THE 1926-27 CRISIS OF Action Française was a stumbling block on which many famous friendships fell in pieces. The friendship between Georges Bernanos and Jacques Maritain, which had just begun when the papal condemnation fell on Action Française, was one of such casualties. However, the rift between the two intellectual leaders was far less serious than would seem to be indicated by Bernanos' occasional fulmination and caustic asides at Maritain's expense, which built a wall between the two that was broken down only with great difficulty and after a long time. But beginning in 1935, the names of Bernanos and Maritain became more and more associated in the public eye because of their common position on many political and social questions, and after the Second World War, it was through the good offices of Jacques Maritain that Bernanos met Dominican Father Raymond Bruckberger, who was to produce the movie version of his *Dialogue des Carmélites*. It was the same Father Bruckberger who wrote to Maritain, after the war, begging him to intercede with the authorities in France to help bring Bernanos back to his homeland.[1]

When Bernanos finished the manuscript of his novel *Sous le soleil de Satan* in 1926, it was to Maritain that he confided it for criticism and for possible publication. Maritain was enthusiastic; he hailed Bernanos as the first in a new generation of Catholic authors who would renew the religious and literary inspiration of France. Despite the numerous conversions among literary figures during the early twenties, no first-rate Catholic novelist had appeared on the horizon. Psichari and Alain-Fournier were dead, and many considered Mauriac too lenient toward the sins of the flesh. The novels of Paul Bourget and Henri Bordeaux had missed the heart of the matter, confusing religion with the religious issue and with the bourgeois conservatism of the complacent pharasaical Catholics of the French middle class, whom Bernanos called the *bien-pensants*. Bernanos went directly to the point in his probing analysis of passion, sin and evil, though there were political overtones in the novel, to be sure. Bernanos said that he wanted to throw a saint (Abbé Donisson) in the face of the idiotically jubilant politicians who shouted their slogans of victory after the First World War. Disillusionment with the men of 1920, he claimed, drove him to write the novel.[2] But these political overtones, in Maritain's estimation, in no way lessened the artistic merits of the novel.

Sous le soleil de Satan was in a sense a *succès de scandale* in 1926, not so much because it expressed, through fictitious characters, the author's contempt for real statesmen who imposed on the nation the slogans and sentiments of a false patriotism, but because it portrayed the Devil as a living, active, personal force for evil. Abbé Donisson actually meets Satan one night, passing through the fields. A generation of cynics could only respond to such a naive conception of evil with contemptuous smiles; but for Bernanos, evil was a person, "alive and squirming," and he spoke from a conviction of absolute faith. Maritain shared this conviction, and the first edition of *Sous le soleil de Satan* appeared in April 1926 in Maritain's *Roseau d'Or* collection.

Maritain had been anxious about the effect of the novel in certain Catholic circles. Pius XI, following the example of Leo XIII, had shown himself quite favorable to the liberal Catholic camp, and too bold a criticism of the liberal position at the moment when the pope was attempting a *rapprochement* with the Republic might not be well received in Rome. On the other hand, the novel applied the goad unmercifully to the hypocritical consciences of the *bien-pensants*. Bernanos, who enjoyed nothing more than scandalizing these complacent Catholic pharisees, was slashing right and left. Uneasy at the boldness of Bernanos' attack, Maritain suggested certain changes, which Bernanos accepted out of respect for their friendship, and he wrote to Massis about Maritain's fears:

> I just received a letter from Maritain; he has suggested several corrections that I am going to try to make out of love for him. . . . Maritain's affectionate confidence does me a great honor and I will try to return it as best I can.

Nevertheless I find his scruples a bit exaggerated. Undoubtedly God appears in my book as a rather hard taskmaster! So what? What can we say about Him who is found at the root of every one of our sufferings and almost always absent from our joys?

But then, how could I avoid scandalizing certain little effeminate souls? That's a part of my very nature. The blood of the cross frightens them.

Perhaps a single drop of it is enough to redeem them. For my part, I must plunge myself in it completely. Alas! I still haven't begun to work out my salvation with much care and attention![3]

No sooner had the novel appeared than Maritain heard rumors that Bernanos was running the risk of censure in Rome. Maritain communicated his anxiety to Massis, whom he asked to get in touch with Father Garrigou-Lagrange and to pass on to the latter the judgment of Father Gillet, master general of the Dominicans, about the novel. Father Gillet had told Maritain personally how much he would deplore the censure of a novel which he esteemed so highly,[4] and Maritain knew that the opinion of these two men would weigh heavily in Rome. At any rate, the book escaped censure, Bernanos was grateful to Maritain for such efforts in his behalf, and *Sous le soleil de Satan* made such an impression on the literary world that Frédéric Lefèvre considered Bernanos worthy of an interview for his regular column in *La Nouvelle Revue Française*. In answer to a question about intellectual cowardice, Bernanos chose Maritain as an example of intellectual integrity and courage:

In order to take the place due to him [Maritain], besides the visible sign of the highest predestination, he needed that unflagging patience, that kind of heavenly stubbornness which comes to the surface in his eyes like the reflection of another world.[5]

Nevertheless, the beginnings of friendship between the two men did not last long, for within a few months Bernanos' expressions of admiration were to change to vitriolic abuse. When Maritain took a position in favor of Rome against Action Française at the end of the year, Bernanos turned upon him with the full violence of his wrath.

In many ways, Bernanos' attitude toward Action Française, just prior to the condemnation, was very similar to that of Jacques Maritain. In fact, Bernanos' sudden, passionate defense of Action Française in the the face of Rome's fulminations was more unexpected than Maritain's submission. In 1920 Bernanos had already given up his membership in Action Française. He had become disillusioned with Maurras and his tactics, but the fact of his resignation and his reasons for it do not seem to have been widely known at the time. Bernanos was by no means intellectually and spiritually detached from the ideals which had first attracted him to the movement, such as monarchism in politics and anti-Modernism in religion. As a matter of fact, he continued to write for *Action Française* and its sister publications, and he continued on terms of intimacy with friends who maintained active collaboration with Maurras. But he no longer believed in the restoration of French *élite* under the leadership of Maurras, who for reasons of expedience had linked himself with the self-centered conservatism of the moneyed middle class. According to Thomas Molnar, Bernanos held Maurras responsible for Action Française's betrayal of the common people:

> Bernanos accused Maurras precisely of having abandoned the proletariat and sacrificed it to his concept of order; he felt that Maurras respected what was "respectable," that is "useful." He did not attack injustice and lies, but the revolt that injustice and lies call forth. What was particularly abhorrent to Bernanos in Maurras' thought was the attitude implicit in a short social parable, *Les Serviteurs*, which Maurras wrote before the war. In it the god Mercury announces to Crito, Socrates' rich and noble friend who is now in the Elysian fields, that Christ has arrived for the liberation of slaves. When Crito's own slaves hear the "good news" they throw themselves at their master's feet, imploring him not to set them free but to keep them in his service and under his protection.
>
> Bernanos understood what is profoundly immoral in this paternalistic approach, and impractical in it in the modern world which simply does not accept such an attitude.[6]

Likewise, Bernanos had begun to find his membership in Action Française incompatible with his intellectual independence. In a public letter to the editors of *Comoedia* (Sept. 1926), he stated that a certain *"scrupule d'indépendance"* was his reason for resigning from the movement.[7] It was about this time that Maritain had begun to speak of Maurras' *"caporalisme intellectuel."*[8] Not content with simply leaving the movement, Bernanos found it necessary to send Maurras a formal letter of resignation, which he wrote with great care after much thought and consultation.[9] Why did Bernanos feel compelled to write such a letter to a man he had approached only four times in thirty years, if not to make perfectly clear to Maurras the fundamental differences which separated them and the gravity of the errors he found in the movement?

On several occasions during the few months that preceded the public condemnation, Bernanos, like Maritain, called for obedience and proclaimed his willingness to submit to an official decree of the Church — the same filial submission to Rome that Maritain called for in his *Opinion sur Charles Maurras*, which appeared on the same day.[10] In fact, Bernanos wrote a letter to Massis declaring his agreement with Maritain, that what was to be avoided at all costs was a half-obedience unworthy of a Christian.[11] He begged Rome to make an unequivocal and definitive statement to deliver Catholics from the agonies of doubt.[12] One could hardly find a more orthodox expression of the spirit of obedience.

If Bernanos was sincere in these protestations, how is one to reconcile them with the fact that when the pope finally pronounced an unequivocal and definitive judgment, Bernanos took a position directly opposed to Maritain's and obstinately refused to submit to Rome, even while he was attacking Maurras publicly in his books? There is some truth in the explanation offered by Thomas Molnar in his *Bernanos, His Political Thought and Prophecy*, that Bernanos' independent and chivalrous temperament forbade him to accept imposition from however exalted a source, and that he feared that the condemnation of Maurras would encourage the left and open the gates to anarchy.[13] These elements certainly entered in, but they are not a sufficient explanation.

A more fundamental reason for Bernanos' position can be found in his vocation of "prophet," and Molnar hints at such an explanation when he speaks of certain prophetic qualities in Bernanos' style which lessened his effectiveness as a polemicist. He lists such qualities as indignation over the spiritual state of the world; vociferous denunciation of *"les imbéciles"* and the builders of the earthly paradise; indomitable hope, by which he overcame the temptation to despair and which led him to proclaim, in season and out, the road of a radical regeneration; and a deep sense of forgiveness, which forever welcomed his prodigal brother back into the Father's tent[14] — and, one might add, a tendency to see everything in the light of a unified apocalyptic vision of the human condition, in its most essential elements.

These qualities of Bernanos are much more than mere stylistic mannerisms. In a very real sense, in the case of Bernanos, the style is the man. He wrote as a prophet because he *was* a prophet. Charles Plisnier compares him to Savonarola, shouting malediction in the prosperous streets of Florence.[15] He was another furious and inspired Bloy, awakening the Church to its vocation as the spotless Bride of Christ and all men to their vocation to be saints, and exposing the lie, imposture and hypocritical connivance with evil. Mauriac calls him an old molossus with bloodshot eyes, biting at the shins of fat sheep and foolish ewes. In 1946 he wrote of Bernanos: "Atrociously unjust with regard to individuals, he was not so with regard to his times."[16] Charles Plisnier remarks that this characteristic prophetic injustice toward individuals is, in a strange way, the result of his profound love: "This man happens at times to be unjust, for injustice can be a kind of exigence, and exigence is the active form of love."[17]

The excess of Bernanos' vituperation seemed in direct proportion to his compassionate love as a prophet for his people, whom God had sent him to castigate. Against which of his masters or comrades did he not turn, from time to time, with a kind of inspired fury? Whom did he not, in turn, first adore, then burn? Mauriac asks.[18] But he adds that not one of the victims of Bernanos' outrageous treatment harbored a grudge against him, because their relations with Bernanos were "in the nature of an intercession."[19] Bernanos' vocation to be the prophet of his time is probably the most essential element in the uniqueness of this author, and it is this sense of prophetic mission which best explains his paradoxical position on the Roman condemnation of Action Française.

If the Vatican's condemnation was not dictated by political considerations, it was certainly timed by them. It was not surprising that the movement should be condemned — what was surprising was that it had not been condemned much earlier. The reasons given by the Church in 1919 for the condemnation of Sillon applied as well, perhaps even better, to Action Française at that time. And the reasons given for the censure in 1926 were equally evident sixteen years before. The difference was that in 1910 it had not been considered politic to condemn Action Française.

> Unlike the Action Française [writes Eugen Weber] which took pride in its Machiavellian opportunism, the Church could not admit its own. It could not say that it suited its book to do now what might, on moral and doctrinal grounds, have been done before; and it cut a rather pitiable figure under the criticism of unrepentent victims who were able to cite repeated praises of the very thing now suddenly brutally reproved.[20]

In 1926 Bernanos resolved to cry from the housetops the things that could not be said out loud in 1910.

Bernanos' cries of indignation were dictated not by anticlerical hatred but by a profound love of the Church. It was the same love of the Church which had led St. Catherine of Sienna to strike a pope in the face. The public condemnation of Action Française was, to all appearances, timed to give to the French republic assurance of loyalty in ecclesiastical circles. The pope's addition, on his own initiative, of the paper *Action Française* to the list of Maurras' works to go on the Index would result in the destruction of a political movement that could have been perfectly acceptable to the Church once it was purged of Maurrassian errors. Bernanos, resolved to unmask the lie in this connivance of the spiritual with the secular, also wanted to expose the measure of the Church's responsibility, through its tardy *clairvoyance*, for the disobedience of so many Catholics.

Nor would he limit himself to speaking out. When he saw the object of his love and faith compromising her essential spiritual dignity, he seemed to have felt it his personal responsibility to be a sign of contradiction in himself. In protest of the condemnation, he continued to read and to write for the newspaper *Action Française*, even though this meant he would be denied the sacraments of his Church. Likewise, he lectured at meetings and at the Institut de l'Action Française, which Maurras had established. He criticized the movement from time to time during the years when Action Française was under interdict, and sometimes quite violently;[21] however, he insisted that it was only *after* the lifting of the papal ban in 1939 that he began his open and relentless attack.[22] During these thirteen intervening years, he remained without the sacraments. He could have received them

surreptitiously, as did many another stubborn Catholic collaborator, or he could have done so with the connivance of a
priest who was sympathetic to Action Française, who defied the
orders of the pope to refuse the sacraments to anyone who persisted in associating with the movement or reading the paper.
There were many such priests in France. But Bernanos obeyed
this order of the pope. He recognized the spiritual authority of the
pope, although he was protesting what he considered the improp-
er exercise of this authority.

We get some idea from the following of what it cost a man
(for whom *"tout est grâce"*) to be cut off these years from the
channels of grace in his Church:

> The only advantage which remains to me of that so black
> period of my life is to be able today to speak with Maurras
> face to face. Whatever Charles Maurras may say or write
> about me, he will not be, he will never be a stranger to us;
> he holds us too close, he holds us by our very souls. He has
> been, he is, he will be, in this world and in the next, the man
> for whom we saw ourselves deprived of the sacraments,
> threatened with a final agony without a priest. His debt to
> us infinitely surpasses the value of his own person; we will
> never deign to demand anything of him.[23]

The writings of Bernanos during these years give the dis-
tinct impression of being not so much a defense of Maurras as an
attack on the political machinations of the Vatican and of the
"faithful" Catholics who rallied to the defense of the papal position. The attitude of those who obeyed the papal injunction to the
letter, or attempted to justify it in their writings, filled him with
disgust. Among these was Maritain, whom Bernanos had come to
look upon as a great philosopher who could "christianize" the
ideas of Maurras. But Maritain's defense of Rome struck him as a
"desertion" and his admiration turned to bitterness and scorn.

The main source of the myth about the irreconcilable differences between Maritain and Bernanos is a series of letters which
Henri Massis exchanged with Bernanos and with Maritain, which
he quotes at length in his book *Maurras et notre temps*, as well as a
series of private conversations he had with the two authors,
which he reproduces from memory in the same book. It is Massis'
unscrupulous use of these letters and conversations and his tampering with quotations from them (to suit his own purposes) that
give a falsified impression of the rift between Bernanos and Maritain. In the period immediately following the condemnation of

Action Française, it was Maritain who had to be discredited for defending the papal position, and Massis used Bernanos as an authority to do so. Years later, when Bernanos turned against Maurras and his movement openly, it was *his* turn to be discredited. In 1951 Massis did not find it inconsistent to claim, within a few pages of the attack on Maritain in *Maurras et notre temps,* that the judgment of Bernanos was devoid of authority since his reason was forever clouded by the instability of his character and the violence of his passions (pp. 127 – 250). Apparently Bernanos' fulminations against Maritain at the time of the condemnation were the product of calm, clear and collected reasoning whereas his judgments on Mussolini's Ethiopian invasion, Maurras' election to the Academy, the Spanish Civil War, the fall of France, and Vichy — all of which disagreed with those of Massis — were products of passionate bias and psychological instability. The facts indicate that the differences between Bernanos and Maritain were greatly exaggerated.

Maritain and Massis had been close friends for a long time. That Maritain expected Massis, in consideration of a friendship that should have been able to transcend political differences, to reject the untruths and exaggerations in many of Bernanos' attacks on him is clear from a letter he wrote to Massis — and the tone of the letter seems to suggest that Maritain suspected that Massis was closing his eyes to the injustice of these attacks, if not encouraging them:

> I know that your friend Bernanos is also spreading lies about me everywhere. . . . But Bernanos is hawking calumnies that he knows are calumnies. And it is a good thing for you to have your attention called to the quality of some people who claim your friendship. . . . What makes my heart sick, my dear Henri, is the fact that you seem to be more and more involved with them.[24]

Judging from Maritain's remark, Bernanos would seem to have taken part, along with many others, in a concerted effort of vilification. From what I have been able to find in print, Bernanos' part in this campaign must have been limited almost entirely to speech and private correspondence. Strangely enough, Maritain's only apparent source for what Bernanos was "saying in public" and "writing in private" is Massis. In none of the published correspondence or in the *mémoires* of either Maritain or his wife Raïssa is there any discussion of his difficulties with Bernanos.

Bernanos' remarks about Maritain in the public press were confined to an article in *Action Française* and an occasional sarcasm. Such asides continued long after Bernanos began his attack on Action Française and after the positions of Bernanos and Maritain on many political issues had begun to coincide. In 1939 Bernanos wrote in *Nous autres Français:*

> I am perfectly capable . . . of honoring Mr. J. Maritain at the same time that I deplore his effeminate daydreams about the Jews and about democracy, which win him public acclaim at the Théâtre des Ambassadeurs.[25]

In *La Liberté pourquoi faire?* (1951), Bernanos wrote:

> We have known many other literary conversions almost as resounding [as that of Paul Claudel], though often less solid, that of Mr. Cocteau for example, signed by Jacques Maritain (literary conversions, you know, can be signed like the paintings of the masters), or the conversion — carrying the same signature — of that unfortunate Sachs who, for his part, went as far as the seminary and who had his first cassock cut *chez Paquin.*[26]

These remarks are typical of what Bernanos wrote publicly about Maritain, and most of them have no direct connection with Action Française. What Beomanos *said* in public may have been far more violent than what he *wrote* for the public. It is possible that this was also the case with his private speech and private correspondence. Massis' account is filed with quotations from his private correspondence and conversations with Bernanos. The accumulation of bitterly anti-Maritain texts in these few pages (which Massis purports to have culled from Bernanos' private letters and conversations) makes the reader wonder if the rift between Bernanos and Maritain may not have been much deeper than can be imagined from the public writings of the two men. But after careful examination of Massis' use of these texts, the reader begins to woner if the differences were not grossly overstated.

According to Massis, Bernanos decried the "theological jargon" by which Maritain pretended to defend Rome's decree. Bernanos scorned the intellectual meetings at Maritain's home in Meudon, from whose attendants Maritain picked his collaborators for this defense:

What is Maritain getting at? He and his lay brothers, who surround him with their pallid faces, certainly do what they can, that is to say, nothing — unless they go sniveling in the waiting rooms of prelates, stammering *yes* or *no, doubtless* or *perhaps*. . . . I don't give a tinker's damn for their intentions and their scruples! But one thing is certain, my friend, it is not with their unsightly distinctions between the abstract and the concrete that these poor devils, green from fear and from the drying up of all their glands at the thought of losing the support of Msgr. Baudrillart or of being condemned by Jean Giraud, will regain any intellectual authority! . . . I wonder by what disgrace, by what curse the Catholic intelligencia has been so reduced, that in order to instruct its flock, it should find its nourishment among the disciples of Bergson and Cocteau, made up as Thomists! . . . Cocteau, the conversion of Cocteau and his little "fairies" from *Le Boeuf sur le toit;* come now, is this what they call the "Catholic Revival"?[27]

According to another quotation, Bernanos accused Maritain of speaking of morality and politics "in a lingo that mixes the true and the false, to send us all to the devil — let him wallow in it alone!" Concerning Maritain's *Pourquoi Rome a parlé* and *Primauté du spirituel,* Bernanos is quoted as saying:

Ah! I feel so sorry for these new theologians! They confuse *primary* and *priority, prius* and *primum* for they don't even know their Latin any more. . . . Do you mean to tell me that it's up to us to remind Maritain, that great philosopher, of such elementary things? And now poor Jacques has taken it into his head to justify the Pope by his tangled *"distinguos"* between "direct power" and "indirect power," and pretends to teach us *why Rome has spoken!* Maritain had better watch his step. . . . I predict that he as well will have his turn, that he too will end up "condemned," unless of course he turns coat another time! . . . But then this is habitual with him. Ripe for any capitulation, Maritain is ripe for all the honors.[28]

And so on and so on. The accumulation of text upon text within these few pages gives this chapter of Massis' book the ring of historical authenticity; and this is precisely the impression that many readers carry away from Massis' account. Thomas Molnar, for example, who frequently quotes from Massis in his book *Bernanos, His Political Thought and Prophecy,* introduces one of his quotations with the remark that Massis "was well-placed to watch the entire parade of this generation." Or to present a view of Jacques Maritain's relationship with Action Française that contradicts that of Raïssa Maritain, John Hellman, in his *Emmanuel Mounier and the New Catholic Left, 1930 – 1950,* sends his readers to Massis' *Maurras et notre temps.*[29]

However, a careful reading tends to lessen confidence in these pages as an impartial, objective account. From time to time Massis seems to let slip the mask of the calm and impartial peacemaker, who steps down, now and then, from the heights of serene wisdom to patch up or pass judgment on the stupid, childish quarrels between his friends. Behind this mask, one begins to suspect the presence of the talebearer and the sower of discord. For example, after recounting a long and intimate conversation between himself and Maritain, in which confidences were exchanged which one would expect to have been honored with secrecy, Massis wrote:

> When I communicated to Bernanos the consultation I had with Maritain, Bernanos exploded in a terrible laugh that came from the depths of his rancor.[30]

And later he quoted Bernanos:

> But getting back to what Maritain told you about these political and moral situations. . . . [31]

It may well have been Massis' remarks to Maritain about what Bernanos had said or written that occasioned Maritain's reference to the "calumnies" of Bernanos. If it were a question of public calumny, Maritain would almost certainly have defended himself publicly. He was always ready to answer his public critics publicly, and in fact felt a responsibility to do so. Yet his writings contain no reply to any criticism by Bernanos. Even in his *Carnet de notes* and in the *Journal de Raïssa* there is not a single reference to his difficulties with Bernanos. It is very probable that Bernanos' public criticism of Maritain went no further than one article in *Action Française* and such occasional caustic remarks as those in *Nous autres Français* and *La Liberté pourquoi faire?*

If the hint of talebearing on the part of Massis raises some suspicion about the historicity of his account of the rift between his two "friends," the revelations of Albert Béguin discredit not only the historical objectivity and correctness of these pages but even the personal integrity of their author. Albert Béguin, who was a friend of both Bernanos and Maritain, was entrusted by Bernanos with the posthumous publication of his private documents and the texts that were not published before his death. Béguin knew intimately the sources from which Massis compiled his pages on Bernanos: a number of unedited texts, which Béguin published in *Cahier du Rhône* and *Bulletin des "Amis de Bernanos,"* and especially twenty-four letters which Massis received personally from Bernanos and kept in his possession. Béguin never saw the original letters, but had to content himself with a version that Massis copied out for him in longhand.

In his attack on Bernanos and Maritain in *Maurras et notre temps,* Massis made such unprofessional use of these letters that Béguin felt obliged to expose him in an article in *Esprit* entitled "Henri Massis, historien." To defend the reputation of Bernanos, Béguin had to make public certain passages from his copy of Bernanos' private letters to Massis, which Béguin had promised Massis he would not publish before the death of Maurras. Since Massis himself made these letters public while Maurras was still alive, in order to destroy the reputation of Bernanos, Béguin felt released from his promise and morally obliged to make public his version in order to expose Massis' misuse of these documents. He prefaced his use of these letters with the following reservation and judgment:

> Nevertheless [let us suppose] that Massis is more scrupulous in copying than he is in quoting! The use he makes of these twenty-four letters received from Bernanos in the course of their ephemeral intimacy (Aug. 1925 – Nov. 1928) is really stupifying.[32]

Béguin noted that these letters were reduced to more than fifty fragments which were quoted without the slightest concern for their dates, their chronological sequence, or their literal exactness. Often texts from letters that were written months apart were quoted end to end, as if from the same letter. Of the fifty fragments, twenty were either cited inexactly, contained interpolations by Massis, or were applied to an object to which the original had no application whatever. The purpose of Béguin's article was to defend Bernanos; however, in a footnote he remarked: "I am convinced that his procedure is the same in whatever concerns Maritain."[33] Béguin cited several cases in which the misused texts twisted the rift between Bernanos and Maritain out of proportion. For example:

> In a letter of November, 1928, speaking of a chapter of *Joy* on which he was working, Bernanos writes: "I would have torn out my hair, my tongue and everything else, I still couldn't finish in two or three days the dialogue I had begun." According to Massis, p. 211, at the end of a long harangue against Maritain which Bernanos is supposed to have declaimed in 1926, the reader sees this pseudo-citation stand out in italics: " 'It is enough to make me tear out my hair, my tongue and everything else,' he cried, fuming with rage."[34]

Béguin found such tampering with texts "difficult to excuse by inadvertence." Massis' conduct could not be explained solely by a sense of impunity from exposure for his liberties due to the fact that these texts were unavailable to the public, for what Béguin called his "congenital incapacity to quote exactly" extends even to quotations from the best-known works of Bernanos.[35]

If Béguin found it difficult to excuse by forgetfulness or inadvertence the misuse of the texts he noted in his article, what kind of judgment would he have passed on the following case? In a passage quoted above, from *Maurras et notre temps*, we find that Maritain and his friends at Meudon "go sniveling in the waiting rooms of prelates, stammering *yes* or *no, doubtless* or *perhaps* . . . green from fear and from the drying up of all their glands at the thought of losing the support of Msgr. Baudrillart" (p. 211). These words are cited, without italics (Massis' usual way of indicating that he is quoting), from what purports to be, according to Massis, a letter or conversation of 1926. What a surprise it is to pick up *Nous autres Français*, after reading *Maurras et notre temps*, and find that these words (inexactly quoted, as is so often the case) were written not in 1926 but in 1939, and above all to find that this telling sarcasm was directed in its original context, not against Maritain but against — of all people — Massis himself. Here is what Bernanos actually wrote:

> Then M. H. Massis, green from anguish and from the drying up of all his glands at the thought of losing the royalist subscribers to *La Revue Universelle*, went sniveling in the waiting-rooms of prelates, stammering *yes* or *no, doubtless* or *perhaps*.[36]

It is inconceivable that Massis could have forgotten that he himself was the target of these cutting words. If he quoted them from memory in 1951, twelve years after they were written, he may be excused for having forgotten that Bernanos used *angoisse* instead of *peur*, but not for having forgotten that the words were directed at Massis and not at Maritain. And if he was not quoting from memory, but had the book at hand for reference, he could not have missed "M. H. Massis" as the subject of the sentence he was "quoting." No, it was hardly a matter of inadvertence; there was method in Massis' madness.

> What is of utmost importance to Massis [wrote Béguin] is to give the impression that after 1926, Bernanos [and Maritain too, I might add] was no longer capable of writing anything sensible.[37]

These two men had to be discredited and their intellectual integrity called into public question at all costs *"par tous les moyens"* — a slogan which Massis seems to have learned well from his master Maurras. In 1951, when Massis' book appeared, Maurras was in prison, condemned by the French government (whether justly or unjustly is not clear) for complicity with the enemy during the occupation. Massis' master's reputation had to be restored, even if the reputation of others had to be unjustly destroyed in the process.

In the 1971 publication of Bernanos' unedited correspondence are a number of letters he wrote during these crisis years to both Massis and Maritain which give a far different impression from the one left by Massis. In November 1926, Bernanos wrote a letter to Massis expressing his fear that, out of zeal for the strict ordering and purity of doctrine, Maritain, who had recently made public his reservations about Maurras, might compromise the possibility of effective political action for all of them.[38] A few days later he wrote again to Massis, referring to Maritain as one of "the specialists in duty whom the Pope's message has put in a state of effervescence" and taxing Maritain for his hypocritical self-righteousness in urging on others the submissive obedience which he accorded the pope's condemnation.

Bernanos wrote of his fear of doing harm to the innocent consciences of simple Christians by counseling defiance because of Rome's overstepping the bounds of its authority, but, he said, such a public outcry from a multitude of outraged Catholics would have two desired results. First, it would teach Rome the limits of its right to interfere in national politics, and second, it would make Catholics aware of their considerable independent force in Action Française. It would also make clear the indispensable distinctions that Maritain had called for and thus bring about the necessary spiritual renewal of which Maritain had said Action Française was much in need.

> I have tried, according to my paltry means, to create a scandal, just as in certain diseases a doctor encourages fever. I had wanted, at any cost, to draw Catholics out of their intolerable silence. From the moment the Pope spoke, Maurras should have stepped into the background, or rather (I express myself badly) it should have been we alone who made ourselves heard. Our cries of anger and pain would doubtless have brought about some clarifications, some indispensable precisions. . . . The multitude of Catholics of Action Française would then have become conscious of themselves as an independent force, and the theoretical project of Maritain would have become a living reality. This could have been the beginning of a spiritual renewal that Action Française certainly needed, for that organization suffers from a deplorable lack of an interior life. And here we are back again to *"politiques d'abord"!*[39]

Between the brochure *Une Opinion sur Charles Maurras et le devoir des Catholiques* of 1926 and the publication of *Primauté du spirituel* in 1927, Maritain's attitude toward Action Française evolved considerably and he felt obliged to break with Massis and the directors of *La Revue Universelle.* For the 1927 publication of *Pourquoi Rome a parlé,* Maritain also wrote a chapter entitled "Le Sens de la condamnation." Bernanos reacted to these 1927 publications with controlled exasperation. On April 21, 1928, he wrote to Maritain in a rage:

> . . . What bullshit!
>   For a long time I have wanted to say this to you: a wager like yours could be made only by a saint. Our souls have already paid for a good part of your illusions. Your work will pay for the rest. It has already been knocked to the ground.
>   As for me, you know, I am nothing but a poor sinner, so sad and so ugly that Our Savior alone has the courage to look at me; but what I begrudge you is that you don't love men. No! You don't love them! . . .

The enthusiastic cries of a small number of esthetes and epileptic Jews are of no avail. . . . You speak well, you speak too well, you speak like the friends of Job . . . with useless palinodes you have dishonored the very notion of obedience and the humble submission of hearts.[40]

With characteristic gentleness, Maritain replied (Apr. 27, 1928):

And if after all, my dear Bernanos, I were there in the name of Our Lord Jesus Christ to testify in His behalf? If it were out of love for Him and for *you* that I do what I am doing? Can you at least imagine this hypothesis, and then picture for yourself what there would be of evil, if such is the case, in your manner of treating me? Because it is possible, after all, that you may be mistaken.

That I am a very poor instrument I know better than you. But it is not the instrument we must consider, but rather Him who moves it.

In truth, as you mistreat me I feel that my friendship for you is taking on new life and sensitivity. Are you praying for me? Do you really wish me *well?* Examine your heart, Bernanos. Is it not filled with disdain? There are more difficult things. If my work is on the ground, as you say it is, you must believe that I love God more than my work. You have constructed for yourself a purely fictitious image of me — absurd, specious and lying. Be careful that in spreading this phantom image in the minds of our friends, you do not lay upon him whom it pictures a heavy weight of injustice that you will regret later on.

For the moment you are led and tortured by the spirit of the world. How can you not recognize the ways of this world in the hateful and lying hypocrisy of Action Française?

It is not a question of politics, or of election, or of clericalism, or of human conniving. It is a question of the Gospel, of the fullness of Catholic truth to which the Vicar of Christ calls back his children. If we want to be with Jesus, we should look to Jesus and to him who teaches us in His name. For the rest it is a question of worldly prestige.

Believe in my affection for you in the Lord Jesus.

JACQUES MARITAIN

If you want to see me I am at your disposition. For my part, I would be happy to see you.[41]

Bernanos replied a few days later (May 2), asking Maritain what made him think he had received the "mission" to speak to Catholics:

> I let Another than myself be the judge of your intentions. If you are here, as you say you are in behalf of Our Lord Jesus Christ, I have no way of knowing, and He cannot hold my ignorance against me. For He deigned to furnish proofs of His mission, and He permitted His saints to give proofs of theirs. Where are your proofs? You haven't received the slightest hierarchical delegation of authority.
>
> . . . The role of volunteer justiciary, or volunteer executor, perhaps does not become you as much as you suppose.
>
> And it seems to me that I could prove it to you.
>
> I love you with all my heart. I ought to love you more than anyone in the world, because no one in the world has done me more harm than you.[42]

During the following months Bernanos' anger mounted, and in August 1928, in a letter to Maurice Bourdel, he referred to Maritain as *"Jacques de la lune"* (moonstruck Jacques). It is interesting to note that during this period, in the letters he wrote to Massis, Bernanos did not make a single reference to Maritain. By the end of the year, Bernanos could control his exasperation no longer, and on November 15 he published in *Action Française* a vitriolic and insulting article about Maritain which resulted in a complete break between the two. The rupture continued until March 1930, when the death of Bernanos' mother became the occasion for bringing them back together. Bernanos sent an announcement of his mother's death to the Maritains, and since Jacques was absent at the time, his wife Raïssa, who had always been close to Bernanos, sent a short message of condolence. Bernanos wrote back an indignant letter, asking how it was possible for "friends" to send only a card in such circumstances. Raïssa then sent him the following letter.

April 4, 1930

Sir,

If the card I sent you in the absence of Jacques caused you pain, I am infinitely sorry. But could I possibly have thought that you would wish that someone whom you had publicly accused of teaching to his friends the science and the delights of mortal sin partake of your sorrow? My first reaction was to write you; but then I said to myself that someone who has not ceased to misconstrue all the intentions of Jacques could not do otherwise than receive coldly any expression of friendship from us. And so, to what seemed to me a secretary's error, I answered with a conventional formula of condolence. That this formula was ridiculous, and I too who sent it, is of no importance. If I write you today, it is because at the end of a cold letter you ask Jacques to pray for you. This has moved me deeply. Believe me, sir, we have lost a friend whom we have not ceased to love. All the pain is ours.

RAISSA MARITAIN[43]

According to Jean Murray, Bernanos replied with a very beautiful letter — unfortunately lost — by which the friendship with Jacques and Raïssa Maritain was definitively renewed.

A letter of August 7, 1930, shows the sincerity, even tenderness, of this renewed friendship, and perhaps a bit of the regret Bernanos felt for having treated Maritain so harshly. He excused himself for having left two of Maritain's recent letters unanswered, and he asked a favor:

My dear Maritain,

You have perhaps learned from the newspapers of the death of Abbé Sudre, killed in the mountains last month. I would like . . . I would be pleased if you would write a simple little note to Jacques Sudre. . . . I realize that you most probably have never met this *"frère Jacques"* and that my request, most certainly indiscreet, is doubtless ridiculous as well. But André loved you *very much.* He even defended you in front of me (and against me too) to the ultimate limit of possibility (or at least what he believed to be such. Don't be angry!) So it seems to me that this little note of condolence that you may write to his twin brother — who is as like him as his shadow — it is the Abbé who will receive it.

Do, naturally, as seems best to you. Naturally, too, I will speak of this to no one.

Excuse me for not having answered your two letters. I was too sick. It seems to me that you do not know me very well. But that's what they all say. And then I'm not so sure, after all, that I know any more than you about this same subject. So it seems to me best for us to put up with each other such as we are, patiently, or even joyously (for we both have our comic sides) waiting to be covered by God's gentle mercy.

Give my best and very particular respects to Madame Maritain, with my affectionate regret for sometimes causing her pain.

And be good enough to think of me in God's kindly presence.

G. BERNANOS[44]

How different an impression these letters of Bernanos leave from the one left by Massis.

What Maritian had said in the late twenties about Maurras and Action Française had been correct, and during the early thirties Bernanos came more and more to realize it; after 1939 he began to say so vociferously. The lifting of the papal ban on Action Française made the prophetic protest of Bernanos' continuing external adhesion to the movement and of his refraining from open criticism quite pointless. It was the political machinations of ecclesiastical diplomats, who thought they could further the spiritual interests of the Church through involvement in partisan politics, that Bernanos had been attacking until 1939. Bernanos remained away from the sacraments and under the condemnation of the Church for thirteen years as a symbolic and prophetic protest. In the thirties the tactic of *rapprochement* with the Republic was no longer in order under the new conservative Pope Pius XII. With the menace of communism looming on the horizon, it was thought that the interests of the Church could best be served by a *rapprochement* with the right, even in its extremest forms in the totalitarian states. Bernanos wrote in 1939:

> Doubtless I have no right to either approve or condemn those in the Church who believe themselves clever enough to make off with the pea in the totalitarian shell game, as they boasted of doing recently in the shell game of the democratic republic.[45]

He could now continue his protest against *"les gens de l'Eglise"* and, at the same time, give vent to the criticism of Action Française that he had been stifling for years. Immediately he began to cry aloud what he had been thinking and suggesting since 1928. His criticism was all the more explosive, perhaps, because he had forced himself to suppress it as long as the papal ban had been in effect, and perhaps too, because Maurras and Massis had come to represent for him (as Béguin suggests at the end of his article in *Esprit*) that evilest of dragons, against which Bernanos forever lowered his lance, and whose services Massis used so unscrupulously in his battle against his former friends: *le mensonge* (the lie).

The reasons Bernanos gave for attacking Maurras and Action Française were surprisingly similar to the reasons given by Maritain for the Vatican condemnation of 1926. One could easily mistake his calmer passages of criticism for quotations from Maritain's *Pourquoi Rome a parlé*.[46] But Bernanos had never really said that the Church was wrong; he had simply accused the Church of the gravest of sins, according to T. S. Eliot: doing the right thing for the wrong reason. One could easily arrange parallel quotations from Maritain and Bernanos concerning the intellectual dictatorship of Maurras; the subordination of religion (and everything else, for that matter) to political objectives; the need for a new economic order, based on social justice; or the defense of the proletariat. Maritain and Bernanos agreed in almost every detail in their judgments of Maurras and Action Française; the only difference was in the tone of their criticism. Maritain made his points frankly and firmly, but with gentleness and discretion. Bernanos, swinging the two-edged sword of sarcasm and irony with complete abandon, slashed through every chink in the enemy's armor, and into the gaping wounds poured the vitriol of derision and scorn.

This similarity of outlook extended far beyond the personality of Maurras and his political movement. Both recognized their basic accord, for even though the bitterness of the three or four years that followed the condemnation of Action Française made it impossible for them to resume the burgeoning friendship of the years of *Sous le soleil de Satan*, Bernanos and Maritain did not hesitate to quote one another from time to time to support their positions on public matters, particularly during the Second World War.

The fact that the two men reacted so differently to the condemnation in 1926 does nothing to destroy their basic agreement. Maritain saw in the condemnation an expression of the will of God. In becoming a Catholic he had accepted the Church, however weak and fallible she might be in her members, as the means that God had chosen to communicate infallibly to man his inscrutable divine will. He accepted the fact, agonizing as it may have been at times, that "God writes straight with crooked lines." So Maritain submitted to the papal decree with anguished obedience. Bernanos accepted this proverb as readily as Maritain, but he refused to ignore the fact that the lines were crooked. If they were crooked, it was not God's doing. It was therefore a matter of honor to put the blame for the crooks in God's handwriting where they belonged. For this reason, Bernanos revolted against the papal decree with prophetic indignation. Whose position was the better one?

Words which he wrote to Massis seem to suggest that Bernanos feared, even before the condemnation, that the course was fraught with grave dangers:

> I am far more profoundly disturbed than you think by this frightful and stupid preaching, this sort of farce in which, nevertheless, *God actually* plays a role, even though we cannot clearly distinguish Him among the abject troupe of players who smirk at us and spit in our faces. Suppose one of our blows should happen to fall on His bleeding Face!
>
> Tell Maritain again and again that I love him. A "negative" obedience is certainly unworthy of us. It leaves too much bitterness in the heart, it does *too much harm* to be really blessed. But then if the evident injustice of the Archbishop of Bordeaux belongs, such as it is, to the plan of Divine Providence, wasn't our witnessing in behalf of this great soul [Maurras] that has been crushed likewise in the plans of God? I have a certain right to present this objection, I who never had for Maurras any more than an admiration void of any tenderness, as you well know. Alas! We are not monks . . . and the line between submission and cowardly retreat, between the heroic solution and the lazy one, is diabolically uncertain.[47]

Massis, of course, quoted only the first paragraph of this letter in his *Maurras et notre temps*. To quote the whole would not have helped his campaign to discredit Maritain. A few lines in *Nous autres Français* seem to hint that, after thirteen years without the sacraments, Bernanos may have come to think that perhaps Maritain had chosen the better part:

> What a tragic mistake [he said of those who refused to submit to Rome], of which God will be the judge, to have

opposed to one another what no French heart could ever disjoin, obedience and honor. And in the land of Corneille! . . .
I was one of this group, I was one of them.[48]

Charles Plisnier says that Bernanos "in disobeying the Church in his time, did a service to the eternal Church."[49] Whether Maritain compromised his honor in the service of obedience, or whether Bernanos compromised his obedience to God's will in the service of his own honor and God's honor, must be left to the judgment of someone who can scrutinize with certitude the labyrinthine ways of the human heart.

The break of Maritain and, later, of Bernanos with Action Française merely confirmed in each case what might have been expected from so disparate a relationship. Action Française had always borne the stamp of Maurras' personality and ideas, and the connection of either Maritain or Bernanos with the movement was essentially incongruous. Thomas Molnar says of Bernanos:

> With the usual idealism of generous men, Bernanos had attributed the *values* he believed in and the *qualities* he possessed to the Action Française (in a way like the left-wing idealists who lent the Communist Party their own good intentions until some eye-opening experience.[50]

The same can be said for Maritain. In neither case was there a real attachment to the conceptual universe of Maurras, much less to the practical policies that Maurras advocated and justified, as the troubled decade of the thirties was to prove.

CHAPTER 3

The Decade of Manifestos

THE CRISIS OF ACTION FRANÇAISE, as we have seen, forced Maritain to do some long overdue soul searching about his philosophical indifference to the political realities of life. His political conscience, which had been active during his student days at the Sorbonne but which seemed to have lain dormant during the early years of his philosophical career, was awakened with a jolt. He could not escape his responsibility, either as a philosopher or as a Christian, to take a definite public stand on certain political events, particularly where a question of conscience was involved, and the troubled years of the thirties gave him ample opportunity to exercise this responsibility.

Maritain never completely abandoned the heights of pure speculation. During these years he published some of his most technical philosophical works (*Les Degrés du savoir* and *Le Songe de Descartes*, 1932; *Sept leçons sur l'être et les premiers principes de la raison spéculative*, 1934; *La Philosophie de la nature* and *Science et sagesse*, 1935; *Quatre Essais sur l'esprit dans sa condition charnelle*, 1939). Nevertheless, he turned more and more to the immediate problems of the day. Although the subjects of the Sunday talks at Meudon continued for the most part to treat speculative and "esoteric" problems, the discussions and conversations that followed turned inevitably to the agonizing political turmoil of those years. In 1935, in his *Lettre sur l'indépendance*, Maritain wrote of the duty he felt, as a philosopher, to concern himself with the pressing problems of public life:

> . . . a writer whose essential work is foreign to politics cannot, in the midst of a serious crisis, withdraw into that essential work and close his eyes to the anguish of men in the City. It seems to me that such an obligation concerns the philosopher in a very special way. For there exists not only a speculative philosophy but a practical philosophy as well;

and I realize that it must go down to that final point where philosophical knowledge turns to action.[1]

His responsibility as a Christian, which he shared with many other writers — particularly those who in large numbers frequented his house at Meudon — obliged him to a "more real . . . a more profound commitment."[2]

In print, the first fruits of Maritain's reflection on the world situation and of the lively, even violent, discussions at Meudon appeared in 1933 in his book *Du régime temporel et de la liberté.* Here Maritain discussed such topics as the philosophical basis of freedom, the historical relation between religion and culture, the problem of means in political action, the institution of private property and Gandhi's doctrine of passive resistance. The chapter "Religion et culture" had already appeared as an article in the January issue of *Esprit,* a review which Emmanuel Mounier had founded in October 1932 with Maritain's advice and help.

Mounier was one of the most active participants in the Cercle Thomiste.[3] He frequented the meetings at Meudon long before the founding of *Esprit,* for in the entry for December 17, 1928, in his *Entretiens,* Mounier implies that he had already participated in a number of these meetings.

During these years and into the early thirties, Maritain was in the process of reconverting his political philosophy, divesting it of all the antidemocratic incrustations of the years immediately following his conversion to Catholicism, when he imprudently and naively let his political orientation be formed by his conservative spiritual director, Father Clérissac. His political philosophy, changing in both content and accent, became more and more open to the misery and anguish that troubled the contemporary world. And yet he became almost fanatically scrupulous about making those precious and, for him, fundamental distinctions that he had neglected so culpably during the days of his association with Action Française and *La Revue Universelle.* During these years, according to Etienne Borne, Maritain was in an "astonishing state of intellectual grace . . . and he became for many a master of intellectual rigor and personal commitment, but in a spirit that remained more prophetic than political, all of which accorded perfectly with what was still, in Mounier's case, in a state of desire and anticipation."[4]

So the young Mounier became an enthusiastic *habitué* of the Cercle Thomiste. Here he found refuge from the hostility of the Sorbonne, where he encountered adamant opposition to the subjects he proposed for his doctoral thesis. He seemed to fall so completely under the spell of his new mentor at Meudon that the mentor of his younger days, Jacques Chevalier, who was metaphysically and politically allergic to Maritain, even contemplated bringing Maritain to court for contributing to the delinquency of a disciple (*"détournement d'un disciple"*).[5]

During 1932, private property and its relation to labor and to the dignity of the human person were frequent topics of discussion at the Sunday meetings at Meudon, and Mounier, with Etienne Borne and Father Riquet, gave conferences and led discussions on these topics. Maritain's affection for and interest in the lively young Mounier, the latter's deference and respect for his new mentor and the collaboration of the two were so well known that, in his reporting, Paul Archambault began to pronounce the names of Mounier and Maritain as one word, just as he had with "Massis/Maritain" in the early twenties. In his series *Roseau d'Or*, Maritain published a collective work of Péguy for which Mounier furnished the preface and an essay entitled "La Vision des hommes et du monde." Maritain had known Péguy too intimately not to be particularly interested in this book and to supervise its publication very carefully, and the conversations and letters about these days created very close ties between Maritain and Mounier.

It was natural, then, that Mounier should speak to Maritain about the review he contemplated founding with his friend Georges Izard, one of the collaborators for the book on Péguy. Maritain offered his experience and advice. He also helped provide financial backing; he was instrumental in procuring free office space and secretarial service, as well as inexpensive printing, from his publisher, Desclée de Brouwer; and he introduced Mounier to an extensive group of writers, of established reputation and of the new generation, whose collaboration in *Esprit* Mounier could never have obtained alone.

The rightist press reacted immediately and violently to the appearance of *Esprit*. Maritain and Mounier were labeled *"chrétiens rouges,"* and it was not long before the new review (as in the case of *Sept*) was denounced to the scrutinizing ecclesiastical vigilantes. Under pressure from the papal nuncio, Cardinal Verdier noted official misgivings and asked for a report. Maritain, familiar with the ecclesiastical *milieux* and the intricacies of their internal power struggles, came immediately to Mounier's assistance with advice and action and helped him draw up the report for Cardinal Verdier. The crisis passed, but scarcely a month after the investigation, Mounier was informed that, due to a reorganization of the publishing house, Desclée de Brouwer could no longer furnish office space and secretarial help. Mounier suspected some connection with the investigation. In his *Entretiens* (June 30, 1933) he wrote: "Have they used [Van der Meer's] departure as a pretext for getting rid of a troublesome tenant? Van der Meer insists it is not so, and certainly it's not his doing. But this bourgeois timidity. . . . " This was the end, he thought. To defray the expenses of the essential services that were now suddenly eliminated, he needed a new source of income; so he asked Maritain to help him find a job to keep *Esprit* financially afloat.[6]

The fundamental positions of Mounier and Maritain were the same; together, they protested the same injustices, the same violations of political rights. To the political and economic upheavals of the thirties, both had the same reactions, and they signed a number of the manifestos that appeared so regularly during those years. From Toronto, where he was teaching at the Mediaeval Institute during the spring semester of 1933, Maritain wrote enthusiastically of a group of young students, a good number of them Americans, who were particularly concerned with the social and economic problems of the day. He even spoke of the possibility of publishing an American edition of *Esprit:*

> The same problems have to be confronted everywhere and collaboration between your groups in France and American young people (especially young American Catholics) could have real importance for the future. . . . Some kind of *entente* with *Esprit* seems most desirable; yesterday evening there was even question of publishing an *American edition* of this *international review!* I do not know how you envisage the publication of foreign editions of the review; I said simply that from my point of view there would have to be a common basis obtained, for example, by the translation of a number of French articles — and then a special collaboration to treat the particular problems and current events of the country involved. . . . I am very happy that my sojourn in Toronto may turn out to be the occasion for an American extension of *Esprit.*[7]

But for all the signs of sympathy and unity, Maritain's support of Mounier was not without a certain uneasy reserve. In the very letter in which he recommended extension of *Esprit* to the New World, he included this warning:

The times are difficult and each day I realize more and more the importance of the seed that it is your mission to plant and to bring to life. Be very, very prudent in all that touches *doctrinal* matters; it is here that your enemies seek to find you at fault and to denounce you.

From the days of collaboration on publication of the collective work on Péguy, Maritain was disquieted by Mounier's lack of a traditional, structured theological and philosophical formation. He did not seem to take theology seriously enough. John Hellman remarks that "Maritain, in singling out faults in Péguy, hit on certain tendencies in Mounier: the personification of ideologies in individuals, the abandonment of any conception of absolute truth among conflicting philosophies, the respect for all systems based on strong intuitional conviction." Mounier evidently had not divested himself of the Bergsonism of his long apprenticeship to Jacques Chevalier. "After six years of tenderminded spiritual direction Maritain's whip-like intellect was bracing."[8]

Though deeply religious and firmly convinced that a personal spiritual revolution was a necessary basis for any just and efficacious social revolution, Mounier was determined to downplay the Catholic and spiritual orientation of the new review. He consistently refused to give any evidence, either on the format of *Esprit*, in its statement of policy, or in its programs of publication, of any connection with Catholic teaching. Though the majority of contributors came from the Cercle Thomiste, or were otherwise Catholic writers with an established reputation for orthodoxy, Mounier welcomed uncritically, and without distinction, contributions from writers of all religious and political persuasions, with the strong "intuitional conviction" that men of "good will," in spite of serious philosophical and theological differences — even in spite of grave disagreements over the acceptability of means to be employed — could work together for the achievement of the "new Renaissance." Maritain found this vague ecumenicism naive and foolishly optimistic. He feared a misunderstanding similar to the one regarding his association with Action Française because of his collaboration on *La Revue Universelle*. In response to a short paragraph in the November issue of *Temps*, which contained such a misunderstanding, a notice appeared in *Esprit* (Dec. 1932), under the signature of one of Mounier's collaborators, affirming the mutual independence of Maritain and *Esprit*.[9]

Maritain was

> particularly sensitive to the two meanings, spiritual and
> political, of the word revolution and his friendship became
> all the more watchful, worried and scrutatory of the
> slightest iota, as he had just succeeded in breaking with that
> politico-religious grouping whose idea of order, common to
> both Thomism and Maurrassism, was offered as a justifying
> reason; and now he feared to compromise the freedom of the
> spiritual, so recently achieved, by being linked to other
> covert groups, whose justification this time was the idea of
> revolution.[10]

Maritain was particularly troubled by Mounier's collaboration with two groups that contributed regularly to *Esprit*, and had
even participated in drawing up the statement of its policies and
positions. One was Ordre Nouveau, the other La Troisième Force.
Ordre Nouveau was a French equivalent to the "Black Front," an
ultrarevolutionary group of National Socialists who had been ex-
pelled from the party by Hitler. One of the leaders of Ordre
Nouveau was Mounier's friend Alexandre Marc, who, when he
heard about the project of *Esprit*, proposed a merger with the new
review. He was given an office across from Mounier's at the publisher Desclée de Brouwer, and helped particularly with the review's international development. According to John Hellman,
Marc thought that *Esprit* would be merely a sort of literary organ
for Ordre Nouveau.[11] The second edition of *Esprit* contained an
article by Marc on "revolutionary federalism" and the new order.
Maritain feared Mounier's close association with such self-styled
revolutionaries, who had no religious or doctrinal basis to direct
and control their revolutionary activities. He wrote to Mounier:

> It is my deep friendship for you that urges me to put you on
> guard against what may risk leading your work astray. I
> continue to fear that there is something dangerous and
> equivocal at the origin of the review concerning your posi-
> tion on Catholicism. . . . You are not publishing a *neutral*
> review. And you are lost if you permit, under one pretext or
> another, the slightest germ of neutrality . . . to take root in
> you. Your only true strength . . . is the Faith and the Gospel.
> You must make this evident; you must make this known,
> and you have to be able to say this. . . . Let me convince you
> that the question, God or atheism, creates an inevitable

parting of the waters. Any common action whatever must one day stumble over this question. It will then be necessary either to break with the atheists one hoped to lead into the fold, or else to betray God, as the people at Action Française did. This is why it is of capital importance to avoid all equivocation from the very beginning.[12]

Mounier sent a sample of Marc's "Personalism," in an article submitted to *Esprit* by Arnaud Dandieu, another member of Ordre Nouveau, to Maritain for criticism. Maritain returned the manuscript promptly and firmly rejected both its content and its fascist tone:

If I were in your shoes I would not publish it. . . . It goes against all your most cherished values and the little truth it contains would be the source of numberless errors and confusion. One does not have the right to confuse souls. And then that goose-stepping philosophy. Such a tone is impossible.

Maritain then asked Mounier to publish his article "Religion et Culture" one issue earlier than had been agreed, to help set the tone of *Esprit* as soon as possible, and he insisted that before he contribute his article to the issue devoted to the *"rupture avec le monde bourgeois,"* he be permitted to read, in advance, all the articles that would make up the issue, so that he might know in what company he would be found. "On these conditions alone will I be able to collaborate. . . . These things are too serious to be taken lightly.[13]

Mounier accepted the criticism and the conditions, but he bridled a bit at what he considered punctilious scrupulosity over doctrinal matters. On November 5, 1932, he noted in his *Entretiens:*

A letter from Maritain (about number 2). . . . In general this was his complaint: he had counted on my loyalty. We are betraying our mission by toadying up to revolutionaries, etc. . . . My heart tells me he is completely right. We must proclaim Christ right from the start. I should leave my friends, rather than . . . but he is thinking like a hermit. . . . We are involved in a temporal work, for God's sake, and we know we have to draw our public from all quarters. To flaunt our Catholicism would discredit us in the eyes of a great number as long as we have not furnished proof that we can be at one and the same time both integrally Catholic and sincerely revolutionary.

A few days later he noted (*Entretiens;* Nov. 9, 1932):

> Number 2 displeased him very much not only because of the summary tone of the article from Ordre Nouveau, but also because the idea of Revolution seems to become the primary value of the *ensemble* of our collaborators (and it is true that we let ourselves be carried away a bit). He is afraid that thus being carried away by one value and remaining silent about the others, because of tactical scruples, the Christian and spiritual values, which alone animate our work, are left to waste away in our souls and in our action.
>
> This finds more than a certain resonance in my soul; it is the very source of my vocation.

The second group of collaborators at *Esprit*, which deeply disturbed Maritain, was the "Third Force," a strange, activist fascist movement with extreme leftist tendencies, situated between capitalism and communism. Georges Izard, a collaborator of Mounier's for the book on Péguy, was director and had a regular column in *Esprit* called "Chroniques de la Troisième Force." Maritain expressed his apprehension about the Third Force on frequent occasions and sent Mounier a long letter with seven recommendations to be followed in order to assure the independence of *Esprit*. Since Izard was one of the directors of the review (with Marc of Ordre Nouveau), Maritain in his final recommendation suggested that

> above all you will have to place on your editorial board someone of your age who will represent, not the point of view of the economy, or the revolution, or of some more or less vague spirituality, but the point of view of philosophical and theological rigor.[14]

Maritain suggested three names: Jacques de Monléon, Etienne Borne and Olivier Lacombe.

After consulting Izard, Mounier agreed sufficiently to all the recommendations to satisfy Maritain, and after publication of the "Programme pour 1933" in late December, in which the readers were assured that *Esprit* was the party of the Spirit before it was the party of the revolution, whose primary value was not the revolution, Maritain seemed appeased. However, when the Third

Force joined Gaston Bergery's Common Front against Fascism, a militant ultraleftist anti-Communist organization that sought to draw all the non-Communist left into itself, Mounier's difficulties with Maritain were aggravated. The situation became intolerable for Maritain when, in the seventh edition of *Esprit* (May 1933), Izard's "Chroniques" concluded with the following paragraph:

> Such is the Third Force. It represents the only movement integrally critical of Capitalism. It rejects Fascism as a consolidation of Capitalism and an enslavement to Statism. It is a new deal. It will perhaps at first undertake a collectivist revolution along with Communism, but this revolution will be a simple destruction, an elimination of profiteers. Later it will undertake the Personalist Revolution; and this revolution will be the true one, the building of a new world founded on the personal development of each man.

Maritain's reaction was immediate and vigorous:

> That paragraph from the "Chroniques de la Troisième Force" is completely intolerable. You should not have let that get by you. Perfect "Kerenskyist" foolishness. To carry out a revolution in two stages, first "collectivist" with the Communists, and later "personalist" is idiotic, and is to betray the spiritual values whose defense those young people have taken on as their mission. It is only too clear that between the first and the second stages they will be neatly eliminated — those at least who will not switch joyfully over to Communism. . . .
>
> Here is an equivocation that cannot, must not continue. This Third Force . . . in spite of its good intentions is nothing but Force 2½ which makes use of the prestige of the Communist Revolution, all the while believing it is fighting independently. This was evident from the beginning when it spoke of accepting the Marxist critique: as if the principles of the solution were not already involved in the critique! They want the revolution to succeed; immediately the old betrayal denounced by Péguy begins to function, the betrayal of the "mystique" of the spiritual revolution by the politicians of that revolution.
>
>   . . . in such a case your duty is to break cleanly and immediately. Otherwise you expose yourself to bitter regrets, and your conscience will reproach you one day with

having surrendered through weakness what you have the duty to defend. It is before God that I speak to you of these matters, my dear Emmanuel. . . .

I will not always be able to send you my *"pneus"* [intra-Paris telegrams], nor write you a long letter like this one. I am a little weary of these "remonstrances" which my friendship obliges me to send you, my dear Emmanuel, and which you receive, I know, with equal friendship. I appeal to your courage, to your sense of responsibility. . . . Everything depends on you, on your firmness and your love of truth. You must swear to yourself never to let truth be offended in your review; this will require of you the very burdensome task of a scrupulous and severe editing of each article.[15]

Along with this letter Maritain sent another very formal one, addressed to *"Cher Monsieur"* instead of *"Mon cher Emmanuel,"* which he told Mounier he felt conscience bound to publish in *Esprit* to avoid any equivocation about his connection with the Third Force. Maritain demanded that Mounier break immediately with Izard and his movement and suppress the regular column "Chroniques." Mounier could report the activities of the Third Force, but only by way of information. If Mounier did not comply, then Maritain felt that he himself must publicly break with *Esprit:*

. . . in such a case it is my duty to break off immediately. As far as I am concerned, I insist on indicating to you my complete rejection of a demagogy that threatens to spoil pitifully the important work of renovation undertaken by *Esprit*.[16]

Publication of such a letter by the most prominent liberal Catholic layman of the day, whose unimpeachable orthodoxy gave viability to the new Catholic left, would be tantamount to a deathblow at any time, but now, at the height of the investigation by the cardinal-archbishop of Paris for the papal nuncio, it would certainly entail the immediate suppression of *Esprit.* Mounier had no choice but to comply. In the July 1933 edition of *Esprit* a notice appeared, signed by Mounier and Izard, which declared the complete independence of *Esprit* with regard to the Third Force and the suppression of "Chroniques." But this decision, eagerly awaited by Maritain, and even desired and welcomed by Mounier,[17] did not settle the problem. Though Izard (and Marc, too, of Ordre Nouveau) no longer had any editorial responsibility at *Esprit,* and their activities were reported only by way of information, the new "personalism" that Mounier began to formulate on his own was strongly influenced by the ideas and tendencies he had garnered from his friends in the two movements.

One might think that what seemed like strong-arm tactics by Maritain would have driven Mounier off. On the contrary, the decision simplified their relations and drew them closer together. Maritain's insistence, even at its firmest, was always friendly and understanding, and Mounier accepted it with friendship and deference. Problems and differences continued, and became more clearly defined throughout their continued correspondence because of Mounier's lack of strict philosophical and theological concern, and especially because of his naive eclecticism and uncritical ecumenicism. After Vatican II, Maritain's trenchant criticism of these same characteristics of Mounier's progeny in the new theological left would bring an extreme reaction. Nevertheless, Mounier continued to defer to the attentive counsels of his friend, and Maritain, for his part, did all he could to support Mounier and to introduce him to interesting and lively intellectuals, as well as put him on his guard.

Following the Stavisky scandal in 1934 and the nearly successful *coup d'état* of the extreme right in the February 6 riots in Paris, Maritain and his friends were deeply disturbed by a situation which seemed ripe for establishment of a fascist regime in France. At the February 18 meeting at Meudon, Maritain, Etienne Borne, Olivier Lacombe, Yves Simon and Maurice de Gandhillac shared their apprehension at the imminent danger of a fascist takeover and decided to write a declaration of their positions as Catholics. They planned to solicit the signatures of as many prominent Catholic intellectuals as possible in order to make it clear to the world that Christian France would not permit her cause to be identified with that of fascism. These men felt all the more responsible for making such a declaration because it was very probably true that the majority of French Catholics favored an authoritarian *régime.* Maritain and his four friends published a manifesto, *Pour le bien commun,* signed by fifty-two prominent Catholic writers, artists and scientists. Among the signatories, in addition to the authors, were Charles Du Bos, Stanislas Fumet, Gabriel Marcel, Etienne Gilson, Jacques Copeau, Jean Hugo, Paul Vignaux, Pierre-Henri Simon and Jacques Madaule.

The purpose of the manifesto was twofold. First, it attempted to break down the wall which was being built up between the spiritual and the temporal orders. The Christian is in the world, it stated, and he must become involved in the turmoil of the marketplace. Second, it aimed to preserve the independence of the Church and the Christian. The Christian is *in* the world but he is not *of* the world. He cannot, *as a Christian*, let himself be identified with any particular political party. The very idea of a Catholic political party was repugnant not only to Maritain's group but to the French mentality in general. Nor should any existing party, of either the right or the left, be designated "the Catholic party."

The manifesto noted that France was split politically into two extremist camps: one seeking dictatorial authoritarianism and "order," as an antidote to political corruption and chaos, the other aspiring to "revolution" and a collectivist regime, oppressive of the human person, as an antidote to social injustice; and the Christian had to oppose a "double no" to the two extremes. The way to a just social order does not lie, however, in a synthesis of the two errors. The individual Christian must apply the moral criteria of Christianity to the social problems of his contemporary world. The cement of the New City would be justice and charity. A closing remark of the manifesto called on Christians to pray for all who fell in the February riots, including Communists. At this, a storm of indignation arose, for the *bien-pensants* quoted these lines with shocked surprise. This is the only part of the manifesto that they seemed to remember: Maritain prayed for the Communists.[18] From then on, Maritain was branded as a leftist.

At the time of the February riots Bernanos was living in seclusion at Majorca. Had he been available, he may well have signed with the Meudon group, in spite of the hard feelings that still persisted over the condemnation of Action Française. In a letter dated July 2, 1934, he wrote to a friend:

> I am not marching with the troops of February 6. Where are they going? It strikes me that the movement . . . manipulates a group of good people who will be used, in the end, for the supreme interest of a collapsing bourgeois society.[19]

Though he was not "marching" with the rioters, he was certainly not to be found in the ranks of the leftists. His position was essentially the same as Maritain's.

Henri Massis, Maritain's erstwhile friend, took particular offense at the manifesto's denunciation of the divorce between religion (or morality) and politics. Such a separation was sacred to Action Française. He immediately published an attack in an article, "Sur un manifeste," which he later included as a chapter in his book *Dèbats*. He refused to acknowledge that there was any problem of moral judgment in taking a position on the February riots. For him, the situation was purely political.

> Although the Catholics who signed this manifesto speak only in their own names, their error runs the danger of troubling consciences even more, for this is exactly what happens when Catholics intervene as Catholics in an area that is specifically political, where they could not be concerned personally except from a moral point of view (besides, it would be the role of the Church alone, as guardian of doctrine, to recall in such a situation exactly what the moral law was, if there were an actual case of transgression).

Strange words from a man who had vigorously maintained, since 1926, that the Church had no right to pass moral judgment on Action Française, since this was a specifically political matter.

> For what is the precise question here? It is the need to reform the State, *i.e.* the necessity of a political reorganization capable of furnishing a remedy to the evils from which our country is suffering — evils which the recent scandals have made more evident. It is not as Catholics that they have opinions to formulate and responsibilities to undertake, but as Frenchmen.[20]

Nevertheless, the manifesto made a deep impression. It was the first time that the concerted voice of Christian humanists had made itself heard. It forced the French public, deeply conscious of social problems, to come face to face with the harsh realities of political life and to realize that a political choice about the situation at hand could very well be a moral choice as well.

Pour le bien commun inaugurated a period of collective manifestos. Within the same month, a second manifesto was published by the same group and under Maritain's leadership, entitled *A propos de la répression des troubles de Vienne*. This manifesto protested the machine gunning of rioting Austrian workers in the streets of Vienna under a Catholic government that pretended to be based on the social principles of the encyclicals of Leo XIII and Pius XI, which specifically stressed reconciliation with the working classes. Maritain and his group called the massacre (over 1,000 were killed) a "historic misfortune." They also demanded "honorable treatment" for those workers who had been arrested.

In 1935, when Mussolini, in public and arrogant defiance of international agreements, invaded Ethiopia, Maurras called for murder, by public proscription of all members of parliament who favored sanctions against Italy, if general war were to result from the application of such sanctions. Massis followed a subtler line of action by publishing *Manifeste des intellectuels français pour la défense de l'occident et la paix en Europe,* in which he repudiated "the false juridical universalism [of Geneva] which puts on an equal footing the superior and the inferior, the civilized and the barbarian." He warned against the dangerous fiction that all nations are equal:

> We have before our very eyes the results of this rage to equalize which mixes together indiscriminately all things and all men; for it is in its name that sanctions have been formulated, which, in order to halt the civilizing conquest of one of the most backward countries in the world (where even Christianity remains fruitless), would not hesitate to loose a universal war, to unite all forms of anarchy and every form of disorder, against a nation which for fifteen years now has been affirming, revealing, organizing and strengthening some of the essential virtues of civilized humanity.[21]

He called on "all the forces of the mind" to rally to the defense of Western civilization, and "the forces of the mind" answered his call in great numbers. Within a few days, several hundred signatures were collected, a large proportion of which were the names of prominent Catholics: Msgr. Baudrillart, Henri Bordeaux, Henri Ghéon (who nevertheless continued to frequent the regular Sunday meetings at Meudon and dine frequently at Maritain's table) and Gabriel Marcel (who had also given his signature to Maritain's manifesto *Pour le bien commun*). Marcel now felt, despite his disapproval of Mussolini's invasion, that, to avoid a greater evil and preserve the peace of Europe, sanctions should not be invoked against Italy.[22] Marcel expressed his position with great frankness in *Sept* (Oct. 25, 1935), a weekly which generally favored the opposite position.

This rallying of conservative and nationalist intellectuals inspired two opposing manifestos. Certain intellectuals of the left published a manifesto of their own in *Le Populaire* (Oct. 5, 1935).

Though a number of Catholics gave their signatures to this document, they did not feel that it expressed the reasons clearly enough why they, as Catholics, had to oppose Massis' manifesto. It did not answer the seductive arguments of Massis concerning a general conflagration which had led such men as Gabriel Marcel and Marcel Aymé to lend their signatures. Nor was it sufficient, they felt, to dispel the mistaken impression that Massis' manifesto represented the official Catholic position. This mistaken impression reached Bernanos in his retreat on Majorca, where he became exasperated at reading in the pro-fascist French newspapers reports about Italy's civilizing mission in Abyssinia and about Italian bishops blessing the embarking troops.[23]

Maritain, along with those who had collaborated on *Pour le bien commun*, on October 18, published another manifesto, *Pour la justice et pour la paix*. It was an illusion, he declared, to believe that the peace of Europe could be preserved without respect for justice, or to believe that a Catholic could find any moral justification whatever for calling evil good and good evil, even to avoid the catastrophe of another European war. The manifesto denounced the hypocritical sophistry of Massis about the inequality of races and the "right" of the so-called superior races to impose by force the benefits of their civilization and culture on the lesser breeds. Christianity could no more be linked to Western civilization than to any political party of the right or the left.

The text was given wide publicity; it appeared simultaneously on October 18 in *Sept, La Vie Catholique*, and *Le Petit Démocrate*, and in the November issue of *Esprit*. Once again Catholics were made aware that, conscientiously, they could not remain aloof from the problems of the City and that the position of the bourgeois Catholic of the right did not represent the official position of the Church. The list of signatures contained the familiar names of those in Maritain's circle: Borne, de Gandhillac, Guillemin, Lacombe, Madaule, Mounier, P.-H. Simon, etc. The name of Etienne Gilson, which had appeared on the manifesto *Pour le bien commun*, was conspicuously absent from this one. (It was at this time that Gilson definitively ceased his regular contributions to *Sept* because "he was reproached for legitimatizing the Italian attack.")[24] The Catholic press of the right counterattacked furiously; on the other hand, about a dozen signatories of the leftist anti-fascist manifesto asked that their names be joined to Maritain's manifesto *Pour la justice et pour la paix*. Among these were André Gide, Julian Benda, Jean Guehenno and Henri de Montherlant.[25]

The few Catholics of the right who (like François Mauriac) raised their voices in protest against Mussolini's international gangsterism were soon disavowed by their parties, or they left them in disgust. The Ethiopian War did more than anything else (with the possible exception of the Spanish Civil War) to determine many Catholics to break their traditional ties with the right. In the October 11 issue of *Sept*, Mauriac published a deeply moving article in which, speaking as a Christian, he defended the rights of the Ethiopians and condemned the war in the name of Christ. At the same time, he pointed out the agonizing complexity of the situation. He revealed to the public the anguished conscience of a "committed writer":

> . . . impossible today to write a simple line without having the impression of "bringing one's stone," but for what reason? To build or to stone? We must speak always from a sincere heart, and in the face of each problem we confront, we must not hide a single one of our scruples. To be ourselves, this is our duty, without any second thoughts about the opinion of the publication that accepts what we write.[26]

The weekly *Sept* played a central role in the controversy over the Ethiopian War and an even more important role during the Spanish Civil War. Maritain was closely associated with this periodical, not only (as in the case of *Esprit*) in its foundation, in his frequent contributions, in the societies organized for its support and defense, and in the fact that a sizable portion of its collaborators were regular members of the Cercle Thomiste; he was also closely associated in the efforts in 1937 to prevent its shameful suppression and in the almost immediate resurrection of the publication under the title *Temps Présent*.

The first edition of *Sept* had appeared on March 3, 1934. During its short life (three years) it became probably the most influential and respected Catholic periodical in France, with a circulation enormously out of proportion to its short existence. It could boast that its list of collaborators was made up of approximately forty of the most prominent and respected Catholic writers of the day. It had this advantage, too, that it represented no particular, specialized point of view (*Esprit*, for example, represented for the most part the "personalism" of Emmanuel Mounier). It represented, in general, the new tendency in the Church to put heavy emphasis on social reform, in line with social justice, and to show favor to the democratic and pluralistic forms of social organization. However, it welcomed responsible and intelligent presentation of points of view opposed to its own editorial policies. Thus controversial subjects were frequently treated in its pages. The editorial position of *Sept* did not always correspond with what most Catholics of the time considered the "official" Catholic position, and this readiness of its editors to treat openly and sympathetically a number of questions considered absolutely closed by the Holy Office in Rome was the cause of its untimely demise.

The Dominican editor of *Sept*, Father Bernadot, refused to echo the position taken by the Holy Office and the papal secretary of state, Cardinal Pacelli (the future Pope Pius XII), in favor of Franco in the Spanish Civil War. The Holy Office therefore ordered Father Gillet, master general of the Dominicans at Rome, to order his subject, Father Bernadot, to scuttle the magazine, which fewer than four years before had been founded with his encouragement and at the express request of Pope Pius XI.[27] The last issue of the magazine appeared August 27, 1939. Within three months, however, it reappeared under the name *Temps Présent*, with Stanislas Fumet, a layman and another close friend of Maritain, as editor.

Father Bernadot had been close to Maritain from the first meetings at Meudon. In 1927, when Pius XI asked Maritain to prepare a defense of the papal condemnation of Action Française, Father Bernadot was one of the collaborators whom Maritain was able to recruit among the regular attendants of the Cercle Thomiste. A short time after Father Bernadot had founded the highly intellectual philosophical and theological journal *La Vie Intellectuelle*, he was asked by the pope to found a weekly review on a more popular level, intellectually respectable but wider in its appeal, by which

> *La Vie Intellectuelle* would continue its work in the form of a weekly which could reach a wider public. . . . The attacks which continue to rain on the Church because of the Vatican's position [on Action Française], the absence of any publication capable of bringing to the public the light of Catholic thought founded on doctrine and open to the concerns of the times made the foundation of this weekly all the more desirable and even urgent.[28]

Bernadot found the collaborators who best fitted the requirements of the new periodical (i.e., sound grounding in Catholic doctrine and openness to the preoccupations of the times) in the Cercle Thomiste. On the cover of one of the first editions, in the new and enlarged format which appeared shortly before the Ethiopian War, the editorial staff pictured the eight most important collaborators of *Sept:* Gilson, Mauriac, Claudel, Pourrat, Maritain, Daniel-Rops, Sertillange and Marcel. Of these eight, six were regular attendants with Maritain at the meetings at Meudon or at the discussions at Berdyaev's home in Clamart, or both. (Claudel and Pourrat do not seem to have been *habitués* of Meudon.)[29] In her history of *Sept*, Aline Coutrot gives the following list of "a few famous names" who collaborated on the review: Gilson, Borne, Maritain, P.-H. Simon, Mauriac and Bernanos. In a later list of the forty principal collaborators, thirteen names correspond to names that appear in the diaries of Jacques and Raïssa Maritain in connection with the meetings at Meudon. Many of the others who are listed were close friends of the Maritains.[30]

Statements of the purpose of the periodical can be found in abundance in several manifestos, editorials, advertisements, and propaganda flyers. These definitions, restated periodically during the three and a half years of the weekly's existence, are always couched in expressions that bear the stamp of Maritain. In an editorial in one of the first issues (*Sept;* May 10, 1934), the editors declared their purpose to counteract the "far from happy" influence of the "literary weeklies." More precisely, in a later article *Sept* described itself as

> a homogeneous group working together in union and capable of furnishing an answer equal or superior to that of the writers of the extreme Left who are themselves very active and very homogeneous: Malraux, Barbusse, Gide, Guehenno, etc., as well as to the young writers of the extreme Right . . . for example P. Gaxotte, Th. Maulnier, R. Brasillach, J.-P. Maxence. . . . Both groups have important weeklies and dailies against which *Sept* alone is capable of fighting today with equal arms.[31]

Sept proposed to itself the work of educating the French Catholic mind to the necessity of holding fast to the tenuous but extremely important distinction — but not divorce — between the temporal and the spiritual orders. That the tragic identification of the Church with an individual political system was widespread among French Catholics is evident from the reaction of many in the Action Française crisis.[32] The most popular slogan of *Sept* was "Above Party Politics." *Sept* was "above politics" not because it despised political action, but to preserve that liberty which would make it more effective in public life by its respect for the freedom of political choice among its readers and collaborators. The editors explained their slogan:

> We believe it possible . . . to find above the parties . . . a position which will be the meeting place of all men of good will. Certainly a publication devoted to ideas which refused any personal debate whatever would be a paradox. Such personal debates even seem necessary to us. But we remain above the *mêlée*. Neither of the Right or of the Left, [we are] independent of all politics, the better to serve the City.[33]

In speaking of the purpose and philosophy of *Sept*, Aline Coutrot uses the distinction that Jacques Maritain made in the columns of *Sept* and which subsequently became a kind of touchstone of orthodoxy for Catholic social activity: between *"en tant que chrétien"* and *"en chrétien."*[34] In working in the world *en tant que chrétien*, the Catholic works as a representation of the Church, founding specifically Catholic institutions and undertaking specifically Catholic activities, and in such activity he involves or commits the Church. This had proved effective in the past, said Maritain, but what was needed in the 1930s, in a world that was no longer informed by a single set of religious principles, was the activity of Catholics *en chrétien;* that is, the Catholic as a citizen in a pluralistic society was to participate through activity, informed by Christian principles, in the founding and implementing of specifically secular institutions. The Christian was to act as a kind of leaven in the secular mass. This distinction referred to the whole range of human activity, political as well as literary. It was this distinction that Mauriac was making when he insisted that he was not a Catholic novelist, but a novelist who was a Catholic.

Maritain made another distinction involving the activity proper to official Catholic Action, a movement instituted in the Church by Pius XI, in which these two kinds of activity seemed to coincide. What Maritain was insisting on, and what *Sept* was specifically concerned with, was that the autonomy of a Catholic's secular activity *en chrétien* be strictly respected. Here is how Maritain put it:

> If I turn toward men to speak to them and to act in their midst, let us say that on the first level of activity, the spiritual level, I appear before them *en tant que* Christian,

and by that fact I involve the Church of Christ; and that on the second level of activity, the temporal level, I do not act *en tant que* Christian, rather I must act *en* Christian, involving only myself who happen to be a Christian, who am in the world without being of the world, who . . . have the vocation to infuse the Christian ferment into the world wherever I may be. . . .

It is on a third level, as on the first, that the layman is called by *Catholic Action* to collaborate in the apostolate of the teaching Church. It is on this third level that the Christian carries out a Catholic *civic* action (in the strict sense of the expression) when he intervenes in political affairs to defend religious interests and in the strict measure demanded by such a defense. This is not the same thing as working at a strictly political undertaking directed by a certain conception of the temporal common good to be procured. To "work" properly "in politics" one must be able to distinguish political realities, one must have a concrete idea of the means necessary to assure the common good of the terrestrial City. To defend the interest of religion involved in temporal matters, it is sufficient to be able to distinguish the interests of religion.[35]

This distinction, though it may seem somewhat fine, is a "capital element in the thought of *Sept;* numerous studies are inspired by it," says Coutrot.[36] The distinction caused many controversies as well. When Gilson began to use the term *ordre catholique* in the pages of *Sept*, the editors of *Esprit* warned of certain dangers in such an expression, as well as in certain tendencies of Gilson's thought, which, they said, tended to set up Catholic "ghettos," cut off from the rest of the world and ineffective for the real solution of contemporary problems. Maritain held that a specifically "Catholic order" was no longer either desirable or possible in contemporary pluralistic society. *Sept* adopted Maritain's position and asked H. Guillemin[37] and J. Folliet[38] for articles which would leave no doubt about this in the minds of its readers. "Between Gilson and Maritain," said Aline Coutrot, "*Sept* chose the latter."[39] This choice by the editors of *Sept*, as well as their condemnation of the Ethiopian War, put an end to Gilson's collaboration with the weekly.

A single quotation from the pages of *Du régime temporel et de la liberté*, which appeared about a year before the founding of *Sept*, leaves no doubt about the intimate connection between the thought of Jacques Maritain and the thought of the editors and the majority of the contributors to this magazine:

> It is quite evident that the reforms and revolutions of temporal forms of government are not the affair of the Church, whose ends are not temporal, but eternal and spiritual, essentially above and beyond political and social concerns, and who jealously guards against becoming the vassal of any regime, class or party.
>
> For the same reason such reforms and revolutions are not the concern of what we presently call *Catholic Action. Catholic Action* involves the Church directly. It is concerned with the apostolate of the laity operating under the direction of the Catholic hierarchy. . . . Its object is not the temporal as such. It remains very much aloof from the specific activity of the temporal order and is as little involved as the Church itself in the struggle between parties.
>
> Nevertheless Catholics are not cut off from time or separated by their faith from the affairs of this world. Their faith makes them all the more sensitive to their duties as creatures assigned to a particular point of time and space and involved in the warp and woof of worldly events. . . . How then and by what right will they work directly toward the proper good of the temporal City? Clearly by their right as citizens of that City, citizens having their own particular convictions, their own particular ideals, and above all their own particular religion, their own particular conception of God and the world, — not by their right as members of the Church and citizens of the Eternal City.
>
> . . . There is naturally no reason for Catholics to be centered about one particular party.
>
> [What is needed is] a party, or better, a political fraternity which will not seek to group Catholics together as such, nor all Catholics, but only some Catholics who have a particular conception of the historical ideal to be pursued and of the means to be employed in its pursuit; a party which will recruit its members, not exclusively among Catholics, nor even exclusively among Christians, but among all those who are in fact willing to devote themselves to a certain historical undertaking.[40]

In an article which appeared in *Sept*, Maritain applied these principles to the publishing of magazines concerned specifically with the temporal order, whatever their orientation might be:

political, social, literary, artistic or scientific. In so doing, he gave a perfect description of *Sept* without mentioning it by name, as well as of *Esprit* or *Aube*, periodicals which, specifically temporal in their subject matter, are Catholic by inspiration, not by denomination.[41]

That the numerous literary figures who contributed to these periodicals looked to Maritain for their inspiration, particularly in the political orientation of their thought during these troubled years, is evident from a series of interviews held by Dominique Auvergne with fourteen prominent Catholic authors concerning the contemporary world situation. The interviews were published in 1938 in a book entitled *Regards catholiques sur le monde*. Of the fourteen men she interviewed, one was Maritain, and eight of the others were, or at one time had been, in attendance at the Cercle Thomiste. (Paul Claudel, who at the moment was engaged in biting attacks against Maritain, Mauriac, and Bernanos and anyone else who opposed the "White Crusade" of General Franco, could hardly be expected to make a kindly reference to Maritain's political theory.)

The main point of the interview was the necessity of charity and fraternity among Catholics. But of the other seven (Fumet, Schwob, Marcel, Madaule, Mounier, Mauriac and Ghéon), four referred to Maritain by name to support their opinions; two referred to Maritain's *Humanisme intégral;* four insisted on strict separation of the spiritual and temporal orders, and used Maritain's distinction *en tant que chrétien* and *en chrétien,* and all seven (plus a certain Robert Garric, who seems to have had no direct connection with Maritain) proclaimed, in words reminiscent of the philosopher, the necessity of the Church's remaining *"au-dessus des partis,"* the impossibility of a "Catholic party," and the absolute liberty of Catholics to belong to whatever party they chose, provided they did not compromise Christian principles.

On November 1, 1935, Maritain, in line with his belief that all men of good will, regardless of their religious or political affiliations, could work together for the establishment of a just temporal order, contributed an article to the first issue of *Vendredi,* a politically independent weekly of the far left, which boasted a spread of contributors from Gide to Maritain. The article, which later became the introduction to *Humanisme intégral,* occasioned a rash of bitter attacks against Maritain in the secular and Catholic press and from the Institut Catholique, where he was teaching. These attacks became so numerous that Maritain felt it necessary to publish his *Lettre sur l'indépendance,* in which he reaffirmed his right and duty as a philosopher to intervene on the level of principles in the arena of public action. He was determined to remain strictly independent of either the right or the left.

Maritain's friends came to his defense. Marc Scherer, a frequent contributor to *Sept*, published a warm approbation of Maritain's position in *La Vie Intellectuelle;* Emmanuel Mounier defended him in *Esprit*, particularly against the rabid attacks of Action Française.[42] The nature of the attacks in many cases seems to indicate that the critics were unaware of the contents of Maritain's article, which proclaimed that no humanism is viable unless it takes account of God's existence, of his dominion over all creation, and of the religious needs of men. Maritain explained his reason for placing such an article in *Vendredi* in his *Lettre sur l'indépendance:*

> In the present case, I was thus pleased for a very special reason to write an article in a periodical of the Left; because the reading public of the Left is precisely the one that has the rarest occasion to hear a Christian voice, and among whom very strong prejudices, of a social rather than of a metaphysical origin, are inculcated against Christianity.[43]

Such explanations, along with the publication in the second issue of Maritain's letter to *Vendredi*, expressing his disappointment with the new weekly for not living up to its promise of political independence and for omitting indispensable clarifications concerning the political independence of its contributors, did nothing to abate the frequency and fury of attacks from the right. After his publication of *Humanisme intégral* (1936), they became even more numerous and more violent. Joseph Desclausais published one of them in *La Revue Universelle,* called "La Primauté de l'être, religion et politiques" (June 15 and July 1, 1936). In *La Revue Hebdomadaire*, Louis Salleron wrote a review of *Humanisme intégral* entitled "M. Jacques Maritain marxiste-chrétien" (Aug. 22, 1936). Etienne Borne protested these attacks in *La Vie Intellectuelle*.

Such attacks were not limited to Maritain. After Maurice Thorez announced the Communist policy of *"la main tendue"* in April 1936, Mauriac suggested in the May 26 issue of *Figaro* that

> when it comes to working for social justice, no refusal on the part of a disciple of Christ is possible or even imaginable.

> Against the presumed trickery of the adversary, the [Christian] must oppose that Grace in which the communist does not believe, but which is perhaps all the more powerful for being unknown to him.

In the pages of *Sept* (May 8, 1936), Scherer suggested, in an article entitled "Possibilités de rencontres," that the efforts of Catholics and Communists in the cause of social justice might very well coincide where the two groups "work on the same site":

> At such a crossroad, they can set up camp together, as comrades, without there being any need to raise "divisive" questions. No, when they meet on the work site, they do so in order to work, not to pick quarrels.

He goes on to suggest several practical examples of cooperation: student campaigns for the lowering of university tuition rates, relieving the immediate and pressing needs of the unemployed, and strikes to settle just grievances.

In his interview with Dominique Auvergne, Mounier made this reflection on "the tragic problem of Catholicism's being cut off from the world of the worker":

> We are faced with a dilemma of action: either we have an authentic contact with the masses, we go where they are, and we seem to certain people, by some optical illusion, to be fraternizing with the marxist parties, even though the meeting is only topographical, if I might put it this way; or else we refuse to join the people and as a result lose any effective influence on them.[44]

All these men were subjected to the same abuse that Maritain suffered for having written in *Sept* (June 12, 1937):

> In the temporal order, as members of the terrestrial City, Christians must exist and suffer with [the people] . . . with regard to the temporal aims of the history of mankind, and in order to work with the people for their achievement. . . . if, in a collective fashion and in most instances the temporal groups who claim to be Christian fail to exist in this way with the people, a deep-rooted disorder is introduced into the world which will be paid for very dearly. . . . The strength of the socialists and communists comes less from their ideology than from the fact that they exist with the people.[45]

In 1936, Maritain had signed a fourth manifesto which protested the tactics of slander and vilification of which he and his friends were to be the victims in 1937. Roger Salengro, minister of the interior, scarcely a friend of Catholics of either the right or the left, was the object of a vicious slander campaign of unheard-of malice, which so ruined his reputation that he was driven to suicide. A manifesto, *Pour l'honneur,* offered a public protest against such calumny, and it was published in *Aube* (Nov. 21, 1936) above a list of signatures in which readers could recognize, along with Maritain's name, the names of many others who had signed the three previous manifestos,

Sept and all its collaborators became suspected of communism, and the rumor was spread that the accusation was founded on declarations of the clergy. But this was almost never the case, with regard to the French episcopate or the Roman authorities, at least until the controversy over the Spanish Civil War, when the situation became extremely delicate.

CHAPTER 4

The Spanish Civil War

THE YEARS WHICH PRECEDED the Second World War were filled with political events of international importance. The most crucial of these events, the Spanish Civil War, deepened the division of French public opinion, particularly among Catholics. Mussolini's Ethiopian campaign had forced the general public to face the problem of the morality of a colonial war, with this complication for Catholics: the aggressor was Catholic Italy, a country on good terms with the Holy See under a papal concordat. The war in Spain suddenly, and with piercing sharpness, posed the problem of the morality of civil war.

The analogous political situations on either side of the Pyrenees, the almost identical coalitions of left and right in the two neighboring countries, focused the attention of the French all the more closely on this tragic conflict because, in a kind of prophetic dream, they seemed to be the spectators of their own political drama, played out in advance on the Spanish stage.

The Spanish war became a particularly acute problem of conscience for Catholics because the uprising seemed to take on the character of a religious war. The overwhelming majority of Catholics foresaw in an eventual victory of the Frente Popular the annihilation of Spanish Catholicism and the triumph of the Communist International.[1] The pillaging of churches and convents and the massacre of thousands of priests and religious during the first days of the uprising were interpreted as prophetic signs of what might be expected for all of Europe. On the other hand, a certain number of Catholics disagreed entirely with this interpretation, and this group was made up generally of those who had accepted and defended the papal condemnation of Action Française. Though it contained the cream of the French Catholic intellectuals, it was a decided minority. Since the crisis of Action Française, however, it had grown both in numbers and

85

prestige, due for the most part to the influence and leadership of Maritain.[2]

The latter group saw in the violent outbursts against the Church a sad confirmation of the tragedy pointed out by Pius XI: the Church had lost the allegiance of the working classes. It felt that every effort had to be made to destroy the popular identification of the Church with the *bourgeoisie* and reactionary and conservative politics. It felt that the first efforts of Catholics had to be to establish social justice, with no second thoughts about their own political or social advantage. It felt obliged, therefore, to refuse to support the Franco rebellion.

The situation in Spain was far more complicated than Catholics of the right would allow, with their simplistic distinction between Franco's Christian crusaders, on the one hand, and anti-God Communists, anarchists and gangsters on the other. The presence of the deeply Catholic Basques in the camp of the "Reds" confirmed in Catholics of the left their refusal of total support or condemnation of either side, and the reserve adopted by the French episcopacy, as well as Rome's desire to defend its religious interests without seeming to give its official support (at least in the beginning) to either party in the dispute, left Catholics free to choose sides. Catholic opinion became passionately divided.

The dominant French Catholic writers of the thirties were Claudel, Bernanos, Maritain and Mauriac. All four of these men, deeply involved both intellectually and emotionally, shared the limelight in the Spanish controversy, but Maritain found himself at the very center of the *mêlée*. His involvement meant the solidifying or reawakening of old friendships, the creation of new ones, and the kindling of undying enmities.

The extent of Maritain's involvement in the Spanish crisis would seem rather limited, if one were to judge by what he wrote specifically on the Civil War — only three articles. The first of these, which appeared a full year after the beginning of the war, was his preface for the book *Aux origines d'une tragédie: la politique espagnole de 1923 à 1936*, written by his very close friend Alfred Mendizabal. This preface was published separately as an article, "De la guerre sainte," in *La Nouvelle Revue Française* (July 1, 1937). The second was a letter to the *London Times* in which he explained his position on the Spanish Civil War; it was later reprinted in French in *Temps Présent*.[3] The third was an article, "War and the Bombardment of Cities," written after the bombing of Guernica and published in *Commonweal*.[4]

Two articles and a letter to a newspaper are actually very little, compared to the countless pages that Mauriac and Bernanos devoted to the Spanish tragedy, and yet whenever there is question of Catholic opposition to the cause of Franco, Maritain's name appears. Sometimes his name is linked with Bernanos,[5] sometimes with Mauriac,[6] as representative of the leadership of the liberal Catholic position. In any case, his name is always mentioned.

Maritain's influence in the circles of Catholic liberals was universally recognized. The lengthy and passionate discussions on the Spanish problem, held each week at Meudon after the formal meetings had been adjourned, were no secret.[7] Catholics with rightist sympathies were often at these meetings and at the annual retreats; opposing points of view were freely expressed, and the discussions often became heated. In his journal, Maritain described the retreat of September 1937, at which more than 250 were in attendance, as "darkened by serious political disagreements."[8] Maritain too expressed his views frankly, and the extent to which he gave direction to the thought of the majority of those who were present could not be missed. Father Garrigou-Lagrange, who preached the retreats of the Cercle, tried to forbid Maritain to speak his mind at the meetings on political and cultural history and on current events, especially the Spanish Civil War. The old priest found that Maritain had a very unwholesome influence, in this respect, on the minds of many of the participants, particularly the young. He wanted Maritain to limit his comments to the abstract and speculative problems of philosophy.[9]

Maritain's writing of only two articles (and a letter) that dealt directly with the Spanish problem does not mean that he wrote nothing else about Spain. His book *Humanisme intégral*, as well as numerous articles and conferences, dealt with problems and principles that were directly applicable to the Spanish situation. Maritain, however, restricted himself to formulating principles and treating the problems from a theoretical point of view. Following the course he had set in his *Lettre sur l'indépendance*, Maritain was determined, as a philosopher, to keep his discussion on a professionally speculative level. The immediate applications were evident, however, and he left it to his friends (particularly those connected with *Sept*) and to his enemies to make them. And they did.[10]

Maritain's enemies, especially, attested to the fact that liberal Catholics looked to him for inspiration and leadership. The editors of *Sept* and its contributors, particularly Bernanos and

Mauriac, had been harshly critical of Franco's "Crusade" long before Maritain wrote specifically on Spain. They had been answered, of course, but with none of the horrified surprise and indignation that greeted Maritain's criticism of the Nationalist
Crusade. *Sept* was answered with petulant irritation; Mauriac and
Bernanos were greeted with scandalized surprise, then dismissed
with a kind of self-confident *hauteur*.[11]

It was unfortunate, said the right, that men of such literary
stature should go so far astray; but had not Bernanos already put
himself beyond the pale of orthodoxy by his strange and stubborn
defense of Action Française? And had Mauriac not become suspect because of an apparent complicity with sins of the flesh in
his novels and the rather original and unorthodox reflections in
his *Vie de Jésus*? However, when the judgments and arguments of
these two men were seconded by Maritain, the paragon of orthodoxy, in articles that combined literary finesse and emotional
depth with a philosophical and theological precision that cut
through the sophistries of the defenders of Franco, the Catholic
right concentrated its hysterical wrath on the "traitorous
ringleader" of the "Red Christians."

In the years that preceded the Spanish Civil War, the magazine *Sept*, with Frenchmen in general, watched with anxious interest political events in Spain, which seemed regularly to precede by a very short time almost identical political events in
France. The victory of the CEDA[12] in the Spanish elections of
November 1933, for example, came shortly before the attempted
rightist takeover during the February 6 riots in Paris. The victory
of the Spanish Frente Popular in February 1936 came four
months before the Popular Front victory in France. *Sept* devoted
at least ten articles and a number of editorials to these two
Spanish elections and their significance.

These were the years when Maritain's distinction between
the sacral and the secular order, between political action *en tant
que catholique* and political action *en catholique*, was a subject of
animated discussion, particularly in Catholic circles. *Du régime
temporel et de la liberté* (1933) had just been published, and Maritain's manifesto *Pour le bien commun* was soon to follow. During
the spring of 1934, when *Sept* was founded, Maritain was busy
preparing a series of lectures on the role of Christians in the temporal order and on the nature of the new Christian society for a
course he was to give that summer in Spain at the University of
Santander. (These lectures were first published in Madrid under

the title *Problemas Espirituales de Una Nueva Cristianidad.*) In these lectures, Maritain gave further development to the problems he had treated in *Du régime temporel et de la liberté.* He spoke at length of the new Christian social order, in which the first concern would be the just distribution of the goods of this world. He spoke of the rights of the poor. He severely criticized the injustices and shortcomings of the capitalist economic system. He developed his concept of a pluralistic society. All of these lectures were published separately as articles in various French journals during 1935, before they appeared in book form as *Humanisme intégral.* Their publication caused a rash of attacks against Maritain which persisted through the late 1950s and which earned for him the epithet "Christian Marxist."[13]

From the time of its foundation in March 1934, *Sept* began to apply Maritain's political principles to the Spanish situation. In April of that year, *Sept,* in an article, commented on the electoral victory of the right in Spain at the end of the previous year. It found the promised social reforms of CEDA "quite congenial." CEDA, however, was an avowed Catholic party, and *Sept* commented on the danger of ignoring Maritain's distinction between the sacral and the secular orders. The Church could not afford to let itself be identified with either the right or the left, and *Sept* expressed its reserve about this Catholic victory:

> The fact remains that action undertaken in behalf of the common people has been unable to shake itself loose from outdated political classifications and that, once having been classified as right-wing, it is automatically considered "reactionary" by the working masses. Will such misunderstandings appear again and will religion once more fall victim to political and social deviations? Our Spanish friends have the duty to do everything possible to avoid such a situation.[14]

Sept's fears were more than justified. The promised social reforms were not forthcoming. In fact, the electoral victory of the Spanish right inaugurated a policy of reaction. The measures of expropriation and property distribution, taken under the former regime in favor of the peasants, were revoked. The uprisings in Asturias and Catalonia and the general strikes that followed were repressed with brutal efficiency. Immediately following these insurrections, *Sept* published an article suggesting that the best way to restore peace is the realization of the long-promised social reforms . . . and the practical application of social programs destined to lessen unemployment and settle the agrarian question.[15]

A week later, an editorial appeared under the pen name "Scrutator," begging for mercy on those who had taken part in the insurrection, in words reminiscent of the closing lines of Maritain's manifesto *Pour la bien commun:*

> Those on whom the lable "socialist" has been pasted are a group of people so miserable, so drenched with humiliation and social suffering that they are ready for anything . . . to escape their fate. But these socialists are Catholics without hope, betrayed, troubled, Catholics who do not even realize they are such, and who, naturally, are considered bad Catholics. These are our poor brothers in despair at the indifference which the entire world manifests for their sad fate. Let us not give them a pretext for believing that the Church shares that indifference.[16]

In numerous articles, *Sept* analyzed the veering to the left in the Frente Popular's 1936 electoral victory. It repeatedly expressed the fear of an imminent wave of anticlericalism, since the left now held power and the masses confused the Catholicism of their country with the parties of the right. One of the first of these articles was written by Georges Bernanos, who had gone to Majorca in 1934 to seek peace and seclusion to complete his *Journal d'un curé de campagne*. From Palma de Majorca, he regularly sent *Sept* articles and fragments of his diary containing his reflections on the Spanish situation, which he was able to view directly.

The fact that Bernanos sent these articles to *Sept*, a periodical that was known to be under the tutelage of Maritain (see the preceding chapter) and to reflect his political view, is significant and it confirms the point made earlier: Bernanos was much closer to Maritain in his political attitudes that one is led to believe by the "excess language" of the old monarchist or the biased account of Henri Massis. Though Bernanos and Maritain may have disagreed as to the form that government should take, nevertheless, on a fundamental point — the same point which was at the center of the Action Française crisis — they were in perfect accord. That point was the proper relation between religion and politics.

Bernanos' first contribution to *Sept* came as part of its inquiry into the significance of the Spanish Popular Front victory.

Bernanos made the same distinction that Maritain had been enunciating for years, but, as one might expect, in far more forceful terms. He accused and castigated, explicitly, what Maritain's discretion led him to criticize with suggestion and indirection (see the former's article "Les catholiques ont des torts" [*Sept;* Mar. 6, 1936]). The election was a humiliating defeat, not only for the right but for the Church itself, since the Spanish Catholic Action Party and CEDA were identified with the cause of the Church, which had been far too eager to paint the Spanish political scene in black and white.

> Clerical and anti-clerical, the army of Good and the army of Evil face to face, such was the image by which the faithful could be easily led to abandon their individual political preferences.

In the eyes of Bernanos, Spanish Catholic Action had supported a limited political point of view and had put its supernatural principles in the service of politics. The consequences could prove disastrous for the Church, he said, and the clerics would have only themselves to blame:

> One would be very mistaken to expect the submission of the Spanish people, who have been wounded in their pride and whose betrayed religious fervor changes so easily, even toward their favorite saints, from prayer to abuse. . . . Daniel-Rops was absolutely correct to lay harsh blame on the selfishness of the ruling classes. But Mister Largo Caballero has a perfect right to answer that the class consciousness of generation after generation was formed by religious.

After the outbreak of the civil war, Bernanos wrote down in his journal what he witnessed of the conflict on Majorca, and he sent fragments of this journal regularly to *Sept,* which were later to constitute the first part of *Les Grands Cimetières sous la lune.* The readers of *Sept* awaited these articles with eagerness and enthusiasm, and their literary beauty and emotional poignancy made them a perfect complement to the more "technical" articles *Sept* published on the Spanish problem.

These eight articles of Bernanos are interesting, too, in that they show the gradual change in his attitude toward the Spanish conflict, as well as the intellectual honesty and deep humility with which he recognized the error of his first judgments on the Spanish war.[17] One can follow this change from the first days of the rebellion, when Bernanos thought he was witnessing the *gesta*

Dei per Hispania and gave his blessing to his son, who had volunteered to fight in the army of Franco. Three months later he began to witness on Majorca the purges instigated and encouraged by the clergy and carried out by the *bien-pensant* "hyenas" with the help of a brutal band of Italian fascists. By the end of the year Bernanos had come to consider this "military and clerical revolution . . . a disgusting spectacle . . . a paradoxical mixture of cynicism and hypocrisy.[18] He recognized the same social divisions on Majorca, the same tendency of the Church to tie its interests to those of the propertied classes and identify its cause with the politics of the right, all of which Maritain had been decrying for years:

> Each of these villages is a closed world, with its two parties, that of the "priests" and that of the "intellectuals" to which the party of the workers timidly associates itself. Then there is the lord of the nearby castle, who is rarely seen, except when the weather is fine, but who knows very well who is on his side, and who long ago noted down in the company of his constant companion, the parish priest, all those who are against him.[19]

The island of Majorca is small, and Bernanos knew the people who constituted the purge committees:

> the propertied bourgeois or his overseer, the sacristan, the pastor's housekeeper, a few morally self-satisfied peasants and their wives and finally the young people hastily recruited by the new *falange*, too often converts of only yesterday, impatient to give proof of their fidelity, drunk with the fear that such wretches inspire in their blue shirts and red-pompom caps.[20]

The central theme of Bernanos' articles in *Sept* and the burden of the whole of *Les Grands Cimetières*, repeated again and again, appears a few months later in Maritain's "La guerre sainte" as the principal reason why Maritain could not give his approval to the cause of France: Ends do not justify means, and one cannot call good an evil which, for the moment, happens to be opposed to another evil.

It was from these days that a *rapprochement* between Maritain and Bernanos began, but some of the stones were never removed from the wall that had arisen between them during the crisis of Action Française. Although they may not have agreed on the form that governments should take in the new Christian humanism, they were of one mind on the spirit and principles that should animate the new society. (Helen Iswolsky, who was also intimately involved in the Spanish controversy, says that Maritain had the "warm approval" of Bernanos.[21] In *Nous autres Français*, concerning the ideals for which a young generation in France was thirsting, Bernanos wrote:

> What will you do with these heroic young people, insanely heroic young people, driven toward glory and death? After they have drunk this terrible wine, will you offer them the baby bottle of the Christian humanism of the Jesuits, that Christian humanism which Jacques Maritain said recently "has been tried *ad nauseam*, for it is the world of this particular humanism that God is presently vomiting out of his mouth"?[22]

Yet, in the very same pages where one finds expressions of agreement and admiration, it is disconcerting to find remnants of the "unpleasant mockery"[23] that followed the crisis of Action Française. For example, not far from the passage quoted above, Bernanos wrote:

> I can perfectly well have my opinion of General Franco without at the same time committing myself to the cause of Francisque Gay; I can very well honor Jacques Maritain and at the same time deplore his womanish reveries about the Jews and democracy which bring him enthusiastic applause from the audiences at the Théâtre des Ambassadeurs![24]

Indeed, during these years the two men had the same enemies, suffered the same abusive attacks, were subjected (as we shall see) to the same kind of unofficial ecclesiastical harassment. They were linked, in the minds of many, as the only two prominent Catholics who came through the Spanish affair with intellectual and moral integrity.[25]

The Spanish Civil War also deepened the friendship between Maritain and Mauriac, who had known each other for many years. Though they were always on good terms and always showed profound intellectual respect for one another, one senses that the ardor of their friendship, up to this time, had been tempered by mutual diffidence. Mauriac had been a member of the liberal Catholic political movement, Sillon, condemned by Pius X for its Modernism. Maritain's early campaign against Modernism

and Liberalism in his book *Antimoderne* (1922) and his collabora-
tion on *La Revue Universelle* could not have been reassuring for
Mauriac. The boldness of some of Mauriac's texts referring to the
Catholic faith disturbed Maritain ("terrified" is the expression
Mauriac used).[26]

Mauriac seems to have taken personally Maritain's warning
to novelists against conniving with evil in their portrayal of sin.[27]
During the early years of their acquaintance, the two men met
from time to time when Mauriac came to Meudon,[28] and frequently at the home of Charles Du Bos.[29] At these meetings,
Mauriac usually took the side opposed to that of Maritain. From
an undated letter of Raïssa Maritain (reproduced in her *Journal*)
we find this note:

> I see Jacques at Berdiaeff's before Russian and French phi-
> losophers, at Du Bos' house before Gabriel Marcel, Du Bos,
> Mauriac (and soon Gilson). . . . Everywhere it is to Jacques
> that they look for the true Catholic position, either to accept
> it, or to attack it ferociously.[30]

In spite of such disagreements, Maritain and Mauriac were
quick to recognize how nonessential were their differences. Maritain's objections to Liberalism were based on certain theological
questions, not on political positions, as we have seen. The airing
of their positions on the treatment of evil in the novel revealed
their fundamental agreement. As a matter of fact, each attributed
to the other the origin of the expression "purify the source,"
which both recognized as the key to the solution of the problem.[31]

The fact that Mauriac and Du Bos ordinarily sided with the
opposition to Maritain at the meetings at Meudon and at the
home of Du Bos does not tell the whole story. Du Bos became an
enthusiastic reader of St. Thomas Aquinas, under Maritain's inspiration and direction,[32] and Mauriac, though he never became
an avid Thomist, had this to say about Maritain in a conference
he gave in Madrid in 1929:

> Catholic philosophy is, today, in France, in the forefront of
> an anti-Bergsonian and anti-pragmatic movement, and this
> is so thanks to a rebirth of Thomism of which, among
> laymen, not to speak of eminent theologians both Domini-
> can and Jesuit, Jacques Maritain remains the most illustri-
> ous representative. No doubt if I had been a philosopher by
> profession, it is on this Thomist renascence that I would
> have insisted.[33]

The intellectual influence that Maritain exerted over these two men came from the fact that they recognized in Maritain's Thomism a tolerance and flexibility that were lacking in the narrow, radical Thomism that characterized so many men closely associated with Maritain — a Thomism "that constitutes a bloc," remarked Du Bos, "that must be accepted in the same category as the truths of faith."[34] Mauriac insisted on this distinction as late as 1966. In his regular column ("Bloc-notes") in *Le Figaro*, he spoke of his admiration for Maritain and, at the same time, of his horror of "that sacred monster of Thomism: Father Garrigou-Lagrange."[35] The fact that Mauriac and Du Bos disagreed with Maritain on certain philosophical approaches did not prevent their joining or following Maritain in the positions they took on a great number of political, religious, cultural, and artistic questions.[36]

By 1936 the friendship between Maritain and Mauriac had grown from diffident respect to genuine warmth. It was the Spanish Civil War, however, and the constant collaboration of these two men in their efforts to promote the cause of justice, peace and reconciliation in suffering Spain that solidified and established their friendship once and for all.

At the time of Franco's uprising, Mauriac's first reaction, like that of Bernanos and the French public in general, was to wish for its immediate success. The antireligious excesses of the early days of the conflict seemed to put Franco's forces in the right. Nevertheless, Mauriac refused to take sides, though not as forcefully and unequivocally as later. He wanted an early end to the senseless conflict, and in an article in *Le Figaro*, entitled "L'Internationale de la haine,"[37] he attacked Léon Blum for the apparently imminent French intervention in behalf of the Spanish republic. Such an intervention, he feared, would prolong the conflict and result in the unnecessary shedding of Spanish blood. Throughout the war, Mauriac continued this opposition to intervention, but he felt it necessary to explain in what spirit he had written this article. One notes a tone of apology for having voiced the slightest approval of the cause of Franco:

At the first news of the military uprising and of the massacres at Barcelona, I at first reacted as a man of the Right, and from Vichy, where I happened to be at the moment, I dictated in haste, by telephone, that article, "L'Internationale de la haine."[38]

A series of *billets*, which he sent regularly to *Sept* during the early months of 1937 trace Mauriac's gradual change of position in regard to the Spanish Civil War. In one of these *billets* ("Our Duty as Writers") he took a position identical with that expressed by Maritain one year earlier in his *Lettre sur l'indépendance:* writers could no longer avoid their responsibility to commit themselves on the burning questions of the day, but must situate themselves and their action "above party lines":

> The only *raison d'être* for writers, and especially Catholic writers in the midst of civil wars, is their lucidity; the only merit of which they can boast is to see more clearly than others, to reason more exactly and to out-manoeuvre in their own minds and hearts the machinations of the party spirit.[39]

It may be said that from the autumn of 1936 onward, the positions of Mauriac and Maritain on the Spanish Civil War coincided completely. The particular circumstance that led Mauriac to adopt Maritain's position without reservation was the fall of Badajoz. The news of the cold-blooded massacre of Republicans in the bullring of Badajoz on the feast of the Assumption of Our Lady filled him with horror and inspired one of his most moving articles on the Spanish Civil War:

> The mass execution of the conquered, the extermination of the enemy — as was the law before Christ — represents the most horrible triumph that the powers of darkness know in this world.
>
> The massacres and sacrileges of Barcelona dictated their conduct to the conquerors of Badajoz. They proclaim their allegiance to the traditional religion of Spain. In Seville on the day of her Assumption they honored the humble Queen of heaven and earth, the Mother of all men. . . . They should not have spilled on her feast day one drop of blood more than was demanded by the atrocious law of war.
>
> But these Spaniards, friends of the bulls, accustomed to corraling these furious beasts, could they not have surrounded and disarmed their desperate brothers, and behind fences left them to sober up from the wine of vengeance and hate? Should they not have begun immediately the work of reconciliation and pardon in the name of Her whose feast it was that day on earth and in heaven?[40]

It is easier to judge the justice of a war by the manner in which it is carried out than by the principles which govern it. The atrocities of August 15 convinced Mauriac that the forces of Franco had no right to the title "Crusaders." He could no more give his allegiance to the butchers of Badajoz than to those of Barcelona.

Until the early months of 1937, Maritain had not publicly written his views on the Spanish conflict, though they were well known among his numerous followers and his enemies. For the time being, Maritain seemed content to leave direct comment on the Spanish war to his disciples. However, when Franco permitted Hitler to experiment in Spain with new tactics of war, such as the intense bombing of cities and civilian populations in order to demoralize the enemy, and when Franco made such tactics his own, Maritain could not refrain from public protest. In March 1937, with other French intellectuals, Maritain publicly denounced the bombings of Madrid.[41] Because the Basques, a profoundly Catholic people, refused to join his White Crusade, Franco made them pay dearly. The gratuitous cruelty of the bombing of Guernica, which razed a city that could in no way be considered a military objective, and the barbarous slaughter of noncombatants, either by bombing or by machine gunning from airplanes as they fled the holocaust, moved Maritain and his friends to draw up a manifesto *For the Basque People* and to circulate it for signatures.[42]

> Whatever opinion one may have of the parties that are at odds in Spain, it is certainly beyond question that the Basque people is a Catholic people, and that public Catholic worship has never been interrupted in the Basque country. Under such conditions it is up to Catholics, without distinction of party, to be the first to raise their voices to spare the world the pitiless massacre of a Christian people. Nothing can justify, nothing can excuse the bombardment of open cities like Guernica. We address an anguished appeal to all men of good will, to all countries, that the massacre of noncombatants cease immediately.[43]

The manifesto was published only after the facts about the bombing had been verified. Between April 26, the date of the bombardment, and May 8, the date of the first appearance of the manifesto in *La Croix*, Maritain and Mauriac were busy attending a series of meetings where firsthand evidence was presented by eye-witnesses of the bombing.[44] The rightists either denied that bombs had been dropped or minimized (almost to nonexistence) the damage, or even accused the Basques of setting their city aflame to put the armies of Franco in a bad light. The evidence gathered at these meetings, side by side with the denials and obfuscations of the friends of Franco, was published by Emmanuel Mounier in *Esprit.*[45] As soon as the facts were verified, the manifesto appeared, first in *La Croix* and then in *Sept* and *Esprit.*

Mauriac took particular pains to explain his reasons for signing the manifesto. He had not signed, he said, without agonizing reflection. The fact that no manifesto had been written by Catholics of the left against the atrocities of Barcelona seemed to indicate a blind siding with only one of the parties in the dispute. Likewise, the reasons why the Catholic Basques should ally themselves with the party of anarchy, assassination, rape and sacrilege remained incomprehensible to the foreigner. Nevertheless, he signed in favor of the Basque people because

> we have but one right which is indistinguishable from our duty: to bend over their wounds. As for the rest, God alone is judge.
>
> To someone on the ground, overwhelmed with blows, we ought to spare the "you should have's" and the "why's." During this celebration of the feast of Corpus Christi, let us recall that when one member of the Body suffers, all the others suffer. It must not be that on the day when the Basque people awake from this nightmare, they should be able to claim that only the mortal enemies of the Church helped them. It must not be in their eyes that the priest and the pharisee who passed them by without so much as turning their heads should be Catholics; nor that we should lead them to believe that on the turban of the Good Samaritan there is a hammer and sickle.
>
> This is what led me to make up my mind. I have suffered to have seemed to carry water, or rather blood, to the Communist mill . . . but a Christian people is lying in the ditch, covered with wounds. In the face of their misery it is not playing into the Marxist hand to manifest to all the world the profound unity of all Catholics. This is the vine and these are the branches. One of the branches is threatened with destruction and the whole vine is suffering.[46]

It is interesting to note that Julien Benda, who had rushed to attach his name to the list of signers of Maritain's manifesto

For Justice and Peace, felt obliged to explain himself too — this time, however, for refusing his signature to the manifesto *For the Basque People.* He may be commended for his frankness, but certainly not for his sense of justice and humanity.

> A few days ago, a committee asked for my signature to protest, in the name of humanity, against the massacres of Spanish anti-fascists. I refused.
>
> I refused because if next year the fascists are conquered and all massacred, I will applaud with both hands. I am not for the religion of human life; I am for the extermination of a principle which is incarnated in some human lives.
>
> I am not a humanitarian, I am a metaphysician, which is just the opposite.[47]

The effects of the manifesto *For the Basque People* were far reaching in Catholic circles and extended even to the Vatican. In addition to signing the manifesto, Mauriac had in several articles[48] made specific appeals to the pope to intervene in the Spanish dispute. Maritain used his influence in clerical circles to get his pleas to the pope. In the July 1, 1937, issue of *Esprit,* Emmanuel Mounier quoted an official press dispatch from the Vatican which stated that the cardinal – secretary of state, Msgr. Pacelli, had telegraphed, in the name of the pope, to the archbishop of Toledo, the official representative of the Holy See to the Burgos government, commissioning him to intercede with General Franco and urge upon him the utmost moderation in the conduct of military operations in the Catholic Biscay sector. The dispatch stated that

> this initiative is not the result of the meeting of the Congregation of Extraordinary Ecclesiastical Affairs, which took place last Sunday. It was taken as a result of the intervention of a group of French Catholic public figures.[49]

Mounier quoted this dispatch as a postscript to an article on the efforts of Maritain and Mauriac in behalf of the suffering Spanish people. The identity of these Catholic personalities is unmistakable, because the only really prominent Catholics in France who defended the Basques were Maritain and Mauriac. In an interview with the editors of *Commonweal,* Maritain referred directly to his efforts, and those of Mauriac, to secure the intervention of the Vatican.[50]

In April 1937 Maritain published an article, "Con el pueblo," in the Spanish periodical *Sur.* He felt that the miserable and hopeless plight of the dispossessed proletariat was more dramatically evident in Spain than in any other country of the West.[51] On February 12, 1937, *Sept* published this article by Maritain in French ("Exister avec le peuple"), along with others by Mauriac and Borne, in a special edition devoted to the working classes. It was a remarkable issue, aimed at closing the gap between the Church and the masses.

All of the contributors to the issue were of bourgeois origin, and none of them had any immediate experience of proletarian existence. Mauriac's article was filled with passionate indignation over the injustices imposed on the proletariat by the rapacious *bourgeoisie* and with an anguished sense of responsibility, incurred by his belonging to the "guilty class." Borne's article was full of exultation that the day of retribution had arrived and that nothing could stop the march of the proletariat toward vindication of their rights. But for all the expressions of sympathy, solidarity and enthusiasm, it is not difficult to detect what a reviewer in *Esprit* called a patronizing tone:

> a certain manner of speaking which certainly does not touch the profound realities involved but which, in a way that Catholics who live in a closed social milieu hardly realize, grates on the ears of those they wish and ought to win over.[52]

Maritain's "Exister avec le peuple," on the other hand, was exceptional in that the author seemed to have been able vicariously to identify himself completely with a class to which he did not belong. It was undoubtedly his long and intimate relationship with Bloy and Péguy which made him capable of such an identification. His article insisted that what was needed to win the working classes was not a "love of benevolence" but a "love of unity," a love born of "co-naturality" (as he would put it), of communion and compassion, in the real sense of the words.

> If we love that living and human thing which we call the people, a difficult thing to define, I realize, as are all living and human things, but which is all the more real for that very reason, we will wish first and foremost to exist with them, to suffer and to remain in communion with them.
>
> Before "doing good" to them, and working for their benefit, before practicing the politics of one group or another . . . we must first choose to exist with them and to

suffer with them, to make their pain and their destiny our own.

The philosopher and theologian tried to define the nebulous and equivocal term "people" and determine its precise connotations. He was careful, first of all, to distinguish "people" from "race" or "class." It is rather, he said,

> a community of the under-privileged . . . centered around manual work, characterized by a certain historical patrimony . . . of suffering, of effort and of hope . . . by a certain way of understanding and living out poverty, suffering and pain . . . by a certain way of being always the same ones who get themselves killed.

The "people" cannot be equated with the *plebs* or the *populas* of antiquity, particularly since Christianity has added to "the idea of the little people of God" "the idea of the people of the poor to whom the beatitudes are promised." The nineteenth century had seen take place in the people, claimed Maritain, "a recognition . . . of the dignity of the human person in the worker as such," and the twentieth century had seen the people develop "the consciousness of a personality in a state of becoming, the condition necessary for the future flowering of a personalist democracy." Maritain looked on the people as "the great reservoir of vital spontaneity and non-phariseeism . . . the reservoir of a new civilization."

After distinguishing once again between the sacral and the secular orders of society, Maritain insisted that it is absolutely incumbent on the Christian, as a member of the terrestrial City, to exist and to suffer and to work with the people for the temporal goals of human history. But, he warned,

> if in a collective fashion and in the majority of cases the temporal structures to which we give the name Christian fail to exist in this way with the people, a profound disorder is introduced into the world, which will be dearly paid.

And what was more costly in lives and sufferings than the fratricidal slaughter in Spain? Who, on reading (or writing) these words in February 1937 would not have thought immediately of Spain? Who would have missed the reference to the Spanish catastrophe in these words from Maritain's conclusion?

The strength of the socialists and the communists comes less from their ideology than from the fact that they exist with the people. They believe whole-heartedly that to exist with the people, they must bind themselves to them. But whoever wants to replace in real life the errors of their ideology with a true vision of things must first exist with the people. To apply effectively the social doctrine of the encyclicals, there is one prerequisite condition: to exist with the people.

The unity of viewpoint on the Spanish war, so characteristic of *Sept*, was suddenly broken by the anomalous inclusion in the issue of June 4, 1937, of a poem by Paul Claudel, "To the Spanish Martyrs."[53] The poem was inspired by the declaration of the pope that all the priests and religious murdered by the anarchist factions of the government troops and by the enraged populace during the first days of the uprising would henceforth be included in the official list of martyrs of the Church. Claudel not only celebrated the glory of the 11 bishops and 16,000 priests who "in a single burst of flame" colonized heaven; the poem was likewise a lyrical expression of allegiance to General Franco (without pronouncing his name) by the way in which Claudel opposed the anarchist assassins on the one hand to the martyrs for the faith on the other. The poem was considered an epic of the new White Crusade, despite the fact that the word "crusade" does not appear.

In this hour of your crucifixion, O holy Spain, on this
    day, my sister Spain, which is your day,
My eyes filled with ardor and with tears, I send you my
    admiration and my love.
When all the cowards proved false, you, once again, you
    alone did not accept.
As in the days of Pelagius and of the Cid, you have once
    again drawn your sword.
The moment has come to choose and to unsheath one's
    soul!
The moment has come to look the infamous proposition
    in the eye and to take its measure!
The moment has finally come when we shall show the
    color of our blood!
Many people think that their feet, all by themselves,
    make their way to heaven, by an easy and pleasant
    path.

But suddenly the question is posed, the call to
    martyrdom rings out.
Heaven is in one hand, hell in the other, and we have
    forty seconds to choose.
Forty seconds is too long, my sister Spain, O holy
    Spain; you have already chosen.
Eleven bishops, sixteen thousand priests massacred,
    and not a single apostasy!
Ah, would that I could, like you, one day at the top of
    my voice give such witness in the splendor of the
    southern skies.
Sixteen thousand priests! The battalion formed in a
    single moment, and behold, heaven is colonized in
    a single burst of flame.
Why do you tremble, O my soul, and why vent your
    anger against the executioners?
I only join my hands and weep and I say that it is
    beautiful, that it is good.
And you too, O stones, holy churches brought to ruin, I
    salute you from the depths of my soul.
Statues broken under hammer blows, and all those
    venerable paintings, and that ciborium before it
    was crushed under foot,
Where the C.N.T., grunting with delight, roots with
    slobbering snout!
What good are all these objects of piety? The people
    have no need of them.
What the impure beast detests as much as he does God
    is beauty!
Burn the great libraries! Once more Leviathan is
    wallowing and from rays of sunshine has made
    himself a lair of filthy straw and dung.
We must make room for Marx, and for all the bibles of
    imbecility and hatred!
Kill, comrade, destroy; get drunk, make love! For this is
    human solidarity.

Whether the poem was published by *Sept* "to add a little
yeast" to the controversy (which seems highly improbable, since
the controversy was already far more heated than was desirable
among Catholics) or because of a desire to assure the collaboration of a renowned figure like Claudel, whom a refusal would

have turned away from the periodical,[54] the poem's appearance did not constitute an about-face in the viewpoint of the magazine. Only one other article (which we shall have occasion to speak of later) departed from the line of thought generally held by *Sept.* Nevertheless, the repercussions of Claudel's poem were considerable. Mauriac appealed to Claudel to honor

> with a single verse, with a single line of poetry, the thousands and thousands of Christian souls which the leaders of the "holy army," which the soldiers of the "holy crusade" have introduced into heaven.[55]

It may well be that Maritain felt obliged to do what he could to counteract the prestigious influence of the great poet in the formation of Catholic public opinion. Or perhaps he wanted to avoid the trap of equivocation in which he had been caught once before, during the days of his collaboration on *La Revue Universelle.* Whatever the reason, shortly after the appearance of the poem, Maritain published a long and impressive article, "De la guerre sainte," in *La Nouvelle Revue Française.*[56] For the very first time, Maritain, in this article, departed from the policy of limiting his discussion to the general philosophical level and made his first direct reference in print to the Spanish Civil War.

Maritain's article attacked the theory that the war in Spain was a holy war. This claim of the White Crusaders had already been contested by Mauriac and Bernanos, particularly from the point of view of the means used in the conduct of the war.[57] Maritain too gave prime importance to the "problem of means" in the Spanish conflict:

> This problem of means, on which we continue to insist, is of absolutely central importance. It involves all morality; it is morality itself. It is on this point that Christianity, if it does not wish to abdicate its role, will have to affirm its evangelical folly in the sharpest possible manner against the doctrines of force for which all means are good and which prove it by moving from one success to another — toward death.[58]

The horrors perpetrated by the "Reds" did not excuse or render less evil the means employed by the "White Crusaders." The passages in which Maritain expressed his pity and compassion for the poor of this world, who are invariably the first victims of the Machiavellian tactics of the powerful, are among the most beautiful and moving passages written on the Spanish Civil War:

> We forget . . . that evil is evil, and that it is growing at the present time, and that the horror that is done remains done and that the despair of men and their suffering or a single tear, a single cry torn forth by injustice, that all these things can be abundantly compensated for (that is why Jesus died), they can never be effaced, they never will be effaced, never. . . .
>
> . . . it is a horrible sacrilege to massacre priests, even if they are "fascist" (they are the ministers of Christ), out of hatred for religion; and it is another sacrilege, just as horrible, to massacre the poor, even though they are "marxists" (they are the people of Christ), in the name of religion. It is an evident sacrilege to burn churches and the images of the saints, sometimes in blind fury, sometimes, as in Barcelona, with cold anarchic method and in a spirit of systematic madness; and it is also a sacrilege (of a religious nature) to decorate Muslim soldiers with badges of the Sacred Heart so that they might kill in a saintly manner the sons of Christians, and to claim that God shares their own passionate hatred which considers the adversary unworthy of any respect or pity whatsoever.
>
> . . . A man who does not believe in God might think: after all, this is the price of a return to order and one crime deserves another. A man who believes in God knows that there is no worse disaster. It is as if the bones of Christ, which the executioners could not touch, were broken on the Cross by Christians.[59]

However, Maritain's original contribution to the discussion of the "holy war" was to consider it from purely philosophical and theological points of view. He examined the intrinsic value of the idea of a "holy war" in itself and in relation to historical reality. Maritain admitted that in the past,

> with regard to the forms of civilization "sacral" in themselves, like that of the ancient Hebrews, or the Muslims or the Christian civilization of the Middle Ages, the notion of a holy war, as difficult as it is to explain, could make some sense.[60]

He offered the Crusades of the Middle Ages as an example of such a holy war in a "sacral" civilization, but he hastened to add that the Crusades failed in their principal goal. Any of the medieval Crusades,

> given the manner in which they were carried out, and all the impurities they involved, could they have pleased God as much as was thought?[61]

Whatever opinion one might have of these ancient holy wars, the reality of civilization in the 1930s was entirely different:

> With regard to forms of civilization like our own, . . . (and this comes from the teaching of Leo XIII on this subject), the temporal is more perfectly distinguished from the spiritual and, henceforth being quite autonomous, no longer plays an instrumental role with regard to the sacred. In the typically profane civilization the notion of a holy war has no meaning whatsoever. Just or unjust, against a foreign power or against fellow citizens, from now on a war remains necessarily what it is in itself and by its essence, something profane and secular, not something sacred: not only something profane, but something open to the world of darkness and of sin. And if, defended by one side and attacked by the other, sacred values happen to be involved, they do not render the whole profane complex either holy or sacred; it is rather these sacred values which, with regard to the objective movement of history, are secularized by the war, and dragged into its temporal finalities. The war does not become holy; rather it risks blaspheming what is holy.[62]

Maritain did not condemn the use of force or violence absolutely, but, applying the philosophical and theological axiom that "the order of means corresponds to the order of ends," he concluded that temporal history justifies a Christian in setting above the means of violence a whole world of other means, and that, though violence might in certain cases be capable of justification in defense of religious values, it remains, even in the temporal order, the least good of possible means. In the present context of secular civilization, however, the idea of a holy war must be excluded

> by the very virtue of the transcendence of the sacred order; for no longer being the work of the temporal state (a thing

which was possible only in the case where the temporal
state was constituted in a sacral manner), the holy war, if
one wished at any price to maintain the idea as a formative
idea, would pass for the work of the sacred order itself act-
ing by the means proper to it, which is an absurdity: the
means proper to the kingdom of God not being force and the
shedding of blood. Let people invoke, if they wish, the justice of a war they are waging if they believe it just; let them
not invoke its sanctity! Let them kill, if they think they have
a duty to kill, in the name of the social order or of the nation; that is already horrible enough; let them not kill in the
name of Christ the King, who is not a military leader, but a
King of grace and charity, who died for all men, whose
kingdom is not of this world.[63]

Emmanuel Mounier praised the article highly in *Esprit* and
invited its readers

to give to this article the resounding publicity that it merits
if it doesn't get the attention it deserves on its own, by that
sort of serene and rigorous audacity which is characteristic
of each of Maritain's sorties in what I might be permitted to
call the actuality of the spiritual.[64]

The article, of course, received widespread circulation and
comment. It fell like a bomb in the rightist camp, whose theologians' arguments defending Franco's cause had, until now, been
unopposed by a respected professional Catholic philosopher.
Panic and hysteria followed. Paul Claudel and Vice Admiral
Joubert led the Catholic press into the breach.

On July 1, 1937, the very day on which Maritain's "De la
guerre sainte" appeared, the Spanish bishops published a collective letter to their fellow bishops throughout the world in order to
enhance the prestige of the Nationalist cause and counteract the
rising chorus of opposition. The letter, composed by Cardinal
Goma and signed by the majority of Spanish prelates,[65] took the
position that the Franco uprising had been a "civic-military" venture on the part of the healthiest and best-qualified civilian elements of the nation, as well as the most dependable members of
the military. Although a victim of anticlerical legislation, the
Church, according to the bishops, had counseled respect for constituted authority, whereas the authorities had permitted acts of
violence against the Church and acts of criminal revolt among the

populace in the general chaos of the spring of 1936. The Church had not wanted war, but it was grateful for the protection it received from the Nationalists.

In the Republican zone, on the other hand, persecution was rife. In order to give theological backing to their position, the bishops quoted the principles of St. Thomas Aquinas concerning the right of legitimate self-defense. To conform to a stipulation of St. Thomas, that a revolution is not justified unless the harm caused by the revolt is far outweighed by the harm that would result from continuation of the *status quo,* the letter referred to what it called "irrefutable" documentary evidence that the rising had forestalled a long-planned Soviet revolution in Spain.

Besides being circulated in France in pamphlet form, the letter of the Spanish bishops was also published in *Sept* (Aug. 13, 1937). It is difficult to explain the appearance of the letter other than by an order from an ecclesiastical superior, for *Sept* continued doggedly in its editorial policy of refusing to recognize the civil war as a holy war. (In the very next issue [Aug. 20, 1937], one finds an article by P. Raymond that is far from indulgent toward the Spanish hierarchy.) Perhaps *Sept* was determined to prove its objectivity by publishing material that went directly contrary to the editorial policy it had always held and would continue to hold, but not a word of editorial comment accompanied the letter of the Spanish bishops.

Sept could easily have dispensed with publishing this letter, for even the official Vatican newspaper, *Osservatore Romano,* passed it over in silence. A far more probable explanation is that the Dominican editor, Father Bernadot, either was ordered, under obedience by a religious superior, to print the letter, or he may have had an inkling of the imminent ecclesiastical suppression of the magazine and therefore published the letter in an effort to forestall such an eventuality. One may speculate also that this premonition may partially explain why Maritain's "De la guerre sainte" appeared in *La Nouvelle Revue Française* instead of *Sept.*

Claudel hailed the letter of the Spanish bishops as a theological refutation of the arguments adduced by Maritain against the holiness of the Franco uprising. In an article entitled "L'Anarchie dirigée" (*Le Figaro;* Aug. 27, 1937), Claudel denounced that segment of the Catholic press which, by disfiguring or misunderstanding the events in Spain, left the reading public in a troubled and hesitant state of mind.[66] This article was the first open attack by the great poet on Maritain in the public press. The letter of the Spanish bishops, claimed Claudel, justified the Nationalist uprising by theological arguments "which are as valid as those of Jacques Maritain."[67] He concurred with the letter in protesting

> with energy against the repeated attempts, never more often repeated than by certain Catholic pens, to balance the occasional abuses which could possibly have been committed by Franquist troops and the systematic exterminations which have been carried out according to the anarchist order of the day . . . and against the extravagant projects of mediation put forth by a number of ideologues, as if it were possible to come to any agreement whatever with men whose principles are the very negation of moral and social order and aim directly at the disruption of the state.[68]

He considered attempts to establish the possibility of mediation as "incongruous inventions in favor of the red allies with regard to certain imaginary scandals."[69]

Maritain and Claudel now became, in the public mind, the leaders of the two opposing Catholic camps and symbols of the two conflicting points of view. Vice Admiral H. Joubert, in his pamphlet *La Guerre d'Espagne et le catholicisme* (published as a refutation of Maritain's article "De la guerre sainte"), recognized the great moral influence of Maritain. He opposed Maritain to Claudel, and declared his allegiance to the latter:

> The position taken by this philosopher with his Catholic name tag, the influence he exerts on the younger generation, make it impossible to pass over such an article without indicating its specious content and the sophisms it feeds upon. . . .
> To the equivocal attitude of Mister Maritain, to his suspicious oscillation between irreconcilable principles, to the baseness of those who never know how to take a side, I prefer the Catholicism of Paul Claudel.[70]

A letter to the editor of *Commonweal*, which had published an article favorable to Maritain's position, contained this paragraph:

> Now that you have definitely opened the doors to the "radical Thomists" you can be sure of much material in corroboration by the growing army of Maritainites![71]

The projects of mediation to which Claudel referred were likewise due to the initiative of Maritain. Early in the summer of

1937, Maritain and his friend Alfred Mendizabal founded a Committee for Civil and Religious Peace in Spain. There were Spanish, British, and French branches of the organization, and Maritain was president of the French branch, of which Mauriac and Bernanos were members. The committee set several objectives for itself: (1) to cooperate, as occasions might arise, with any steps to make the consequences of the war less inhuman and whenever possible to initiate such steps; (2) to work, in the event of victory for either side, to spare the population from reprisals; (3) to do whatever might be possible, through the formation of public opinion, to influence governments to offer their help to mediate a peace as soon as the opposing parties might make such a step possible, and to study carefully the problems raised by such projects of mediation, particularly with a view to avoid meddling with the internal political and social life of Spain, so as to permit the Spanish people freely to realize its own will.[72] Maritain was able to report some considerable accomplishments of this committee to the editors of *Commonweal* in February 1939:

> We have been able, particularly thanks to the intervention of the Vatican, to save many human lives. We have also worked at arranging means for harboring Basque children . . . [and at] supplying food and medicine to the starving children of Catalonia. Then also the idea of a peace of conciliation has the support of the majority of French public opinion and has likewise made noticeable progress in international public opinion.[73]

Claudel remained vocally aloof from this "majority." We have already seen what he thought of "ideologues" like Maritain, with their "extravagant" and "incongruous" projects of mediation. Maritain found it incomprehensible that, after more than two years of slaughter and horrors, some men still could not see that the greatest evil was to continue the war and to refuse to consider the possibility of a peace of conciliation:

> A peace of conciliation on a purely Spanish basis is what one must hope for if one desires that Spain should resume its characteristic mission in the world. If this does not take place, we must expect, in the political order, tragic results; and perhaps, in the spiritual order, an appalling religious crisis and an entire evangelization to be undertaken from the foundation. . . . What will be the results in the future of the historic wound caused by a war of extermination for

which many (and not only in Spain, alas) have tried to make religion jointly liable? Anyone who cares about the evangelizing of souls can think of this only with profound sorrow.[74]

It was this repeated insistence on peaceful mediation that led Mauriac to join Maritain's committee and to become one of its most indefatigable workers. Mauriac wrote:

Whatever side we lean to in this atrocious war, whatever our preferences may be, it does not seem possible that Catholics be free not to desire some mediation; and this is why I have agreed to join the Committee founded for this purpose by Jacques Maritain.[75]

Bernanos, too, joined Maritain's committee — the first time that Bernanos publicly gave his name to one of Maritain's projects. (The measures taken by pro-Franco Catholics to silence these "red Christians" indicate the extent to which Maritain and his friends were successful in their efforts to form public opinion.)

On the afternoon of September 26, 1937, Maritain was called to Paris to take part in a meeting to discuss the crisis of the Dominican weekly *Sept*. The editors had received a telegram some weeks before from Father Gillet, master general of the Dominican order, saying: "Last issue, economic reasons, take up later under new form. Best wishes." "Economic reasons" was certainly a subterfuge, and it offered Bernanos another occasion to tilt his lance at his old enemy, *le mensonge* (the lie).[76]

Three days after the telegram, Father Gillet, pressed by M. F. Charles-Roux, the French ambassador to the Vatican, for a more satisfactory explanation, adduced another reason: the interior discipline of the order was menaced by the division resulting from the position *Sept* took on the Spanish affair, particularly in its religious aspects. Bitterness and rancor were certainly engendered among Dominicans throughout the world because of opposing points of view; but there is enough evidence to indicate a strong probability that the suppression of the magazine was demanded and imposed by the Holy Office in Rome.[77]

Complaints flowed into Rome in abundance from the vigilantes of orthodoxy in both the conservative and progressive Catholic camps. The ambassador of France to the Vatican complained in his *memoires* of the mania at Rome among Catholics of different political persuasion, particularly French Catholics, "to denounce one another to the Holy See."[78] Magazines like *Sept* and

the writings of intellectuals like Maritain were objects of special
scrutiny by the Holy Office, the guardian of doctrinal purity, and
its membership was dominated by conservative clerics. Moreover,
there were conservative Catholics in abundance who were eager
to keep the censors of the Holy Office apprised of the "dangerous
tendencies" in the writings of Maritain and his friends at *Sept*.

> From time to time there appeared . . . an article taking sides
> in the Spanish Civil War, whitewashing the reds or redden-
> ing the whites. Without fail, the article was pointed out to
> the Vatican and incriminated as scandalous either by the
> Spanish Franquists, the Italian Fascists or by the French
> Conservatives.[79]

Ambassador Charles-Roux, however, did what he could to prevent
the ax of censorship from falling on the heads of such writers and
thinkers:

> If I found out that *Temps Présent* or *Sept* or some *avant-garde*
> theologian gave the Roman readers attacks of the tic, I did
> my best to parry the blow.[80]

The members and friends of Action Française, who never
forgave "the deserter" Maritain or those who followed him, were
particularly active in these denunciations.[81] Sensing a shift
toward the right in the Vatican's political orientation in the last
years of Pius XI's reign, when the Church felt itself menaced by
international communism, Action Française took every opportunity to strengthen its position by denouncing its enemies, new
and old.

Bernanos had already run the danger of censorship at the
Holy Office for his novel *Sous le soleil de Satan*. For years he had
been under suspicion for his obstinate defense of Action Française. In the middle thirties, when he turned against the movement, it was Catholics of the right who began to study his writings for signs of doctrinal aberrations. The appearance of *Les
Grands Cimetiéres sous la lune* in 1938 caused a furor and seemed
to provide an occasion for censorship. The archbishop of Palma
de Majorca, of whom Bernanos had been especially critical, sent a
letter to *Action Française* denouncing *Les Grands Cimetiéres*.[82] Another Spanish prelate denounced the book as containing grave
calumnies about Spain and ideas which could rightly come under
suspicion from the point of view of the faith.[83] Pius XI, however,
seems to have read Bernanos' book with great interest, and Bernanos seems to have had evidence that *Les Grands Cimetiéres*

would have been put on the Index had it not been for the express opposition of the pope.[84]

The campaign of denunciation at Rome against Mauriac began during the Spanish Civil War. Mauriac had always caused uneasiness in conservative Catholic circles for what was called his complacency toward sins of the flesh. In spite of the fact that his *Vie de Jésus* (1936) carried an *imprimatur*, it was the object of severe attack in Rome. Father Garrigou-Lagrange underlined the disquieting side of Mauriac's portraits of Christ and his Mother. Mauriac's conception was too personal, Father Garrigou-Lagrange said, and was without documentary justification in that it attributed to Christ characteristics that would be more typical of a character in a novel.[85]

Maritain, formerly the champion of orthodoxy, now became "an *avant-garde* theologian," "a second-hand theologian." Henri Massis lumped Maritain, Mauriac and Bernanos together as equally insensitive to the wishes of Rome:

> Some Catholic writers who formerly passed for "men of the Right," men like Bernanos, Mauriac and Maritain, denounced at their pleasure the "Franquist atrocities." . . . And Jacques Maritain was there to take his stand against the "abominable heresy" of the Spanish Nationalists, painting the violence of the Whites with the most frightening colors.
>
> . . .To Maritain, as to Bernanos, a voice from Rome replied immediately. It is not lawful to speak with wrath of the errors and failings of those who wish to rebuild a Catholic Spain, and remain unmoved in the face of a barbarian tyranny which has tried to turn Spain into another Russia and to overthrow the West.[86]

Such "voices from Rome," of course, did not constitute the voice of infallibility, whether they came from a group of Spanish bishops (as Maritain was careful to point out)[87] or from an occasional contributor to *Osservatore Romano*, or even from a member of the Holy Office. But the swelling chorus of denunciation was enough to establish a climate of suspicion in the conservative Catholic press of almost every country of Europe and the Americas. In South America, particularly in Argentina, Maritain became the object of a campaign of defamation and slander that continued into the 1950s. In England, Reginald P. Dingle expressed the conservative sentiment when he accused Maritain and his followers of a "species of Tolstoyism" and pointed up the "essentially morbid character of his attitude" toward the Spanish crisis. Dingle warned his fellow Catholics that Maritain "hovered at times on the 'dangerous edge' of material heresy."[88]

The 1937 annual retreat at Meudon, on the weekend of September 25 – 28, had the largest attendance on record, but the atmosphere was charged with tension. The conservative Father Garrigou-Lagrange, who habitually preached the annual retreats, was in a testy mood over the article "De la guerre sainte." Maritain's position on the Spanish Civil War was decidedly too much for the great theologian (as, later, Maritain's position on the Vichy regime would likewise prove to be). Father Garrigou-Lagrange arrived on Friday the twenty-fourth, and the evening turned out to be extremely difficult. It was one of the very rare occasions when Maritain, who was known for his gentleness and consideration, gave vent to his anger. He notes in his diary for that day:

> Father is extremely angry with me; he goes so far as to reproach me, a convert, for wanting to give lessons in the spirit of Christianity "to us who have been Catholics for three hundred years" (and why not since the Crusades? He forgets that he too was converted by reading Ernest Hello). It seems that they put the blame on Raïssa and Vera [Maritain's wife and sister-in-law] for using their influence to lead me astray. (They're Russian Jewesses, aren't they? They who detest these political quarrels and would have been so happy to have me remain aloof from them, if I had not seen in them a witness I had to bear to the truth.) I find myself in a black fit of anger, which I cannot hide. . . . Father Garrigou would like to forbid me to speak on the philosophy of history and to judge current events and to influence young people in this regard. (He is not the only one in Rome to think this way, I know very well, and to tremble at the thought of "Maritain in politics.") Only metaphysics! But he doesn't hesitate to pronounce in favor of Franco and to approve the Civil War in Spain.[89]

It was on Sunday afternoon of this retreat that Maritain was called to Paris concerning the suppression of *Sept.* By Monday the air had cleared somewhat. Maritain noted in his journal:

> Mass by André Baron. Father Garrigou has finally gotten off my back a bit. Up till now he has remained only in places where groups have gathered.

Arthur and young Borgeaud remarked that something must have been wrong, a concealed tragedy that blocked everything. Father is obsessed by Spain.[90]

It must be remarked, in justice to Father Garrigou, that however profound his feelings were in this matter of Spain, his public conduct and utterances were always governed by the strictest justice and by rational responsibility. This eminent theologian, who was quick to point out the idiosyncracies in Mauriac's portrait of Christ and Mary, could have (and certainly would have) pointed out any doctrinal errors in Maritain's writings, if there had been any. Father Garrigou realized that the controversy over Spain had nothing directly to do with doctrine, but that fallible human prudence determined the positions in either camp. Though he may have disagreed strongly with Maritain on political questions and blamed him severely, as a spiritual father, for the scandal he thought Maritain was causing, when it came to doctrinal purity, he publicly and staunchly defended Maritain's orthodoxy before his accusers at Rome.[91]

The purpose of the meeting Maritain attended in Paris over the *Sept* crisis was to discuss the future of the magazine. The weekly had been suppressed, the final issue had appeared; but the words of the telegram, "take up later under new form," left the door ajar. It is doubtful that Father Gillet had in mind anything like the *forme nouvelle* that evolved from the meeting. After the meeting, a month had barely passed before a new weekly, *Temps Présent*, appeared. (The full title of the new periodical was the subtitle of the old *Sept: Hebdomadaire du Temps Présent*.) The list of collaborators was identical, the position of the magazine was identical, as was the list of subscribers. The only thing new about this *forme nouvelle* of *Sept* was the fact that it was entirely under the direction of laymen. This move was made, evidently, to avoid the dangers of "committing" either the Church or a religious order because of the magazine's position, as well as to avoid suppression by the unilateral decision of an ecclesiastical or religious superior. The new editor was Stanislas Fumet, a close friend and admirer of Maritain and a longstanding attendant at the Meudon meetings.

To one of the early issues of *Temps Présent*, Maritain contributed an article entitled "Are You a Barbarian?" He put to the reader three questions, to which he wrote, "if you answer yes you should be considered a barbarian." Here is one of the questions:

> Do you think it is permissible to *put to death,* in order to
> affirm a principle or to carry out a plan of either social revo-
> lution or of national renewal, an *innocent man* (innocent of
> all but believing in this principle or of not participating in
> this plan)?[92]

No one could mistake the reference to Spain. This question
in particular stuck in the throats of pro-Franco Catholics. Mr.
Dingle had this to say about what he called the "most painful"
article to date in *Temps Présent:*

> It would be puerile to pretend that M. Maritain is not think-
> ing throughout the article of Spain and that he has not the
> intention to pillory the great majority of European Catholics
> as *"barbares."* We are entitled to believe that, on any subject
> on which his vision was less distorted, the unfairness of his
> method of presenting the question would be immediately
> apparent to the eminent philosopher.[93]

Maritain's question is certainly a leading one, but justifiably
so. It led the reader down a road where he was forced to view
certain aspects of Franco's campaign, a thing which Catholics of
the right stubbornly and angrily refused to do.

A slanderous and defamatory attack on Maritain came from
the minister of the interior of the Spanish Nationalist government
at Salamanca, Luis Serrano Suñer, who published an article
entitled "Maritain, Judio convertido." Mauriac, who wrote a
warm defense of Maritain, thanked Señor Suñer, "who does me
the honor of naming me" in the same article with Maritain. The
attack was directly on Maritain; nevertheless, Mauriac took this
occasion to explain his own position on the Spanish Civil War. An
attack on Maritain, in this respect, was an attack on Mauriac, so
completely were they of one mind. The article is particularly no-
table for the warm tribute Mauriac pays Maritain:

> First of all the Spanish minister's attention must be called
> to the fact that here, in France, Jacques Maritain, tenderly
> loved by his friends, is also respected by his enemies. For
> many who cannot share his views on Thomism, nor approve
> all his undertakings and all his ways of doing things, he has
> remained and will always remain this "loveable Jacques."
>
> Jacques Maritain is not a "converted Jew," as the
> Minister of Salamanca assures us. If he were, he would not
> seem to me less worthy of being admired and loved, but

after all he isn't. We believe, however, that she to whom God
has joined him has certainly helped him become the
exemplary Christian who, like his Master, makes no distinction of persons, but venerates in each single person a re-
deemed soul, and on the faces of all races, recognizes the
features of the same Father. There are many today, whom
one would believe lost in despair, who know that all is not
lost for them as long as there exist in a house at Meudon,
where God himself dwells, that man and that woman, whose
look and whose voice bring them more than a promise: the
visible presence of Mercy.

    . . . Jacques Maritain, in taking his stand, with all the
power of his logic and all the fire of his charity, against the
pretention of the Spanish generals to be waging a holy war,
has rendered to the Catholic Church a service whose importance is measured by the fury it unleashes.[94]

Mauriac had published, some months before, an equally eloquent
tribute to Maritain in *Temps Présent:* "L'Exemple de Jacques Maritain."

    In one of his *billets* to *Temps Présent*,[95] Mauriac called the
attention of his readers to a quotation from Maritain's
Humanisme intégral:

As long as modern society secretes poverty as the product of
its normal functioning, there can be no rest for the Christian.

The words caught the eye of Claudel, for they called into question
the ethical basis of the capitalist economic system, a system particularly dear to Claudel. Statements about the immorality of certain aspects of capitalism were as hateful to Claudel as were critical remarks about certain aspects of the Spanish war. Such things
were better left unsaid. But in Maritain's mind the Spanish war
was the inevitable result of an inherent weakness in the contemporary social structure, of which capitalism was the economic
framework.

    What Maritain wrote about the Spanish Civil War was spe-
cifically concerned with the morality of the war, but his references to the evils of capitalism as one of the prime causes of the
war, though they were indirect, are unmistakable. In his article
"De la guerre sainte," he referred his readers twice to his book
Humanisme intégral, from which Mauriac had taken the text to

which Claudel objected so strenuously. In one of the passages to which Maritain referred the readers of his article, he spoke of the new social-economic structure which must replace the present one, and in this new structure, he said,

> there are certainly both rich and poor, and how much poverty, but the existence of a class reduced to the rank of a tool or of marketable work, the existence of the proletariat in the strict sense of the term, is then inconceivable.[96]

In another footnote to his article "De la guerre sainte," Maritain equated the causes of the Spanish Civil War with the causes of the general political, social, and economic unrest in the Western world by referring the reader to two articles he had published two months before in Spain.[97] One of these articles was "Con el pueblo," of which we have already spoken; the other was "De un nuevo humanismo," a kind of summary of *Humanisme intégral.* The English version of this article was used as the first chapter of Maritain's book *Scholasticism and Politics,* in which he claimed that communism and "industrial rationalism or capitalistic materialism" work ultimately to the same end. On the social significance of the new humanism, which he felt must replace both communism and capitalism, he wrote:

> I will simply say that in my opinion it should assume the task of radically transforming the temporal order, a task which would tend to substitute for bourgeois civilisation, and for an economic system based on the fecundity of money, not a collectivistic economy, but a "personalistic" civilisation and a "personalistic" economy, through which would stream a temporal refraction of the truths of the Gospel.[98]

"This is specious!" cried Claudel in *Le Figaro.* He claimed sarcastically, in attacking the first part of the statement quoted by Mauriac ("the normal product of their functioning"), that the great philosopher seemed never to have heard of what the Scholastics called *per se* and *per accidens.* He declared that the words of Maritain implied that poverty and destitution are the end for which society exists. He concluded:

> He is unjust, and I would go so far as to say guilty, of loading [capitalism] with all the responsibility. Poverty is not "the normal result of the functioning of human society." All

one can say is that it is the sad sign of its inherent imperfec-
tion.[99]

Claudel then proceeded to Maritain's second *"clausule"*:
"there can be no rest for the Christian." Claudel interpreted this
phrase as meaning that

> from the moment we become Christians, we are in a state of
> obligatory and permanent mobilization against social evil;
> in other words in a state of revolutionary mentality.

Claudel denied that the Christian has any *obligation* to work for
the renewal of the social order. Justice, he said, is not involved.

> We have the right to be moved to the very depths of our
> being by the spectacles of distress, scandal, stupidity and
> injustice that surround us. We have even the right (but not
> the duty) to propose, with all possible modesty, our little
> ideas. But if we bring passion and fanaticism to the affair,
> we run the risk not only of folly and ridicule, but of positive
> evil and of sin. Here the domain, no longer of justice, but of
> our personal desire, is confused with that of our capability
> and our competence.

Claudel suggested that instead of going beyond his compe-
tence by seeking the universal causes of misery in the world, the
good Christian should occupy himself, first of all, with his "duties
of state as father of a family, head of an industry, civil servant,
military officer, diplomat, priest, etc.," and then, if one has the
inclination to do so, to occupy himself, out of a sense of charity,
not justice, with the immediate social problems at hand, such as
alcoholism, prostitution, pornography, the family, housing and
strikes. He urged prudence and caution upon the Christian. The
most dangerous thing in society, he said, is

> ideology, uncontrolled sentimentality and blind confidence
> in our own powers and our own lights, which is found in
> bookish people and theoreticians.

Summoning up the ghost of Robespierre, Claudel warned
Maritain of bringing on a second Reign of Terror by his well-
intentioned but inept fanaticism:

> This is what happens when busy-bodies have the leisure to
> create careers for themselves and when "Christians" suffer

from that disease which in Lyon is called *"tracassin"* [meddling].

Maritain defended himself in a letter to the editor of *Le Figaro*. His customary patience was ruffled and one notes a tone of sarcasm. The *ad hominem* character of much of Claudel's argument, and the fact that Claudel admitted to not having read the book, or even the context in which the sentence in question was found, irked Maritain.

> I suppose that to the opinions put forth by Mr. Paul Claudel, pontifical pronouncements alone would constitute worthy rebuttals. This is why I take the liberty here to offer a few citations from the encyclicals. However, even a professor, a busy-body, indeed one infected with the disease of *tracassin*, has the right to common justice (if not to that fraternal charity of which Mr. Paul Claudel abundantly spreads such moving examples).[100]

Maritain answered the first of Claudel's charges by insisting that what he had said was that modern society secretes *"la misère"* as a product of its normal functioning, as an ever present by-product, not that modern society has as its end to produce *"la misère."*

> It is enough for me to indicate that since the time of the sweat shops to that of the great crisis of unemployment which we have before our very eyes, the activity of modern economic society in the pursuit of its objectives (of which the famous *"Enrichissez-vous"* expresses one of the principles) has been regularly accompanied by a state of destitution for a great number of men.

Concerning the second *clausule* of his statement, Maritain maintained that the Christian, whether he works to remedy certain disorders of a vitiated social structure or the causes of these disorders, is certainly in a state of permanent mobilization, but he refused to admit that this constitutes revolution.

Maritain next proceeded to back up his assertion with numerous quotations from the papal encyclicals. Concerning the first part of his statement contested by Claudel, he quoted Pius XI from *Quadragesimo Anno:*

> It is important to give to each one what belongs to him and to regulate, according to the demands of the common good

or the norms of social justice, the distribution of the resources of this world. The flagrant contrast between a hand-
ful of rich and the multitude of the destitute calls the attention today of any man of good will to very serious disorders
in this regard. . . . From the free play of competition one
cannot expect to arrive at a well-ordered economic system.

Concerning the duty of Christians to give themselves to the
task of reorganizing society on the basis of a more equitable distribution of wealth, in order to remedy the situation which had
lost the working classes to the Church, Maritain quoted the words
of the same pope:

The soul of each worker is of infinite value, and as long as
we have not brought them all under the influence of Christ
and the Church, our mission is not over; you cannot take
your rest.

Maritain concluded:

When one claims that some statement is false, one holds
that the opposite is true. If Mr. Paul Claudel holds as true
that in the face of poverty "secreted" by the functioning of
modern economic society a Christian can take his rest, may
he excuse me for having involuntarily troubled his repose?

Claudel passed over the texts from the papal encyclicals
with the facile remark:

Mr. Jacques Maritain has thrown at my head a number of
quotations from the encyclicals, where the Pope points out
with severity certain imperfections of society, not only today's society, but yesterday's and tomorrow's too, I fear.
When have I ever said the contrary?[101]

The rest of the article consists of putting words into Maritain's mouth or of forgetting words he said. For example, dropping the phrase "as long as modern [economic] societies" from
Maritain's sentence, Claudel replaced it with the simple word
"society," so that, according to him, Maritain held, along with
Rousseau, that society as such is evil. Nothing could be further
from the sense of the sentence, to say nothing of the context. Nor
did Claudel attempt to answer the points Maritain made in his
letter to the editor of Le Figaro. Claudel's letter to the editor simply reiterates what he had said in his original article:

I deny for my part that poverty is the normal product of society, nor is it a by-product; that society, any civilized society at all, considers as its own well-being the misfortune of any of its members and that it takes pains to produce and maintain this misfortune. If the misfortune exists, as is only too evident, it is the result of a deplorable deficiency, but an accidental one, and not of an organic defect.

Maritain, who had never said that the object of society as such is to produce *le malêtre* (misfortune) of any of its members, explained carefully, with examples, what he *did* say. Claudel did not bother to take up the idea that Maritain had intended to express — however badly he may have done so, in Claudel's opinion. Nor did he show how Maritain's statement of the thought could not mean what it was intended to mean. Claudel said simply:

> Mr. Jacques Maritain . . . maintains that he did not want to say what he said. I congratulate him, but all the same he did say it.

Maritain's reply to Claudel — that the Christian's being in a state of permanent mobilization against the evil principles that animate a society or the evils that flow naturally from these false principles does not constitute revolution — received the same treatment. Claudel begged the question, declaring once again that Maritain was inviting the working classes to bloody revolution in the Marxist tradition. He purported to bolster his begging with theological principles:

> It is not beside the point to recall one of the cardinal principles of moral theology: it is never permissible to procure a good by means of an evil. But then in the case of social revolution, the immediate evil, the harm caused to one's neighbor, is certain and the good only eventual. That's why the Church is so severe with regard to revolutionary movements.

The dispute was getting nowhere. Maritain published an article in *Temps Présent*, "Les points sur les 'i' " (July 14, 1939), in which he tried to clarify the issue and put an end, once and for all, to the controversy. He methodically reiterated his position on all points in the dispute. He pointed out that Claudel could have easily found clarification for his misconceptions himself, if he had taken the trouble to read in *Humanisme intérgral* a few pages before and after the place where the text in question was found. Maritain ended his letter, as well as the exchange, with these words:

> Let him who is tired and wants to sleep go to bed; but let him stop up his ears, for there are many cries in the world that risk troubling his repose. After all, the Apostles fell asleep on the Mount of Olives during the agony of the Father of the poor. To tell the truth, we are all asleep. What good does it do to calumniate and to vilify those who try to shake off a bit of their drowsiness? They won't bother the sleepers for very long. Let them be permitted to watch one hour with the poor and the downtrodden — that hour during which a human life runs its course and is quickly gone.[102]

At the time of Claudel's attack on Maritain, Mauriac and his son Claude were entertaining Gide at Malagar, their estate near Bordeaux, and Claudel's article in *Figaro* came up one evening in conversation. Mauriac remarked that he had learned how deeply hurt Maritain had been by Claudel's attack. He expressed his surprise to Gide that no one had come to the defense of "that little sentence, so beautiful and so true, of Maritain's," which he himself had quoted and inadvertently brought to the attention of Claudel. He regretted that he could not do so because he owed too much to Claudel, the light of his youth. He had "too many things in his heart to tell him what he had on his heart."[103]

Later that evening the conversation turned again to Maritain and Claudel, and Claude Mauriac suggested that Gide take up the defense of Maritain. The friendship and gratitude which Claude's father, among many others, owed to Claudel kept him from doing so. "But you, nothing holds you back," he said. Gide replied somewhat enigmatically: "I have thought about it. But I'm afraid of . . . of compromising Maritain." Claude Mauriac wrote:

> His face was suddenly aglow with both pride and humility. A triumphant irony deformed his features and gave them a slightly comic appearance, very agreeable and a bit, a very little bit, devilish. He continued: "That's it. They will say: 'Naturally! It's Gide who defends Maritain, Gide! The opposite would have surprised me.' Poor Maritain . . ."[104]

A few days later Gide conceived the diabolical scheme of having Claudel, in spite of himself, contribute money for a fund in behalf of Spanish intellectuals who had sought refuge in France and were without means of support. Gide proposed to do this by selling a manuscript of Claudel's which Claudel had confided to him long before and which was worth 20,000 francs. He had written an article to accompany the sale. The project, however, never got off the ground, probably because of François Mauriac's cool reception of the plan.[105]

The unconditional surrender of the Spanish Republican forces on April 1, 1939, put an end to the civil war. The German occupation of Czechoslovakia on March 15 had already initiated a series of events that would shift the center of focus from the Iberian Peninsula to Central Europe. The Spanish tragedy proved to be a prelude to an even greater catastrophe.

The close of the Spanish war likewise brought an end to a decade that saw a change in orientation among Catholic literary figures. It was during this decade that Catholic writers, largely under the influence of Maritain, became what would shortly be called *"écrivains engagés."* The great figures of the Catholic literary revival during the thirties, Bernanos, Claudel, Mauriac and a host of lesser figures, felt compelled in conscience to "commit" themselves, through their writings and practical action, to the social and religious problems involved in the Spanish Civil War.

Not a single democrat went so far, and in so absolute a manner, in condemnation of the imposture of Franco as the old monarchist Bernanos. He wanted to restore — everywhere on earth and immediately, even in social institutions — the kingdom of God and his justice. He poured cataracts of sonorous and violent invective on all who placed obstacles in the path of such a restoration. He wrote without equivocation, without hesitation, making enemies on all sides, caring only that such things be said. But his violence and excess were never ridiculous, because they were animated by his profound faith and by a secret but all-encompassing love of mankind.

The articles Mauriac wrote as a "committed" author did not have the power of those of Bernanos. Mauriac did not have the same sense of historical continuity or the same prophetic insight, but he had the "genius of the moment," a feeling for his times. And he added to this sense of immediate historical relevance his incomparable gifts as a moralist. His extraordinary intuitive knowledge of the human soul made his articles far more efficacious, if less prophetic, than those of Bernanos. He denounced the hypocrisy of the White Crusade with artistic economy, implacable precision of thrust or flash of wit, and a depth of feeling that convinced rather than angered. He never resorted to eloquence. His pinpoint irony did not require a tirade. He had no need, as Bernanos did, to gather momentum and soar into flight. He preferred the editorial and the short, condensed article.

Maritain united in his articles and books the prophetic vision of Bernanos with the convincing intimacy and genius for the moment that characterized Mauriac. Like Bernanos, Maritain had a burning desire to restore the kingdom of God on earth, but his sense of immediate historical relevance made him realize that the reform of social institutions is a slow, laborious and ungrateful struggle. His prophetic vision was announced with patience and serenity rather than with apocalyptic fury. Like Mauriac, Maritain persuaded rather than angered and alienated. His contribution, in this respect, was complementary rather than identical to that of Mauriac. Though at times his writings exhibited a depth of feeling comparable to that of Mauriac, what he contributed most to their common cause was intellectual and doctrinal respectability and integrity. If Mauriac won men's hearts, Maritain won their minds.

Claudel, on the other hand, more attached by his traditional and dogmatic temperament to defense of the established social structures and political powers, loudly defended the White Crusade. He offered a certain artistic respectability to a cause that already enjoyed the respectability of numbers in Catholic circles; but he came off so poorly in the controversy with Maritain, Bernanos, and Mauriac that in the future he proved far more cautious in his espousal of political causes.

However much the "Catholics of the left," under Maritain, were outnumbered at the time, the years of the Spanish controversy saw them grow in numbers and prestige. Maritain contributed greatly during the decade of the thirties, and especially during the Spanish Civil War, to a movement which had begun years before, under Lammenais, Blondel, Laberthonnière and Sangnier, whose object was to establish relevance between the Church and contemporary society. Maritain did more than any other Catholic writer to give direction to and make doctrinally acceptable a movement which, though distrusted and even stifled at times by the Church, gained momentum during the Second World War and the postwar years and culminated in the *aggiornamento* of Vatican II.

CHAPTER 5

The Jewish Question

ONE OF THE MOST troublesome and tragic problems to confront the conscience of the Western world in the first half of the twentieth century was the "problem of the Jew." At the end of the nineteenth century, a wave of anti-Semitism began to wash over the world; it reached its crest in the middle thirties and broke over Central Europe in the violent hatred and coldly calculated genocide of Nazi Germany's "Final Solution." For all her devotion to justice and liberty, France was by no means exempt from anti-Semitism. The new tide of anti-Jewish sentiment began to run in France after the publication of Edouard Drumont's *La France juive* in 1886. Reaching its peak during the Dreyfus Affair, at the turn of the century, it was held at its crest by the ultranationalist propaganda of Action Française, the conservative opposition to the Blum government and the collaborationist policies of the Vichy regime.[1] It did not ebb till the liberation of France in 1943.

From the earliest days of his career, Maritain showed a particular interest in the Jewish Question. The problem of the Jews was, for him, a problem of predilection. Long before he became involved, on the level of principles, in the contingent problems of the political scene, he had been working, through lectures and articles, for a practical Christian solution to the Jewish Question. There is probably no other problem that he approached with such ardent commitment. He brought to it a sympathetic understanding that was perhaps shared by no other scholar of his time, particularly among Catholics. Even the positions of Bloy and Claudel, who gave evidence of extraordinary insights into the place of the Jew in the history of the Western world, were colored by certain lingering prejudices. The readiness of the general Catholic public and of a great number of the clergy to accept without question the "facts" marshaled by Drumont in *La France juive,* as well as the propaganda of Action Française, was one of the religious scandals of the century.[2]

The extent to which anti-Jewish prejudice was entrenched in many Catholic minds can be judged from the difficulties encountered by the Church during the Second Vatican Council (1965) in attempting to eradicate such prejudices even from some of the council fathers. The original conciliar *Statement on the Jews* expressed almost point for point the position Maritain had been maintaining in the face of strong Catholic opposition as far back as 1921. This conciliar document, however, could not gain the acceptance of the assembled bishops until it had been watered down to allay the prejudices of certain council fathers, to placate Eastern Catholics, and to avoid offending the Arab world. Maritain's position as a Catholic on the Jewish Question put him far ahead of his time.

Three people whom Maritain met within a period of a few years at the beginning of his career profoundly influenced his position on the Jewish Question. In order of importance they were probably Raïssa, his wife; then Léon Bloy, his godfather; and Charles Péguy. Chronologically, it was doubtless Péguy who first influenced Maritain on this question. He inspired in Maritain a zeal for justice due to the Jew as a human person. Raïssa brought him immediate and very personal experience of what it meant to be a Jew — the culture and traditions of this people and its religious, social and political aspirations. It was Bloy who introduced him to the Jew under the aspect of the mysteriously central and continuing role of this unique people in God's plan of salvation.

Maritain first met Péguy in 1901, shortly before the opening of the bookshop of *Cahiers de la Quinzaine* on the rue de la Sorbonne. The two men soon became very close friends. They got along famously from the very beginning and understood each other remarkably well. Péguy took the young Maritain (who was nineteen at the time) as a collaborator in the role of *"reviseur et correcteur attitré des Cahiers,"*[3] and the young disciple was in daily contact with his master during this period of collaboration. Péguy considered Maritain a younger brother who would help and, later, succeed him to carry on his work with *Cahiers de la Quinzaine.*[4] Péguy affectionately dubbed Maritain and his *protégé's* two friends, Ernest Psichari and Maurice Reclus, with what the latter called "the tenderly ridiculous" title *"les trois dauphins."*[5] Maritain's admiration for his master was so enthusiastic that he insisted that his mother, Geneviève Favre, meet Péguy. Accordingly, he brought Péguy to one of the Thursday evening meetings at her home, and Péguy became an even more regular habitué of these meetings than Maritain himself.

In his boundless enthusiasm for the work of Péguy, Maritain gave generously not only of his time, but also of his money. In 1905, when Péguy had to interrupt the publication of *Cahiers* because of financial difficulties, Maritain advanced him ("evidently without any security," says Reclus) the considerable sum of 10,000 francs, which he had inherited from his recently deceased father.[6] This generous and completely disinterested gesture is proof of Maritain's faith in the causes espoused by Péguy.

One of the causes most ardently espoused by Péguy during the early days of his friendship with Maritain was justice for the Jews. In the very first year of Maritain's collaboration with Péguy (1901), the second series of *Cahiers de la Quinzaine* appeared, in which considerable space was devoted to persecuted peoples, particularly Jews. *Cahier* number nine of the sixth series contained a lengthy article, "La délation aux Droits de l'Homme," a *dossier* on the Dreyfus Affair and its aftermath. In July 1910, Péguy published *Notre Jeunesse*, a reply to the anti-Semitic Edouard Drumont, who had taken the publication of *Le Mystère de la charité de Jeanne d'Arc* as a disillusioned Péguy's rejection of his former position on the Dreyfus Affair and as a confirmation of the thesis of *La France juive*.[7]

It was at the bookshop of the *Cahiers de la Quinzaine* and at the Thursday *soirées* of his mother that Maritain was introduced to Péguy's position on the Jews. The impressionable young Maritain absorbed from Péguy a passionate zeal for justice for the Jew, considered not as a member of the Jewish race but as a member of the human race, with the inalienable dignity of a human person. For Péguy, the horror of the Dreyfus Affair was not that such an injustice was done to a Jew, but that such an injustice should be done to any man. Dreyfus happened to be a Jew, and his condemnation had trampled in the mud certain truths dear to Péguy, namely, the sacredness of Christianity and the honor of France. In *Notre Jeunesse* Péguy wrote:

It was precisely our Christian *mystique* that corresponded so perfectly, so exactly with our French *mystique*, with our patriotic *mystique* in our *Dreyfusard mystique*, that what must be recognized, and what I will proclaim, and what I will put in my confessions, is that the point of view that we took was no less than that of the eternal salvation of France.[8]

By the time Maritain met Péguy, the Dreyfus Affair had been settled in court. In Péguy's mind, however, the affair was far from dead. He wanted it kept alive in the *Cahiers* and in the minds of Frenchmen until its very last potential had been exploited for the "eternal salvation of France."

Péguy spoke on occasion of the Jews as a race. At such times, however, he did not consider the Jewish race from the point of view of its election by God for a unique spiritual destiny. When he spoke of the strange permanence of the Jewish race in the face of so many Christian attempts to wipe it out, of the tremendous cost in suffering required for this survival, of the prophetic mission of this people, he was either preparing a symbol of "that race, the only chosen one among all modern races, the French race"[9] (with its own *mystique* and its own prophetic mission in the modern world), or his references to the sufferings of the Jewish race tended to denote primarily a sympathy for the suffering individual victims of injustice who constituted the race.

> I know this people well. On their skin there is no single spot that does not cause it pain, where there is not some old black and blue mark, some ancient contusion, a silent pain, the memory of a silent pain, a scar, a wound, a bruise from the East or the West. They bear their own and those of others.[10]

Péguy lost no love on the Jews as a race. He loved this Jew or despised that one. He did not understand the Jews; he knew and understood certain individual Jews, some of whom he loved for their spirit of poverty, their piety, their fidelity and friendship, others of whom he despised for their degrading avarice, their willingness to sell one of their own (Dreyfus) in exchange for a little peace and economic security.

Insight into the peculiar vocation of the Jewish race, which he considered the fundamental reason for the social and political injustices perpetrated against the Jews, Maritain would get from others, as well as his love for this unique people. What he got from Péguy was a sense of justice for the Jew as an individual human being, a sense of justice unencumbered by the slightest prejudice.

Maritain met Raïssa Oumansoff shortly after he had been introduced to Péguy. Born on the banks of the Don in a Russia of another epoch, the young Jewess had come to Paris with her family as a very small child; so her entire education was French. Despite the secular, positivist character of this education and the fact that her pious parents, uprooted from the religious milieu of the Russian ghetto, had abandoned their strict external adherence to the public practice of the Jewish religion, she remained profoundly attached to the religious life and the spiritual traditions of her pious Jewish ancestors: admirable, saintly ascetics, nourished on the wisdom of the Book — pious *hassidim*, radiating a sincere and simple charity. Though as a young woman she may no longer have prayed to the God of Abraham, Isaac and Jacob, she retained her belief in a transcendent, personal deity.

Like Maritain, she was subject to a vague adolescent dissatisfaction which quickly turned into a kind of metaphysical anguish. In her search for answers to her questions about existence, the nature of God, the meaning of man, the basis of morality, and the inescapable problems of evil, suffering and death, she seemed to confront an impenetrable wall. One summer day in 1903, in the Jardin des Plantes, Maritain and his *fiancée* Raïssa made a solemn pact to continue for a certain time their search for a meaning in life, and if, after that lapse of time, they had found no deliverance from the nightmare of a sinister and useless world, to commit suicide together.[11]

For Raïssa, the tension and anguish of this period of doubt and despair were all the greater because, as a poet, she was endowed with a more than ordinary sensitivity which brought her intuitive understanding of the ancient, endless sufferings of her people. Robert Rouquette calls her "a tiny individual made to suffer and to understand through sorrow."[12] These intuitive insights into the meaning of Judaism and the role of the Jew in history became conscious and explicit for her through the reading of Léon Bloy's *Le Salut par les Juifs*, and particularly, wrote Madame Maritain, through her subsequent conversion to the Catholic faith:

> Suppose that a Jew should, as is so often the case today, have become altogether a stranger to the Mosaic Faith and hence indifferent to the destiny of Israel. If such a Jew becomes a Christian he begins only then to understand the depths of his debt to Judaism — the idea of a God at once transcendent and personal; the revelation of the supernatural universe, the roots of his new theology, the beauty of

his new liturgy; and only then does he do justice to his people's greatness, and become proud to belong to it.[13]

Madame Maritain communicated this profound sensitivity to all things Jewish to her husband. Two years after their marriage, while he was studying science at Heidelberg, Maritain decided to write a life of his wife. He completed no more than an *Introduction à la vie de Raïssa*, but from this short text (which he reproduced in part in his *Carnet de notes* in 1965) it is easy to see what a central role she played in his understanding and love of the Jewish people. What began as a tribute to Raïssa ended as a lyric tribute to the Jewish race. She was, for him, the exemplar of the traditional virtues, the refinement and the nobility of an ancient, privileged people.

> In her passion for concrete certitude, in her respect for wisdom and her love of Justice, in her unshakeable good humor and her readiness to question, as in the ardor of her blood and the precision of her instinct, everywhere she carries about with her the nobility and the privilege of the race from which she comes, of that Elder Race, to whom God entrusted Himself and who contemplated his angels, who alone is at home in heaven, alone the depository of the promise, is at home everywhere on the earth, will perish only when the world does, and who has the right to consider all other peoples as guests, but late-comers, in its patrimony, as uncultured and without a past, heirs of the Lord by adoption, not by birth. *Puella hebraeorum!* Her native pride marches before her; I have heard Jews declaim on the purity of her type. *Ecce vera Israelita, in qua dolus non est.* But does anyone know how deep plunge the roots of a true Jew? We know that the true Jew is not the carnal Jew, bitter at contestation, chained to the pride of this world; do we realize fully enough that the true Jew loves Poverty and Tears, is Pure of Heart and Merciful, hungers and thirsts after Justice and suffers persecution and death for Justice's sake without ever surrendering? The true lineage of Abraham, an indomitable and faithful people, obedient and tenacious, resisting every hardship, who, sword in hand, constructed the Temple and who fell by the thousands to defend it, patient and charitable men, strong and pious women, whose hope watered the miraculous Stem, worthy at last of God Himself, who did not despise a Virgin's womb, or to

make Himself their descendent, or to choose them as his fellow-citizens.[14]

After a few years of strained relations with Raïssa's parents, due doubtlessly to the fact that their new son-in-law was a gentile and that Raïssa had been baptized a Catholic along with him, Maritain was accepted completely into the Oumansoff family, where he became intimately acquainted with Jewish cultural traditions.[15] In 1906 Raïssa's sister Vera came to live with them in Heidelberg, and henceforth always remained with them. She, too, added to Maritain's appreciation of the Jewish character. In the chapter of his *Carnet de notes* devoted to "Notre soeur Vera," he had this to say of his wife and his sister-in-law:

> They had that same quickness of mind, that same delicate sensitivity, an almost airy perceptivity, that same sense of humor in the midst of tears which comes among the children of Israel not from the blood or the flesh, not from racial heredity, but from a kind of refinement or sharpening of nature which from the time of Abraham and Moses grace has brought about in this people and its culture. Such a quality, which is also a particular susceptibility to suffering, can easily become exacerbated in certain cases, but in others is the seal of a kind of royal dignity.[16]

So important, even from the point of view of the formation of his own character as a human person, did he consider this happy union of the traditions of spiritual refinement, of innocence and of nostalgia for the absolute which he encountered in Raïssa and Vera, that he proclaimed himself a debtor to Israel and expressed his desire to become a Jew by adoption:

> Thus I consider myself a debtor to Israel. Moreover, I do not like the vulgarity of the gentiles: I would prefer to be as little as possible a *goische kop*, I would prefer to be a Jew by adoption, since I have already been introduced by baptism into the dignity of the children of Israel.[17]

The final words of the preceding quotation, written in 1965, concerning the fact that the spiritual life of grace in the Christian finds its origin in the ancient dignity and calling of the Chosen People, express an idea which is central to Maritain's thought on the Jewish Question. He was first introduced to this idea sixty years before by Léon Bloy, whom the Maritains met shortly after their marriage.

Moved by Maurice Maeterlink's praise of Bloy's *La Femme pauvre*, they decided to read it, and were so impressed that they wrote Bloy a letter expressing their admiration and telling him of their religious difficulties. They included a small gift of 25 francs to help relieve the destitution from which Bloy and his family were suffering.[18] *"Le Mendiant ingrat,"* deeply touched, sent a letter of gratitude, and two of his books, and a few days later invited the Maritains to visit him. They did so on June 25, 1905. During the weeks that followed, the Maritains came into possession of *Le Salut par les Juifs*, which Bloy had written in 1892. They read it together, while vacationing in the country in August, after Maritain's completion of the *agrégation de philosophie*, and were overwhelmed. Their ignorance of the relation of Judaism to Christianity, and of Christianity itself, made them totally unprepared for the shock of this revelation. Though much of the book completely mystified them, they immediately recognized its beauty, its startling revelation that the Jewish Question, even in its social and political aspects, was basically a religious problem based on the ancient and irrevocable calling of that people. It expressed the longing for justice, truth and charity which they felt in their own hearts.

On their return to Paris, they visited Bloy to discuss the book with him and have him explain its obscure passages.[19] The reading of *Le Salut par les Juifs* was one of the decisive factors, not only in determining the focus of his thought on the Jewish Question, but in bringing Maritain into the Catholic Church. He wrote in 1927:

> *Le Salut par les Juifs* is undoubtedly, along with *La Femme pauvre*, Bloy's masterpiece. At a time when we knew nothing of the Christian faith, this book — along, of course, with the help of actual grace — was like a supernatural thunderbolt for us, the blinding extension of the prophets and the Figures, the revelation of the divine meaning of human history, and of that permanent witness to which Israel is implacably constrained, proving in spite of itself the authenticity of the Church's message.[20]

Maritain considered this book so important that he decided, shortly after reading it, to have it republished at his own expense as a gift to Bloy. The new edition appeared in January 1906, only five months after Maritain picked it up for the first time,[21] and Bloy dedicated it to Maritain's wife:

To Raïssa Maritain
I dedicate these pages
Written for the Catholic glory
of the God
of Abraham,
Isaac
and Jacob

Until Bloy died, in 1925, he and Maritain visited each other frequently. Maritain helped the old man financially whenever he could, even pawning his microscope for 20 francs to have something to give to his destitute godfather.[22] At these meetings, Bloy and Maritain spoke often of the Jews. Sometimes Maritain would submit his thoughts on the Jewish Question to Bloy for criticism; sometimes he would note down phrases from Bloy's conversation which struck him with particular force.[23]

There were many aspects of the Jewish Question on which Maritain did not agree with Bloy. He recognized that Bloy — even more, perhaps, than Péguy — did not really understand the Jew:

> Bloy had a congenital incapacity to see or to judge individuals and particular circumstances in themselves. He did not make distinctions. From this . . . came the unrestrained excess of his violence which was, in reality, aimed at *something else*. In his violence one must see, first of all, the effect of a very special kind of abstraction, not philosophical certainly, but artistic, or, if you will, an abstraction of typification; every event, every gesture, every individual, given *hic et nunc*, was instantaneously transposed, uprooted from its contingency, from the concrete conditions of the human environment which explain it and make it plausible, and transformed, under the terrible visionary, into a pure symbol of some devouring spiritual reality.[24]

Bloy's excoriations of the Jews remind one of Bernanos' invectives against the Church. Both men were motivated by a profound love; both men were cast in the same prophetic mold. It was Bloy's mission to re-proclaim a divinely revealed mystery which the clergy and Catholic writers of France seemed to have forgotten. His unpleasant caricature of *"Les Trois Vieillards de Hambourg,"*[25] his conception of the extent of Jewish guilt for the Crucifixion, his strange exegesis of certain scriptural texts, which led him to consider the Jews responsible for "keeping Jesus on the cross" and obstructing the arrival of the Parousia, "the third kingdom,"[26] which he longed for with all his prophetic and apocalyptic heart: these excesses and aberrations did not prevent Maritain from recognizing the essential genius and justice of Bloy's vision. Raïssa Maritain, with gentle understanding excused Bloy's harsh and excessive words against the people of her fathers because she knew that even these words were dictated by the excess of his love.

> To this particular man, among all the others, much will be pardoned because he loved much, and because all that he thought of what is divinely true, he was able to express with incomparable beauty. We pardoned him all the dross in favor of the grandeur of his intentions and the magnificence of his words. And then, after all, he didn't know the Jews — at least at the time when he wrote *Le Salut*. . . . Instinctively on our guard in his favor, we pardoned him as children sometimes pardon adults who have hurt them, because the children understood very well that adults know not always what they say, or, according to the testimony of God Himself, what they do.[27]

Despite the book's shortcomings, Maritain knew that Bloy was right in calling *Le Salut par les Juifs* "the most considerable of my books" and "without any doubt, the most energetic and the most urgent Christian testimony in favor of the Elder Race, since the eleventh chapter of Saint Paul to the Romans."[28] The essential message of *Le Salut par les Juifs*, that the Jewish problem is fundamentally a religious problem; that this remarkable race is a people set apart, not only from every other people but from all other peoples taken together; that their uniqueness stems from their election by God for the special mission of providing the world with a Savior; that the gifts of God are without repentance, so that, despite their infidelity, the Jews remain the Chosen People, whose salvation is closely linked to that of the Church, and that the destiny of all mankind depends in great measure on the destiny of this unique people — all these ideas of Bloy became the guidelines of Maritain's reflections on the Jewish problem.

Bloy had couched his visionary intuitions in the mystical language of hyperbole and parable. He did not propound philosophical and theological truths through ordered rational discourse. He sought, rather, to produce the "sensation of mystery and its effective presence." Bloy spoke in a mystical language which made use of reason in a manner

that was more experimental than demonstrative, to express
the real in the very obscurity that joins it to their feeling . . .
[a mystical language which] has as its purpose to make us
guess at reality as if we could touch it without speaking of
it.[29]

Maritain took the truths of Bloy's revelation and, in a philosophical language, "[which] attempts to say it without touching
it,"[30] to express, according to the imperfect mode of human concepts, what it is possible for us to know rationally of the mysterious problem of the Chosen People.[31]

His whole literary effort [said Maritain of Bloy] was, — while
waiting for the day of vision — to project into the mirror of
enigmas and similitudes the rays of that substantially
luminous night. . . . Read according to his intentions, *Le
Salut par les Juifs*, it seems to me, takes on more easily its
true proportions.[32]

Maritain set for himself the task of explicating these
enigmas and similitudes in the ordered language of rational discourse. He felt that Bloy, without being able to express it clearly,
had *touched* a mystery which he himself was attempting to express *without* having touched it.[33] Raïssa Maritain, like her godfather, had most certainly *touched* this mystery, in her case
through poetic experience. It would seem safe to assert that
Jacques Maritain too (though perhaps in lesser degree) *touched*
the mystery in the person of his wife.

In 1945 Charles Journet,[34] one of Maritain's closest friends,
wrote of Bloy:

When put to the proof, the shortcomings of *Le Salut par les
Juifs* will perhaps appear, from a theological point of view,
to be considerable. Five or six affirmations will remain
completely original. But they are the truest, the most important, the most divine, that is to say, the most truly forgotten.
They are royally, splendidly clothed and their clarity is
blinding. This is not a common treasure, worthy of disdain.
It is well worth the trouble to extract it.[35]

He expressed regret that Bloy lacked the facts and the clarifications necessary to grasp, in full reflective and explicit consciousness, the significance of his prophetic intuitions. It was
specifically this lack that Maritain set himself to supply.

Maritain recognized that the principal merit of *Le Salut par les Juifs* was in its treatment of the Jewish Question from the only perspective from which it could be understood, the religious perspective. Bloy had reestablished it on the "infinitely high" plane of theology and supernatural faith, where St. Paul had put it in his Epistle to the Romans. The Jewish Question was not a problem to be solved but a mystery to be contemplated.[36] Charles Journet maintained that it was inane to ask if Bloy had solved the Jewish problem, since for him there was no solution, at least in an earthly historical sense. His mission was to cry out in the desert a divinely revealed mystery which Christianity had forgotten.[37] Maritain was probably the first to heed Bloy's prophetic cry.

Maritain made his first public utterance on the Jewish Question in 1921, when he was asked to deliver a lecture *"à propos de la Question Juive"* at the Semaine des Ecrivains Catholiques.[38] His debt to Bloy is unmistakable. He began by stating that the Jewish Question could be considered either from the political and social aspect or from the spiritual and theological aspect. To his brief consideration of the social and political aspects of the problem and of certain governmental measures taken to alleviate the problem, not solve it, Maritain appended this footnote to the printed version of his text:

> It is impossible for anyone to understand or to judge with complete justice the history of the Jews and their place in the world without taking into consideration the point of view of Revealed Truth. Christians alone are capable of ferreting out the true meaning of the history of Israel.[39]

That is to say, those who consider the problem from a purely temporal, a-religious point of view, whether it be political, economical, racial or social, miss the point entirely. Such interesting and objective, even noble and generous studies, such as the one undertaken by Batault and mentioned by Maritain in his footnote, or Sartre's *Portrait d'un antisémite*, must necessarily remain, in the judgment of both Bloy and Maritain, fundamentally deficient.

Bloy had written, long before Maritain's 1921 conference, that *Le Salut par les Juifs* was not a counterblast to all the racial, cultural, social and financial accusations hurled by Drumont against the Jews. Nevertheless, the mention of Drumont and his anti-Semitism frequently threw Bloy into a rage:

> I was angered to see this colossal question of Israel debased
> to the most abject of financial investigations, and I resolved
> to speak out, for my part, in order to express what others
> cannot or dare not say.[40]

However, he maintained that, essentially, his book had nothing to
do with Drumont:

> The anti-Semitism stirred up by Drumont and his cronies is
> first and foremost a low-down trick. It is at the same time an
> imposture, in the sense that one thing is perfidiously substi-
> tuted for something else, that is to say, an accessory put be-
> fore the public in place of what is essential. This is not the
> question at all. What is the financial power of the Jews com-
> pared to that of the Protestant multi-millionaires? The root
> of the Jewish Question lies elsewhere and it is profound in
> an entirely different sense.[41]

Another way in which Maritain, in his very first text on the
Jews, establishes his debt to Bloy is by using the Epistle of St.
Paul to the Romans as the proof that the Jewish problem is in
truth a mystery of supernatural origin. St. Paul wrote in his remarkable chapter 9:

> The result of their false step has been to bring the Gentiles
> salvation. . . . Why then, if their false step has enriched the
> world, if the Gentiles have been enriched by default, what
> must we expect, when it is made good? . . . If the losing of
> them has meant a world reconciled to God, what can the
> winning of them mean, but life risen from the dead? When
> the first loaf is consecrated, the whole batch is consecrated
> with it; so, when the root is consecrated, the branches are
> consecrated too. The branches have been thinned out, and
> thou, the wild olive, hast been grafted in among them,
> sharest, with them, the root and the richness of the true
> olive. That is no reason why thou shouldst boast thyself bet-
> ter than the branches; remember, in thy mood of boastful-
> ness, that thou owest life to the root, not the root to thee. . . .
>
> I must not fail, brethren, to make this revelation
> known to you; or else you might have too good a conceit of
> yourselves. Blindness has fallen upon a part of Israel, but
> only until the tale of the Gentile nations is complete; then
> the whole of Israel will find salvation. . . . In the preaching of
> the Gospel, God rejects them, to make room for you; but in

His elective purpose He still welcomes them, for the sake of their fathers. God does not repent of the gifts He makes, or of the calls He issues. You were once rebels, until through their rebellion you obtained pardon; they are rebels now, obtaining pardon for you, only to be pardoned in their turn. Thus God has abandoned all men to their rebellion, only to include them all in His pardon.

How deep is the mine of God's wisdom, of His knowledge; how inscrutable are His judgments, how undiscoverable His ways!

However degenerate the unfaithful, carnal Jews may prove, they are still the race of the prophets, of the Apostles, of the Virgin and of Christ. They are the olive tree to which all Christians have been grafted by their baptism.

This fundamental notion, that the Jewish Question is incomprehensible and incapable of explanation other than as the divine *mystery* revealed by St. Paul, is basic, as it was in the case of Bloy, to everything Maritain wrote on the Jews. He insists on it again and again. In 1937 he wrote that the Jewish Question could not be considered a racial problem, however much the Nazi propagandists might make use of this idea, because the Jews, strictly speaking, are not a race, whether considered biologically, nationally or geographically.[42] However, by the fact that they are all nourished by the same spiritual and moral tradition and answer to the same calling, the Jews are indeed a *people:*

the people *par excellence,* the people of God. They are a consecrated tribe; they are a *house,* the house of Israel. Race, people, tribe, all these words used to designate them ought to be held sacred.[43]

In 1939 he wrote:

The central question of our study remains a question of a sacred order, and for us the Jewish Question is first and foremost (I do not say exclusively) a mystery of the theological order; and we must continue to affirm that a Christian is incapable of judging the Jewish Question either speculatively or practically unless he takes the point of view of Christian doctrine and unless he is inspired by the Christian spirit.[44]

To consider the Jewish Question "as such," purely and simply from the natural point of view through the observation of con-

crete facts and independently of religion, he said, is to fall into
the trap of *Maurrassisme.*

In 1965 Maritain published a collection of his texts on the
Jews, *Le Mystère d'Israël,* that takes its title from the principal
essay. Of the eighteen selections chosen for the volume, seventeen
refer directly to St. Paul's Epistle to the Romans, which Maritain
said Bloy had revealed to him in a "supernatural lightning bolt."
Maritain agreed with Bloy that no "final solution" to the Jewish
Question could be found before the great reintegration announced
by the apostle Paul:

> To want to find, in the pure and simple sense, in the decisive
> sense of the word — a *solution* to the question of Israel, is to
> seek to arrest the movement of the world.[45]

Bloy's conclusion to *Le Salut par les Juifs* and to the premise
he seems to establish there, of the apparently congenital sordid-
ness of almost all the Jews, seems to be that, since the condition
of the Jews is willed by God, there is nothing a Christian can do
either for or against the Jews. At this point, Maritain went beyond
Bloy by maintaining that there are practical decisions to be made
and steps to be taken toward a partial and provisionary solution
to the question.

The naturalist or positivist solution of simple and complete
assimilation of the Jews, Maritain rejected as specious. Because of
their holy calling, which according to St. Paul is "without repentance," the Jews would always be a people apart. Economic, political and social assimilation, Maritain maintained, is simply a
question of justice and an end toward which society must work.
But this is no solution to anti-Semitism. Nowhere in the world, he
claimed, were the Jews more fully assimilated than in Germany;
yet this is precisely where hatred of the Jews found its most violent expression. The Jews had been assimilated there in every respect except *spiritually,* and this is precisely the point of the
difficulty.

> The Jew becomes lost if he becomes established, I mean *be-*
> *comes established* as a spiritual phenomenon, as a loss of
> that stimulus of restlessness and as a failing in his vocation.
> *Assimilation* concerns an entirely different problem, of a
> political and social order, not spiritual. . . . [Assimilation]
> will always incur a risk . . . the risk for the Jew of becoming
> established, of becoming *like the others,* I mean in the

spiritual sense, of losing the vocation of the house of Israel. It is then that their God strikes them, even by the vilest of instruments.[46]

This is the dilemma of the Jews: if they refuse to be assimilated spiritually, the wrath of the anti-Semites falls upon them; if they let themselves be assimilated spiritually, and deny their divine calling, they fall into the hands of the Living God. "Jews who become like the others become worse than the others."[47] Maritain goes so far as to maintain that, even if after political, social and economic assimilation, the Jews would accept Christ as their Messiah, they would remain, even among Christians, a people set apart — this time, however, in a place of signal honor, for they would remain the Chosen People of God who gave the world its Savior, the olive tree on which all Christians are grafted.

To declare that there is no solution, absolutely speaking, until the day of the great reintegration leaves only two courses of action open to the Christian, Maritain declared in 1937:

> an animal way — to enter by violence and hatred, overt or masked, prudent or enraged, into a carnal war directed at the extermination, the eviction or the enslavement of the Jews, a war of the world and of the *animalis homo* against Israel. This is the anti-Semitic position. The other way is one proper to the Christian. It consists of entering through compassion into the sufferings of the Messiah and through intelligence and charity into a spiritual struggle directed toward the accomplishment of the Church and of the *spiritual man* for the salvation of the world and the salvation of Israel; this is the *Catholic* or Pauline position which demands in addition the undertaking in the temporal order of a constant work of concrete intelligence, which cannot resolve or surmount definitively all the antinomies, but at each moment of time discovers the means to put up with them and to soften them.[48]

In his writings on the Jews, Maritain returned again and again to a striking sentence of Bloy concerning the role of the Jew in the temporal order: "The history of the Jews dams up the history of the human race as a dike dams up a river, to raise its level." This conception of the Jews as a goad, continually provoking society toward the realization of temporal justice, was also suggested to Maritain by Bernard Lazare, to whom Maritain had been introduced by Péguy.[49] In 1921 Maritain wrote that an essentially messianic people like the Jewish people, from the instant that it refuses the true Messiah, must play in the world a fatal role of subversion, I do not mean by reason of a preconceived plan, I mean by reason of a metaphysical necessity which makes of the Messianic hope and of the passion for absolute Justice, when they descend from the supernatural to the natural plane, and are falsely applied, the most active of revolutionary ferments.[50]

The conclusions that Maritain drew from this insight in 1921 were very different from those he drew in 1937. They proved embarrassing, it seems, in later years and probably explain in part why this first of his texts on the Jewish Question was never included in his 1965 collection *Le Mystère d'Israël*. From the situation described in the above quotation, Maritain deduced the "evident necessity" of a struggle for the public safety against secret Judeo-Masonic societies and cosmopolitan finance, as well as the necessity for certain "general measures" by government for preservation of the social structure. In support of his conclusions Maritain cited an article, "La Question juive et la révolution sociale," written by the anti-Dreyfusist, the Marquis de la Tour du Pin, and reprinted in 1921 in the collection *Vers un ordre social chrétien*.[51] The marquis condemned the political emancipation accorded the Jews during the French Revolution, and in a series of outrageous simplifications he opposed the Jewish conspiracy to Christian society. The Jews, he said, simply obey a historic fatality in carrying out their corrosive activity against Christian society.[52] He proposed, therefore, to treat the Jews as dangerous foreigners to whom all rights of citizenship had to be refused for the good of Christian society.[53]

It is regrettable that Maritain should have given any credit to such anti-Semitic ideas — but did not, of course, completely accept the position of de la Tour du Pin. Maritain suggested that with creation of the Zionist state in Palestine, the Jews be made to choose allegiance to their country of residence or allegiance to Palestine. If they opted for the latter, they should go to live in Palestine; if they opted for the country of their residence, they should sever all connection with the Jewish political body and receive the rights of citizenship in the country of their choice. In 1943 Maritain protested the Vichy government's depriving all Jews of the rights of citizenship and General Giraud's effective revocation of Jewish citizenship in Algeria by abrogation of the Décret Crémieux.[54]

In his 1921 lecture Maritain did not specify what "general measures" the government should take. Such measures were easier to determine in the days when civilization was officially Christian, but he felt that the equivalent could be found for contemporary society. Maritain was evidently ill at ease in this position, for he concluded his remarks to his audience of Catholic writers with a double warning. First, it was their responsibility, he said, to enlighten public opinion, to which government must have recourse for approval of its "protective measures," and to teach the public to consider the Jewish problem without hatred, for "the passions of the masses and the pogroms have never resolved a single question, indeed to the contrary." Secondly, the Jewish Question must not be permitted to misdirect the social unrest and disillusionment of the day toward the Jews as the *unique* cause of the evils from which society was suffering.

> Whether it is a question of ideas, of men or of institutions, there are others that are guilty, and in particular it would be too easy for us to beat our own guilt on the breast of Israel, forgetting that the failings and infidelities of Christians hold first rank among the causes of the present universal disorder.[55]

If Maritain's remarks about governmental protective measures and their contemporary justification seem to echo Bloy's medieval attitude toward the Jews, they appear to be at variance with Péguy's stand for complete recognition of political rights for Jews.

The incompatibility between Maritain's position on the social aspects of the Jewish Question in 1921 and his position in the 1930s is unmistakable. His 1921 position was doubtlessly due to the intellectual confusion resulting from his efforts to bring his social and political thought in line with what Father Clérissac seems (temporarily) to have persuaded him was the official and exclusive position of the Catholic Church. "A propos de la question juive" was written during the time of his ambiguous and embarrassing adherence to Maurras' Action Française and to Massis' Parti de l'intelligence. By 1937, Maritain did not consider the ideas expressed in 1921 as representative of his position, and in 1961 he seemed openly apologetic for his utterances of 1921. He spoke of a "kind of inattention and brutal simplification due to the coarseness of heart that persists in the Gentiles, even those converted (Alas, I am one of them, I know where I stand in this respect)."[56] He was probably referring to his 1921 article, when he stated (in a note to the *avant-propos* in his 1965 collection *Le Mystère d'Israël*) that he was forced to omit certain texts "treating the same subject and writings from times far different from our own, for a different public."

In his second warning to Catholic writers concerning the responsibility of Christians for the evils of modern society, Maritain's words, "whether there is question of ideas, of men or of institutions," reflect his fundamental incompatibility with the position of Action Française on the Jewish Question, particularly from the point of view of Jewish participation in revolutionary movements. The idea that institutions, as well as men, need reform is a revolutionary concept. Maritain developed this thought more explicitly and more fully in the years that followed, until their full expression in *Humanisme intégral* drew, as we have seen, the concentrated fire of Paul Claudel. As early as 1926, even before his formal break with Action Française, Maritain had protested (in his *Réponse à Jean Cocteau*) against certain young *"bien-pensants"* who had expressed their contempt for a Jewish political figure by shouting *"Abraham! hou! hou!"* According to Maritain, they outraged heaven by smearing the name of a great saint whose paternity embraces all Christians, and he added immediately that it is the duty of Christians to look to the Jews as an example of the social unrest that should give impetus to Christians to undertake the necessary reform of institutions:

> It is on them that we are grafted. How could we be inattentive to the winds that pass over the old trunk? We must follow with much love, vigilance and respect the anxiety that troubles Jewish young people.[57]

When *La Grande Peur des bien-pensants* appeared in 1931, Maritain wrote to Bernanos of his objection to certain anti-Semitic passages and to his (Bernanos') adulation of Drumont. Bernanos replied to Maritain's criticism with a letter that was rather harsh in tone, considering that it was at a time when their friendship was just beginning to be reestablished and when Maritain's wounds from previous abuse were just beginning to heal.

> My dear friend, what a phobia of anti-Semitism! God knows after all the very small place I have given it in my book! But when you write that my book "wounds Christ from the very beginning," I find this a very human view, a truly Jewish

view of the Mystery of the Incarnation. It is precisely for just such flesh and blood reasons that your friends ended up putting Christ on the Cross. It seems to me that in dispensing His very pure Mother from the heritage of original sin, common to all the sons of Adam, Our Lord placed her outside and above all race.

But then don't I have the right to the same opinion of the Jews as did the men of the thirteenth century? . . .

Ask your dear wife, whom I always think of with a respectful, profound and fraternal affection, to forgive me for some of the reflexions I made above. Your friendship is more consoling for me and sweeter than you can imagine. We will speak of it again when we meet in Paradise.

Jacques Maritain does not seem to have replied directly to this letter. He sent it to his wife, who at the time was sojourning in St.-Paul de Vence; and perhaps being out of patience with the irascible and unpredictable Bernanos, and fearing that in replying he might express himself in a way that would compromise the fragile, reburgeoning friendship, he seems to have asked Raïssa (before whose delicacy and finesse Bernanos was incapable of anything but gentle galantry) to answer this disconcerting letter in his place. At any rate, in the Maritain Archives at Kolbsheim, along with the letter from Bernanos, is the rough draft of a letter from Raïssa (dated Pentecost, 1931) which is a point-by-point answer to the letter of Bernanos:

I am deeply touched, more than I can say, by the friendship that you show me. . . . I am trying in the light of this friendship, to situate the very serious evil you have spoken of Jacques; and I understand that you cannot reflect on it when you enter into that region, in some respects sub-human, of polemics whose object is not truth but the battle for a cause in which one thinks it possible to compromise everything, even friendship and justice, because it seems to contain all those things in itself and to take precedence over all.

It is in this area of polemics that your book on Drumont also finds its place.

The passionate love of France, the concrete, vital knowledge you have of that person and his history, all the bursts of flame that run through all those pages, all this is good to feed the flame and spread the fire. But how can we hold it against you? When in fact the straw of certain arguments will have gone up in flames, there will remain the immortal trace of a heart that has loved much.

Nor is it the anti-Semitism of your book which hurts me. As you say, you give it little space. And I haven't the slightest desire to defend the "power of money," even when it is Jewish. After all I personally do not know any rich Jews. My family has always been poor and that is perhaps what enabled me to love the *"mendiant ingrat"* [Léon Bloy]. Nor do I believe that any single one of us can presume on the immense gifts of God to his people. *Populi, populi meus . . .* God Himself calls them back to Him reproaching them for their ingratitude; *Quid feci tibi . . . aut in quo contristavi te?* But these gifts are undeniable.

The privilege of the Immaculate Conception puts neither Mary nor Jesus "outside their race." Otherwise how do you explain that on the day of the Nativity of Mary the genealogy of Christ is read from St. Matthew's gospel? *Liber generationis Jesu Christi, filii David, filii Abraham . . .*

The people who have been charged with the writing of the Old and New Testaments and furnishing the Universal Church with its prophets, its apostles and its evangelists, and its first martyrs cannot be laicized either because of its faults or because of its race.

Excuse me for taking up so much of your time with my thoughts. I would like to speak to you again at greater length, and do you think it necessary that this wait until we meet again in Paradise? Won't you come to Meudon some day?

Later, it was to Raïssa that Bernanos sent a personal copy of *Les Grands Cimetières,* inscribed: "For Madame Raïssa Maritain who protects with her two joined hands a fervent and patient flame from which we light our torches."

In 1937 Maritain published an essay entitled "L'Impossible anti-sémitisme" in the collection *Les Juifs.*[58] By this time Father Clérissac was long dead, any connection with Action Française had been severed, and the shackles these two associations had imposed on his intellectual independence were broken. In this essay he completely repudiates the doctrine of those who (like de la Tour du Pin) claimed that "the Jews are united as one man in a plot to morally corrupt and politically subvert Christianity."[59] He renounces his own contention of 1921, that the Jews should be the object of special restrictive legislation to prevent such subversive purposes. In 1939, he claimed that restrictive legislation, modeled on the Middle Ages, was inapplicable, even in modified form, and completely incongruous in contemporary society. Modern pluralistic society, as he conceived it in his *Humanisme intégral*, was far different from the "sacred society" of the Middle Ages, and no legalistic equivalent respecting the Jews is applicable today.

> It seems that the period into which we are entering is called to try another experiment fundamentally different from the medieval experiment, but which might correspond to it analogically, and which would temporalize, if I might use the term, or would adapt to a "profane" civilization a problem which the Middle Ages envisaged from a social point of view. One could quickly characterize the regime we are thinking of here as pluralist and personalist; and this regime, far from being invented for the particular case of Israel, corresponds in our way of thinking to the type of civilization whose historical ideal is particularly fit for our times. We feel that contrary to Hitler's medieval parody, a pluralism founded on the dignity of the human person, and which, on the basis of complete equality of civil rights and of respect for the liberty of the person in his individual and social life, would recognize in the different spiritual families entering into the fellowship of the temporal City an ethico-historical statute proper to the questions we might call mixed (that is, touching both the spiritual and the temporal) would represent, among other advantages, for those nations capable of this type of civilization, the attempt at an organic settling of the Jewish Question that is best adapted to our historical climate. It is by direct agreements with the spiritual community of the Jews, institutionally recognized, that these questions touching on both the Jewish and the general common good would be resolved.[60]

Maritain had again returned to the inspiration of his old master, Péguy.

In 1937 Maritain developed further the thought he had expressed in his *Réponse à J. Cocteau* eleven years before: in the social sphere, the Christian should emulate the "stimulating restlessness" of the Jew. If the Jew seems to have an excess of that earthly hope which leads to personal commitment in the struggle to achieve the reign of absolute justice, the average Christian has far too little of it. Thus in the history of the world the Jew plays the role of a stimulus:

> In regard to what touches *indirectly* on the salvation of the world, [the Jewish people] obeys a calling on which, in my opinion, we should insist above all else and which gives the clue to many an enigma. While the Church is assigned to the work of the supernatural and supratemporal redemption of the world, Israel is assigned, in the order of temporal history and its proper ends, to the work of *terrestrial activation* of the mass of the world. Though it is not of the world, Israel is there to irritate it, to exasperate it, to *move* it. As a foreign body, as an activating ferment introduced into the mass, it will not leave the world at rest; it prevents it from sleeping, it teaches the world to be discontented and restless as long as it does not possess God; it stimulates the movement of history.[61]

In the same collection in which Maritain's "Impossible anti-sémitisme" appeared, Daniel-Rops, the editor, published three letters by Paul Claudel on the Jewish Question, one of which points up the single aspect of this problem on which he and Maritain were at variance: the historical role of the Jewish *"inquiétude stimulatrice."* For Bloy and for Maritain, this "stimulating restlessness," which raised the level of civilization, was an element of the divine calling of the Jews, whereas Claudel found Jewish involvement in modern social unrest completely negative, subversive, and destructive.

The first of Claudel's letters is one he wrote to the organizers of a World Jewish Congress, who had asked him to submit an article to serve as a kind of preface to this congress. The fact that he was asked is testimony to the widespread recognition of Claudel's love for and understanding of the Jews. In this letter, Claudel denounced the persecutions in Germany of the Jewish people, "that unshakable rock," which "with an heroic courage and an intellectual boldness that would be inexplicable without a vocation from on high . . . had always maintained . . . the idea of a personal and transcendent God." Because of the pressure of his numerous duties, Claudel excused himself from contributing an article, in which, he said, he would willingly have written again of what he had written so often before: his great love and respect for the Jewish people and for their divine calling. The beautiful

lines of Sichel in *Le Pain dur* and of Pensée in *Le Père humilié*
prove this to be true.

Claudel's careful and loving study of the Bible freed him
from the prejudices rampant even among the Catholics of his
time, particularly those of his own political persuasions. Even on
questions of the social evils which pressed on society, he refused
to go along with the right wing, which attributed them wholly or
in great part to the machinations of the Jews. If there were evils
in the world, he claimed, gentiles were far more responsible for
them than the Jews. In his play *Le Père humilié*, Claudel has the
young Jewish girl, Pensée, reply with these words to the question
of Orian about her blindness: "Show me Justice and it will be
worth the trouble to open my eyes." She continues:

> I am a Jewess like my mother, and she thought that the
> Revolution had arrived, and that everything was going to
> blend and become equal, and that you would accept it
> among you, she had so much good will!
>
> But I know better:
>
> Anything is better than a false love, that carnal desire
> which we mistake for passion, and that passion which we
> mistake for acceptance, and then the position which is taken
> up again little by little and becomes foreign to you. . . .
>
> But I, I am like the synagogue of old, such as it was
> portrayed on the portals of the Cathedrals,
>
> I have been blindfolded and everything I wish to take
> is broken. *(Low and fervently)* But you others who can see,
> what do you do with the light?
>
> You who see at least, you who know at least, you who
> at least are alive,
>
> You say that you are alive, what are you doing with
> your life?
>
> ORIAN — But this blood [of God], it was you who
> spilled it.
>
> PENSEE — This God, we are the ones who gave Him to
> you.
>
> Ah, I know, if there is a God for humanity, it is from
> our heart alone that He could come one day.
>
> ORIAN — Didn't He come?
>
> PENSEE — What did you do with Him? Is that why we
> gave Him to you?
>
> In order that the poor be poorer and the rich richer?

In order that property owners collect their rent? In
order that the stock-holders eat and drink well? In order
that half-crazed kings rule over their brutalized people?

There can be no resignation in the face of evil, there
can be no acceptance of the lie. There is only one thing to do
with what is evil, and that is to destroy it![62]

How many ideas important to Maritain are expressed in
these moving words of Pensée: the impossibility for the Jew to
find complete assimilation, rejection of the idea of Jewish responsibility for the death of God, the exalted vocation of Israel to
supply the God-Redeemer, the Jewish preoccupation with the
reign of temporal justice.

The second letter from Claudel in the collection *Les Juifs*,
however, reveals the second point on which he and Maritain disagreed over the Jewish Question. This second letter was addressed to Daniel-Rops, who had written to Claudel for permission to include the first letter in *Les Juifs*. Claudel's reply to
Daniel-Rops shows clearly that the point of his disagreement with
Maritain over the Jewish problem is simply another aspect of the
same discord which inspired the bitter exchange in *Figaro* over a
sentence from Maritain's *Humanisme intégral*.[63] If there are evils
in society, claimed Claudel, they had to be cured by the reform of
individuals, not by social revolution or the reform of institutions.
The structure of society, according to Claudel, had to remain in-
tact.[64] He refused to admit, with Maritain, that the Jews had a
vocation to "stimulate" the movement of history through their
thirst for absolute justice. If, as Maritain recognized, "the world
detests their passion for the absolute and the unbearable stimulus
that this passion inflicts on it," Claudel claimed that Jews who
pursue such a vocation in society were simply receiving their
comeuppance in the persecution society inflicted on them, as it
has a right to inflict on any deluded, meddling humanist.

In his letter to Daniel-Rops, Claudel wrote that his letter to
the Jewish Congress represented only one aspect of the question:

There is another on which for the moment I do not have the
courage to insist. Yet it is a fact that the Jews can be found
everywhere in the front ranks of the parties of social and
religious subversion. Besides, may it not be that in this destructive role they are obeying a kind of providential vocation? But it's not surprising then that this brings about certain reactions.

On the other hand it is surprising to see so much intelligence, such a spirit of generosity and sacrifice, such a vivid sense of spiritual matters, gathered together around something dead and petrified. One would be tempted to say that the Jews no longer read their Scriptures or that they read them without understanding. When I lived in America, from time to time I came upon sermons of rabbis. It was the same disgusting hog-wash that flows inexhaustibly from Protestant books.

"How the gold has been tarnished? How its excellent color has been changed?"

It is sad to see a son of Israel who can no longer be distinguished from a Baptist or a Methodist.

Claudel added this postscript at the end of his letter:

P.S. — There is another text that I cannot reproduce except in Latin: *Qui nubriebantur in croceis amplexati sunt stercora.* This last word seems to me to apply exactly to this disgusting humanism which instead of being attracted to man himself, appreciates nothing but his offal.[65]

In 1938 Maritain delivered a lecture at the Théâtre des Ambassadeurs, entitled "Les Juifs parmi les nations," in which he took up once again the question of revolutionary tendencies among the Jews. He denounced the readiness among fascists, right-wing conservatives and even among large numbers of Catholics to identify Judaism with communism. He sympathized with Jews who were often driven to anarchic and revolutionary activity by the unbearable injustices of a society which then blamed them for their rebellion.[66]

In this address, Maritain classified Louis Ferdinand Céline with Hitler, Rosenberg, Streicher, Goya, Cuza and all those who imputed to the Jews all the plagues of the human race. He considered inexcusable the blind and almost visceral anti-Semitism of *Bagatelles pour un massacre*, in which Céline "seems to have gone to the end of the night only to find the *Protocols of Sion* waiting for him there, left in the filthy darkness by the former Tsarist police."[67] In an article in *Nouvelle Revue Française*, entitled "Les Juifs, Céline et Maritain," André Gide took issue with Maritain's classification of Céline as an anti-Semite; he was astonished that Céline could be so completely misread. The fact that Céline included Cézanne, Picasso, Maupassant, Racine,

Stendhal and Zola among the Jews marked for massacre was indication enough, for Gide, that the whole thing was a joke, calculated to shock the public. "What more do you need? What better evidence that this is nothing but a big joke?" Gide asked. Most people, he said,

> could find unbecoming a literary joke which, with the help of stupidity, risks entailing tragic consequences. As for the question of anti-Semitism itself, it is not even touched upon. If *Bagatelles pour un massacre* had to be considered as anything else but a joke by Céline, despite all his genius, it would be inexcusable to arouse such banal passions with such cynicism and irresponsible lightheadedness.[68]

After this defense of Céline, Gide put down a few personal reflections of a general nature on the Jewish Question, provoked by Maritain's lecture, which he had read as published in *La Vie Intellectuelle*. He spoke of his admiration for this "remarkable conference" and paid Maritain a very generous tribute:

> Here we find that enlightened generosity, that Christian confidence and that wisdom which makes us love Maritain in whatever he writes.[69]

Nevertheless, Gide found the conference disappointing. First of all, he expressed his difficulty in following Maritain's argument that the Jewish Question is not a question of race in the biological sense of the word. Maritain had claimed that if the question could be considered racial, it was only from an ethico-historical point of view. Gide agreed that the continual harassment to which the Jews had been forced to submit in the course of centuries had certainly marked this people, even to the extent of forming certain traits of character which tend to distinguish them from the gentiles among whom they dwell. But one step further, he wrote, "and we will be claiming that it was the blows rained upon them and the sacks of flour loaded on their backs that slowly turned horses into donkeys."[70]

Secondly, Gide disapproved of Maritain's emphasis on the religious aspect of the problem. Even if one day all the Jews, touched suddenly by the inspiration and grace of the Holy Spirit, were to convert to Christianity, he claimed, they would nevertheless remain Jews, because the essential problem was not confessional but racial. He also questioned whether a certain moral relaxation might not follow the disapperance of those racial characteristics which give the Jews their proper specificity. He felt, for example, that if the Jewish passion for law and justice were excessively tempered by Christian charity, something invaluable would be lost, not only to the Jews but to the world. This problem was for Gide but one aspect of the general problem of national and racial minorities. He felt that with the gradual disappearance of minority groups, the West was in danger of losing those contributions to civilization that such groups could offer and of upsetting the delicate balance established by their presence. He ended by expressing his desire that Maritain give more consideration to the positive contribution of the Jewish race. The future, he said, would undoubtedly give Maritain ample opportunity to return to this problem.

Despite Gide's generous compliment, his article irritated Maritain, and in June 1938 he published an article in *La Nouvelle Revue Française*, "Réponse à André Gide sur les Juifs." He stated that it was impossible to cover all aspects of the Jewish Question in a lecture whose subject was the theological significance of the Dispersion and the present plight of Jews in the various nations of Europe. Many misunderstandings could have been avoided, he said, if Gide had simply consulted the text of his earlier lecture, "L'Impossible anti-sémitisme" (to which Maritain had referred his reader, in the text which Gide had read),[71] for a more complete treatment of "this immense and painful subject." Here Gide would have found an anticipated reply to the desire he expressed at the end of his article.

Maritain insisted that to place considerations of race with respect to the Jews on an ethico-historical (rather than biological) basis is by no means to "cause the notion of race to scatter and disappear." Such distinctions were necessary, he said, to get rid of the "pseudo-problems" raised by the biological myths which distract from any real solution:

> Once this authentic sense of the notion has been made precise, many pseudo-problems and myths will vanish, along with the great blond Dolichocephal with blue eyes in whom today so many dark-haired, brown-eyed Germans recognize themselves and to whom they dedicate in their private sanctuaries a kind of totemic reverence.[72]

In the article which Gide had read, Maritain had insisted (after quoting his old master Péguy) that the Jews have a strict right to "the justice and human brotherhood that all men deserve"; but he added that after the distinctions of race resulting from historical injustices and animosities had been eliminated, the Jew would remain a Jew. This was proof for Maritain that the problem was basically religious. For Gide, it was proof that the question was not "confessional" but racial in a biological sense. Gide's choice of the word "confessional" is unfortunate, for it betrays a rather careless reading of Maritain's text. As was the case with Claudel in the *Figaro* exchange, Maritain betrayed his irritation at being accused of saying what he had not said:

> Where could Gide have found that I am reducing the Jewish Question to one that is purely confessional: To say that it has its origin in a mystery of the theological order, and to try to understand it in the perspective of Scripture and of St. Paul, is in no way to make it a simple confessional question. It is Scripture that speaks to us of the Chosen Race; it is the Scriptures that oblige us to see in the Jewish Question a transcendent social question; it is not from a confessional point of view that the Scriptures look at things but from the divine.[73]

Gide should not have missed phrases in Maritain's text which raised the problem far above the mere matter of confessional adherence. For example,

> If the world hates the Jews, it is because it knows very well that they will always be strangers from a *supernatural* point of view; it detests their passion for the absolute and the unbearable stimulus that they inflict on it.[74]

If Gide took Maritain's statement that, according to St. Paul, the drama of love between God and Israel would find its *dénouement* on the spiritual and temporal levels only through the reconciliation of the Church and the Synagogue, as meaning that conversion to the Catholic confession would eliminate all distinction between gentile and Jew, a reading of the text to which Maritain referred him would have indicated to Gide that "when a Jew receives the grace to become a Christian, he is less than ever like the others; he rediscovers his Messiah."[75] That is to say, even after the reintegration of St. Paul, the Jews would nevertheless continue to be the Chosen Race, the priestly people.[76] Gide's statement that if the Jews "suddenly converted all together, they would remain no less Jews for that fact" in no way contradicted what Maritain had said. The difference lay in the interpretation given to the nature of the persisting distinctions. Gide would have considered them racial whereas Maritain would have considered them religious, based on a divine and irrevocable calling.

Maritain was piqued too by Gide's accusing him of considering the racial characteristics of the Jews "uniquely as troubling elements." Maritain claimed that his incessant promotion of pluralism should have prevented such an accusation by Gide. And indeed, Gide must have been cognizant of the furor that arose over *Humanisme intégral.* Gide would certainly have found the concept of pluralism applied directly to the Jewish problem, if he had taken the trouble to consult the text to which Maritain had referred him.[77] But even if he didn't do so, he could have found in the text he *did* read a reference by Maritain to the positive contributions of Jews to the historical process, which was in fact one of the major points of his study:

> The communion of this mystical body is the communion of earthly hope. Israel hopes with a passion, waits, longs for the coming of God into the world, the kingdom of God here below. It longs with an eternal desire, with a supernatural and irrational desire, for Justice in time, in nature and in the City.
>
> Thus, like the world and the history of the world, Israel and its action in the world are ambivalent realities. For the desire for the absolute in this world can take many forms, some good, others bad. This is the source of the astonishing complexity of the human types it presents and who abound at the same time in both good and evil. One can always find reasons to exalt Israel and to debase it. . . .
>
> But what then is this vocation of Israel which continues on in the night, and of which we have just spoken? First of all there is its vocation as witness to the Scriptures. But in addition, while the Church is assigned to the work of the supernatural and supratemporal redemption of the world, Israel, we believe, is assigned in the order of temporal history and its proper finalities to the work of the terrestrial activation of the mass of the world.[78]

Maritain's claim that Gide seemed to have read his article "with a certain distraction" appears quite justified.

To Gide's defense of Céline's "dizzying lyricism" about the Jews, "where his grievances and his ill-temper are exposed to the great amusement of his readers," Maritain answered simply that

today one cannot speak frivolously of the Jewish Question
(could one ever do so) either by complacently giving rein to
one's moods or one's resentment, or with the euphoric trucu-
lence that a jokester uses to describe the victims of his wit.[79]

Maritain ended his lecture at the Théâtre des Ambassadeurs
with an account of the oppression and indignities suffered by the
Jews in Germany, Rumania, Poland and Russia, and practical
considerations of what could be done to alleviate the situation.

Maritain's conference at the Théâtre des Ambassadeurs inspired a rash of abusive attacks from the far right, especially from
the collaborators of Maurras and Massis at Action Française.
François Mauriac came immediately to his defense, and all the
more ardently because the president of the Conseil de Paris con-
nived to prevent Maritain from giving the conference a second
time, as had been planned.

Without neglecting a single one of the crafty arguments of
the anti-Semites and the racists, Maritain breaks through
the walls that hatred strives to build around us, and right
from the start sets himself on the supernatural level where
St. Paul had already placed the Jewish Problem: Israel appears to us a mystery, of the same order as the mystery of
the world and the mystery of the Church. . . . Israel has a
kind of supra-human relationship to the world as the Church
has to the world. . . . In the eyes of the Christian who re-
members that the gifts of God are without repentance, Israel
continues its sacred mission, but in the night of the world,
preferred on what an unforgettable occasion, to that of God
himself.

It was from this time that Mauriac, no longer content to manifest
his compassion for the persecuted people of God in words alone,
joined the organizations which Jacques and Raïssa Maritain had
set up or were supporting for the repatriation of Jewish refugees
from Austria and Germany.[80]

It was likewise this conference of Maritain's at the Théâtre
des Ambassadeurs which inspired Bernanos' barb:

I am perfectly capable . . . of honoring Mr. J. Maritain at the
same time that I deplore his effeminate daydreams about
the Jews . . . which win for him public acclaim at the
Théâtre des Ambassadeurs.[81]

It might appear incongruous that this "anti-Semite from way back," as Gaeton Picon called Bernanos,[82] could have written in the same book:

> Under the inspiration of General Franco, Mr. Hitler might very well have used the following language with churchmen: "I love Semites. Spiritually I am myself a Semite. Unfortunately many Jews have made themselves unworthy to bear this famous name, which, through all the earth, is a synonym for Magnanimous. I will call to judgment at my quick and efficient trials all those Israelites who are dangerous for the faith and morals of our precious members of Catholic Action, i.e., all the Jews who are vassals of Moscow." The German bishops would certainly have given their blessing to this irreproachable good will, except to deplore perhaps a certain excess of zeal and to recommend to those dear judges and dear executioners the practice of jaculatory prayer and of the spiritual bouquet in the exercise of their delicate functions.[83]

This apparent excoriation of Hitler's anti-Semitism is not so surprising, however, if kept in context. What Bernanos was attacking here was not so much the horror of anti-Semitism as the kind of hypocrisy, particularly among the *bien-pensant* Catholics, which was undermining the honor and grandeur of France. In his early book *La Grande Peur des bien-pensants*, Bernanos shows that, like Drumont, in whose defense he wrote the book, he considered the Jews as playing an important role in the conspiracy against the honor of France. Like Péguy's, Bernanos' attitude toward the Jews was formed by his concept of the vocation of France. For Péguy, the vocation of France to be the exemplar of justice in the world demanded that she accord complete justice to the Jew. For Bernanos, however, the ancient values of French culture and civilization were being destroyed by the malevolent machinations of a conspiratorial clique of Jewish foreign bankers and capitalists with unpronounceable, barbaric names. The Jews had taken advantage of the only nation in Europe which had spared them the horrors of the Inquisition and the harassment of the Reformation. The Jews suddenly found themselves masters of a country which had been demoralized by the Revolution and was incapable of resistance:

> The ardent Jewish minority [wrote Bernanos], admirably endowed for all forms of disputation, profoundly indifferent

to Western philosophy, but who see a masterful alibi in the war of ideas, waged with banknotes for weapons, has become in the natural course of events the nucleus of a new France which grows more powerful little by little at the expense of the old France until one day it believes itself big enough to play the decisive role. But in the meantime the other France has died.[84]

Unlike Maritain and Péguy, Bernanos — at least until the last years of the Second World War — could not conceive of the Jew as a Frenchman. The danger to France was all the greater because the Jews, who had been cut off for centuries from the civic and cultural life of France, were throwing themselves on its sick and unresisting body. Besides, the Jews — according to Bernanos — were in great measure responsible for the weakening of the moral fiber of the nation by the strange, demoralizing fascination they held over French youth. He treated with sympathy, for example, Drumont's incapacity to understand how three

> young Frenchmen with blue eyes and blond mustaches, with broad shoulders, built to do battle and to make love [could have preferred for their pleasure] . . . an old Jewess, completely faded, painted up like an idol from India, completely mortuary in her appearance . . . to a beautiful Margot in all her freshness, with lovely eyes and healthy white teeth and a youthful figure.[85]

In his blind admiration for Drumont, his *vieux maître*, Bernanos was incapable of making the metaphysical and political distinctions that Maritain could make even in 1921, when he gave some credence to stories of a conspiracy by "Judeo-Masonic secret societies." Bernanos was never able to rid himself of this blind spot, and it is probably this fact, more than anything else, which prevented the complete reconciliation between the two men, even during their common defense of France against the occupying Nazi forces and the Vichy *régime*.

Bernanos recognized Drumont's anti-Semitism as a political maneuver, a center of focus for political discontent, a starting point for a general offensive:

> Where was anti-Semitism leading them? one might object. Doubtless it is not easy to say — for we will see that it has become in the long run the prey of a certain number of naive fools or clever schemers. But what we do know is that the

thought of its creator leads to a dictatorship of the public
safety, a national dictatorship, impregnated with the traditions of old France and of our ancient public Law, to a traditional and popular *régime* at the same time as to a Christian social order. Maurras was never mistaken on this point;
directly or not, the thought of Drumont leads to the King.[86]

Bernanos accepted uncritically this hypocritical cultivation
of anti-Semitism for political ends, and in 1938 condemned the
papal pronouncement against anti-Semitism. Maritain accepted
the pope's condemnation as unquestionable proof that anti-
Semitism is incompatible with Christianity.[87] Bernanos denigrated the papal condemnation, insinuating that the Jews were
still powerful, or, if not, could easily become so again.[88] He put a
parody of the pope's words, "spiritually we are all Semites," in
the mouth of Hitler: "I love Semites. I am myself spritually a
Semite."[89] Bernanos evidently could not take seriously what Maritain considered the heart of the matter: the religious aspect of
the Jewish Question.

During the early months of 1944, in his weekly messages
from America to the Free French, Maritain emphasized more and
more the essentially religious nature of the persecutions of the
Jews. He gave as the fundamental reason for the sufferings of the
Jews the fact that Israel

> activates and stimulates terrestrial history, and because the
> slave merchants will not pardon the Jews and their Christ
> for the demands that they have introduced into the heart of
> the temporal life of the world, and who will always say *no* to
> the triumph of tyranny and injustice. . . .

> The central fact, and doubtless the most important
> meaning from the point of view of the philosophy of history
> and of the destiny of the human race, is that in our day the
> passion of Israel takes on more and more distinctly the form
> of a cross.

> Jews and Christians are persecuted together and by the
> same enemies: the Christians because they are faithful to
> Christ, and the Jews because they have given Christ to the
> world. How is it possible that so many Christians close their
> eyes to the supernatural meaning of a drama that they alone
> can decipher?[90]

A few days later, Maritain read over the radio to the Free
French an unedited poem of his wife Raïssa on the religious basis

of the Jewish persecutions.[91] In May of that year, Bernanos maintained, contrary to what Maritain had always held, that the Jews are a separate race from a biological as well as from a cultural point of view, and he played down the importance of the religious aspect of the problem:

> I am not anti-Jew, but I would blush to write the contrary of what I think, that there is no Jewish Problem, or that the problem of the Jew is not a religious problem. There is a Jewish race, and that is recognized by evident physical signs. If there is a Jewish race, there is also a Jewish sense of life and death, of wisdom and of happiness. That these common traits — social and mental — are more or less immediately evident, I willingly grant. They exist, this is what I affirm, and in affirming their existence, I neither condemn nor despise them.[92]

Even though in 1943 Bernanos may have taken up in passionate terms the defense of Georges Mandel, a Jewish French patriot killed by the Nazis, in an article in which he put himself squarely on the side of Maritain against the Vichy *régime*,[93] one year later he made some reservations about the possibility of a Jew becoming completely French:

> There is no such thing as a French race. France is a nation, that is to say a human achievement, a creation of man. . . . But there is a Jewish race. A French Jew, incorporated into our people for several generations, will without a doubt remain racist since his whole moral and religious tradition is founded on racism, but this racism has gradually humanized. The Jew who is French has become a Frenchman who is a Jew.[94]

During the war years Maritain began to give particular attention to an aspect of the Jewish Question which he felt was at the root of much of the sufferings the Jews had to endure through the centuries at the hands of Christians. This was the ancient Christian prejudice that the Jews were collectively guilty, as a race, for the death of Christ and that their lot of suffering was the punishment imposed by a just God on a stiff-necked, deicide race. In the August 1944 edition of *The Jewish Frontier*, Maritain published an open letter to a certain Hayim Greenberg concerning Christian teaching about the Crucifixion and the responsibility of the Jews for the death of Christ:

This guilt was that of a few persons, the princes of the priests, and, to a certain extent, the mob of those days, blinded and cruel as the killers of the prophets had been. The Christian, knowing that Christ is the Second Person of the divine Trinity, had good reason to call this guilt a crime of deicide: it was so in fact. But it was not so with regard to the conscience of the judges; if they had known He was the Son of God, they would not have condemned Him, for their fault was essentially lack of faith and blindness of the heart; they did not recognize the One whom the prophets had announced. At this point, Christian teachers should emphasize the saying of St. Peter: "I know that ye did it in ignorance, as did also your rulers" (Acts 3:7), as well as the word of Jesus on His Cross: "They know not what they do."[95]

The concept of collective guilt cannot be applied to the Jews of today, said Maritain. If they have suffered collectively as a result of the spiritual misstep of their ancestors, there is a divine mystery to be grasped. In this case, the idea of corporate atonement can be understood only in a very limited sense.

This concept is valid only from the highest metaphysical and transcendental standpoint, and divine punishment is only the normal, mysterious fructification of human deeds, and the patience of God waiting for man's return. Not only must we point out . . . that every Jew of today is as innocent of the murder of Christ as every Catholic of today is of the murder of Jeanne d'Arc or the imprisonment of Galileo. But above all it must be stated that those who want to punish the Jews, who are in the hands of their and our God, for the murder of Golgotha, make themselves guilty of blasphemy and sacrilege; they stupidly encroach for the sake of their own human wickedness upon the hidden purposes of God, they flaunt the love with which He waits for His people, they offend with their bloody hands eternal wisdom itself.[96]

Such rhetorical commonplaces as "the deicide race," which have been used for centuries by Christians, are pregnant with anti-Semitic possibilities which may burst out at any moment into the worst feelings, wrote Maritain. The Christian teacher has the duty to rule out such expressions, which are definitely nonsense, as well as any similar improprieties due to human and gentile thoughtlessness. For a Christian to consider the Jews, as a race, guilty of the death of Christ is an alibi for his own sense of guilt for the death of his Savior, of which he wants to clear himself. This letter was published in 1944 in the book *Pour la justice* and in 1947 in *Raison et raisons*. It is very probable that Bernanos read this letter, since by his references to Maritain in his wartime writings he showed himself familiar with what Maritain was publishing. In 1947 Luc Estang published an essay of Bernanos, "Dans l'amitié de Léon Bloy," as an introduction to his study *Présence de Bernanos*. In this essay Bernanos claimed that he had as much right to the title of *filleul* of Bloy as did Maritain, and a few pages later, as if to prove that he was more faithful to the thought of Bloy than was Maritain, who was attempting to exonerate the Jews, he wrote:

> Do what you will and say what you will, Christians, the poor [Jew] will not really understand your language unless he is a Christian himself, and the others will end up crucifying you by mistake — as they crucified Jesus Christ. For the poor Jews were no less responsible for his death than the rich. After all, those people of Nazareth — among whom were his own cousins — who spoke to him so cruelly that his heart, painfully disappointed and deeply hurt, refused them any miracles, were certainly not rich stock-holders.[97]

Indeed, in this respect Bernanos is closer to the thought of Bloy, but only in the sense that he is closer to one of Bloy's prejudices. Like the men of the Middle Ages, Bloy was not free of certain spiritual and temporal prejudices about the Jews.

Bloy's attitude toward Jewish responsibility for the death of Christ is linked with his particular interpretation of the words of St. Paul: "What will be their reintegration, if not a resurrection from the dead?" (Rom. 11:15). There are generally two interpretations given to these words, and the first is *historical*. The reintegration of Israel will provoke, in the very course of history, a resurrection of Christian life, an epiphany of the universality of the Church. The second is *catastrophic*. The reintegration of the Jews will be the signal for the end of history, the final judgment and the resurrection of the dead. Bloy chose the second. It suited perfectly his apocalyptic temperament and his passion for the Parousia.

For Bloy, as for Pascal, Jesus was forever suffering on the cross. By their refusal to accept their Messiah, the Jews have become the jailers of the Redemption; Christ and his Church are their captives; they can retard at will the coming of God's glory (*Le Salut par les Juifs,* chap. 23). Jesus cannot descend from the cross until they convert (chap. 23); therefore the salvation of the world depends entirely on them (chap. 33). What kept Jesus from coming down from the cross and the heavens from falling on the earth? Bloy thought he had found the answer in revelation: it was the fault of Israel, whose hardness of heart alone held back the decisive hour of the blessed catastrophe. Bloy's anger and persistent prejudice against the Jews did not come, as it did to some extent in the case of Bernanos, from a consideration of the Jews as collectively guilty of a deicide committed 1900 years ago. He held them all personally responsible for holding back today, by their present hardness of heart, the final end of history, for which he prayed each morning and, in this sense, for keeping Christ nailed to the cross. Thus they have become perpetually the deicide race.

Bloy, of course, did not hold the Jews alone responsible; he said elsewhere that Christians are even more responsible, but the emphasis in *Le Salut* is on the guilt of the Jews. Here Maritain separated himself from Bloy; he preferred the *historical* interpretation of St. Paul's text. The arrival of what Maritain called "the Third Age," in this book *Humanisme intégral,* could only be the result of a long period of slow maturation, of patient labor and suffering.[98] He found this gradual realization of God's plan by men through their patient work of recuperation far more beautiful than Bloy's sudden and brutal catastrophe. God would not substitute his own action for that of man, as Bloy wanted, but would depend on the free cooperation of his creatures. In an address to the thirty-eighth Council of the Union of American Hebrew Congregations on April 3, 1943, Maritain said:

> The development of which I am speaking will take place in the midst of the greatest crises of human history. And the entire fulfillment of our hopes is to be expected only at the end of this tremendous trial. In other words, the age in which we are already engaged is an apocalyptic age. Here I must point out that in my opinion the date of the Judeo-Christian eschatological literature must be interpreted as announcing, not the end of the world, but, on the contrary, a splendid renewal of the world.[99]

Maritain's efforts to exonerate the Jews of collective guilt for the death of Christ, as well as his efforts to rescue them from physical persecution, which he thought derived in great measure from the erroneous concept of a "deicide race," won for him a great honor in 1961. During the war years, Maritain worked indefatigably for the rescue of Jews from occupied Europe; he was especially active in the Emergency Rescue Committee and in the International Rescue and Relief Committee, and was frequently invited to address their meetings.[100] Many of the acquaintances he made in the Jewish community of New York, and of America in general, enabled him to carry on much of the work of reconciliation and *rapprochement* between Christians and Jews, which in 1961 won for him (and for his wife posthumously) the Edith Stein Guild Award for fostering cooperation and understanding between Christians and Jews.

In 1947, while Maritain was French ambassador to the Vatican, he received an invitation to participate in La Conférence Internationale Extraordinaire pour Combattre l'Antisémitisme at Seelisberg in Switzerland. Unable to attend because of his numerous duties at Rome, Maritain sent a long communication to the conference in which he put down his most recent reflections on the Jewish Question and reiterated the necessity of eliminating the expression and the concept of "deicide race" from Christian vocabulary and thought. He also decried the fact that the history of the Crucifixion was frequently taught to Catholic children in such a manner as to excite hatred for the Jewish race. In the same way, careless translations of the *perfidia judaica* of the Good Friday liturgy, which rendered *perfidia* by the words "perfidy" or "treachery" instead of by "unbelief," only reinforced such hatred.[101]

In 1959 Pope John XXIII ordered that the adjective *perfidis* be stricken from the liturgical text and that the anomalous rubric of genuflecting before all the prayers except the one for the Jews be eliminated. It is difficult to determine what responsibility Maritain might have had for such decisions. What can be said with certainty is that Maritain held the position of leadership in a scandalously small group of Catholic thinkers who protested vocally against the term "deicide race" and all the traditional teachings, customs and attitudes that resulted from this concept.

Among the few Catholics who had the courage and the vision to protest the traditional position of Christians on the Jews, a surprisingly large percentage were from the group who frequented the Maritain house and the meetings at Meudon. There were Msgr. (later Cardinal) Charles Journet, with his *Destinées d'Israël* and the periodical *Nova et Vetera;* George Cattaui; René Schwob; Nicholas Berdyaev; Stanislaus Fumet and the editors of *Temps Présent;* Louis Massignon; Jean de Menasce; Joseph Bonsirven; Paul Vignaux and the editors of *Témoignage Chrétien;* and Jacques Madaule, who, though he probably owed as much to Claudel as to Maritain for the formation of his attitude toward the Jews, followed Maritain beyond Claudel in his recognition of the Jews as a stimulus to history in the social as well as the religious sphere.[102] To these men one might add Denis de Rougemont, a Protestant from Switzerland, who was often at Meudon, and Robert Charbonneau, Paul Beaulieu and Claude Hurtubise, the editors of the French-Canadian periodical *La Nouvelle Relève,* which owed its origin and inspiration to Maritain during his stay at the Mediaeval Institute in Toronto and his residence in America.[103]

The slaughter of six million Jews during the Second World War gave impetus to a reappraisal of the Catholic stand on the Jewish Question and culminated in section 4 of the Second Vatican Council's declaration on the *Relation of the Church to Non-Christian Religions.*[104] The text on the Jews reads like a *précis* of what Maritain had been writing years before the war. The position that had gained for him strong opposition and even abuse in many Catholic circles had become, by 1964, a commonplace among the growing number of Catholic liberal theologians. The official position of Vatican II on the Jews was the position that years before had gained Maritain the scorn of Bernanos' "effeminate reveries about the Jews," the derision of a Spanish official, who accused him of being a "converted Jew" whose wisdom had certain "accents which recall those of the elders of Israel and the hypocritical manners of Jewish Democrats,"[105] or the odious attack of the Benedictine abbot Dom Jamet, who wrote that the Jewish Question for Maritain could be reduced to a "domestic problem," since all that Maritain had written on the Jewish problem had been written only to please his Jewish wife.[106] The conservative opposition raised at Vatican II by the original draft of the statement on the Jews was reminiscent of the dissension aroused at Les Ambassadeurs when Maritain delivered his "Impossible anti-sémitisme" in 1938.[107] The conservative element among the bishops at Vatican II was still large and powerful enough in 1965 to prevent passage of the original version. A number of modifications were necessary to gain sufficient votes for the statement, and every modification represented a retreat from a position defended strongly by Maritain.

The 1964 text contained specific proscription of the word "deicide." The word was dropped (and consequently its proscription also) from the final text. (It has already been mentioned that Maritain suggested this proscription in 1944.) His statement in 1965, the year in which the Vatican II final statement was approved, leaves no doubt about which version he would have preferred.

> There certainly was deicide. But no one wished it as such. And the murder of Christ was the work of a handful of men — pharisees, high-priests, bands of fanatics recruited by them to demonstrate before Pontius Pilate — a handful of men who *knew not what they were doing.* To make "the Jews" — in their totality responsible for the death of Jesus — all Jews who were on the earth at the time of Jesus, and all Jews of all times — and to speak of the Jews as a "deicide people" is a bloody absurdity.[108]

The second modification was the dropping of the word *damnat,* the word traditionally used by the Church to condemn heresies. The original statement read: "The Church condemns hatreds and persecutions of the Jews." The final statement contained a specific reference to "anti-Semitism" which was not in the first, but the weaker word *deplorat* was substituted for *damnat.* The stronger expression was certainly more in accord with Maritain's thinking. Christians, he maintained, could be anti-Semites only by obeying the "spirit of the world," which is directly opposed to the "spirit of Christianity." He described anti-Semitism as a "pathological phenomenon which reveals a deformation of the Christian conscience."[109] Spiritually, he said, anti-Semitism is the question of "life or death for the Christian."[110]

Concerning Jewish responsibility for the death of Christ, the 1964 statement read: "What happened to Christ in his Passion cannot be attributed to the whole people then alive, much less to that of today." The 1965 declaration was changed to:

> Although the Jewish authorities and those who followed their lead pressed for the death of Christ, still, what happened in His Passion cannot be charged against all the Jews without distinction then alive nor against the Jews of today.

The phrase "who followed their lead and pressed for the death of Christ" leaves the way open to mental and emotional reserva-

tions. The short and pointed statement of 1964 would have ob-
viated this possibility.

Again, the 1964 statement said: "Even though a large portion of the Jews did not accept the Gospel, they remained dear to
God for the sake of the Patriarchs." The last part of this sentence
is a paraphrase of a statement of St. Paul which is central to Maritain's position. The 1965 version says: "Jerusalem did not recognize the time of its visitation, nor did the Jews for the most
part accept the Gospel — indeed many opposed its spreading."
The negative note introduced into the 1965 statement and the
implication of moral responsibility is exactly what an anti-Semite
would seize upon and remember.

Finally, on the preaching and teaching of contempt for the
Jews, the 1964 statement said: "Nothing in the catechetical work
of preaching should teach anything that could give rise to hatred
or contempt for the Jews in the hearts of Christians." The 1965
statement was changed to read: "All should see to it, then, that in
catechetical work or in preaching the Word of God, they do not
teach anything that does not conform to the truth of the Gospel
and the spirit of Christ." This, of course, leaves the door open to
all sorts of interpretations, since it does not spell out in precise
terms just what the "truth of the Gospel and the spirit of Christ"
is in this particular regard. In his letter to Hayim Greenberg
(quoted above) and in his preface to *La Politique selon Jacques
Maritain* of Henry Bars, Maritain was most explicit concerning
the responsibility of Christian teachers in the formation of attitudes toward the Jews.

Despite the modifications introduced into the 1965 text, the
Vatican II declaration on the Jews represented a giant step forward and a victory for a position Maritain had been in large
measure responsible for founding. Louis Chaigne finds it to Maritain's honor that the position on the Jews, finally promulgated by
the Church as part of its effort at *aggiornamento*, was all found in
the pages of books and articles written by Maritain forty years
before, in a political and spiritual climate entirely different from
our own, and before the abominable crimes of the Nazis.[111]

In this, as in so many other questions, Maritain displayed
his almost unerring ability to see into the heart of the matter,
cutting through all pretense, ambiguity, pettifoggery or self-
interest. His relentless opposition to the errors of racism and his
courageous attack on its unspeakable crimes against humanity
rank among the noblest deeds of Jacques Maritain.[112]

CHAPTER 6

The Second World War
and the Defense of Democracy

DURING THE SECOND WORLD WAR Maritain became even more closely involved in the political problems of the day than he had been during the Spanish Civil War. From the first days of the conflict, in the midst of confusion and despair, Maritain refused to give up hope for the survival of democratic institutions in Europe. He devoted himself, with Bernanos, to the problems of democracy, and of the political reorganization of Europe after the war, on both the practical and theoretical levels. He agonized over the problem of Vichy, but allied himself immediately with the National Committee of Liberation. In addition to his intellectual involvement, he gave himself to the immediate and pressing problems of the rescue of European refugees, weekly broadcasts to the Free French and to occupied France, and the founding of a French university in exile. These were the busiest years of his career.

The years that preceded the Second World War were a period of intense anxiety in France. The shadows of the coming war darkened everything. As far back as the early thirties, the clouds of the coming disaster had hung menacingly on the horizon. The apocalyptic predictions of Léon Bloy seemed about to be fulfilled. Henri Massis attributed this mood of anxiety and apprehension among literary figures to the influence of Paul Valéry and Jacques Maritain.

Massis chose Julien Green as an example of what he considered Maritain's influence as a prophet of doom in establishing a mood of pathological pessimism:

> As for Maritain, whose apostolate among "*avant-garde* literary figures" left him in a state of anxiety and disappointment, he buried himself in the coming apocalypse and waited for the "end of the world." Julien Green . . . noted down . . . in his

> *Journal:* "Maritain's visit depressed me. According to him, the
> world is nearing its end, we are already sliding into the abyss,
> or rather, we are already there. If the war doesn't take place,
> the revolution will take care of annihilating us. Everything is
> falling to pieces." At whatever page one opens Green's *Journal*
> for these years, one finds him everywhere obsessed, haunted
> by the war and the revolution.[1]

This sense of imminent catastrophe was common to almost
everyone in Europe, except those who, like Massis, could see in
the invasion of Ethiopia a defense of Western civilization, in the
February riots in Paris a welcome birth of *Nationalisme Social*,
and in the victory of Franco a defeat of communism. For most
men, these events were but preliminaries to the coming disaster.

Massis misrepresents Maritain with this single, isolated ci-
tation from Green's *Journal*. Indeed he seems, perhaps intention-
ally, to have overlooked the fact that in practically every case in
which Green writes in his *Journal* of his "terrible forebodings" in
relation to Maritain, he invariably concluded the entry with some
remark about the sense of peace and confidence that Maritain inspired in him.[2] And rightly so, for if there was one outstanding
characteristic in Maritain during the years before the war and
during the darkest hours of the conflict, a characteristic which he
shared with Bernanos, it was his refusal to despair.

If Maritain spoke of the "end of the world," he meant the
end of the world as it was before the war, the end of a stage in its
existence. In 1935, in the lectures which later were published as
Humanisme intégral, he spoke of a new age of Christianity about
to begin. By "the end of time" he meant "the end of the actual
period of time," the biblical "latter days," which furnished the
title for the periodical he organized as a replacement for the suppressed *Sept.* This *"temps présent"* represented the days of catastrophe and destruction which would precede a new age of religious and spiritual renewal.[3]

The gatherings at Meudon during the years just before the
war, when Maritain's influence was most widespread in France,
were more numerously attended than ever. The pall of anxiety
caused by the storm which threatened on the horizon could not
dim the hope for the future which animated these meetings. Of
the annual retreat in September 1937, at which almost 300 were
in attendance, Maritain wrote:

> Darkened by serious political disagreements and by the
> twilight of Western Civilization, this retreat maintained the

power, as do all our retreats, of establishing a spirit of communion among all the participants. And, in spite of all the anguish, hope, supernatural hope, remained alive in our hearts.[4]

During the unsettled days of mobilization in 1938 before the Pact of Munich, the annual retreat had to be replaced by "private Thomist study-days," which Maritain says were characterized by "an astonishing spiritual joy and an extraordinary sense of peace."[5]

On February 8, 1939, Maritain delivered a lecture, "Crépuscule de la civilisation," at the Théâtre des Ambassadeurs in Paris.[6] If the Western democracies were not to be swept away, said Maritain, and a darkness fall upon Europe that might last for centuries, it was on condition that they find their vital principle in justice and love, whose source is God.[7] Maritain had no illusions about the immediate possibility of a return to the vital principle. He foresaw with surprising accuracy, in February 1939, the betrayal of this vital principle on French soil in the 1940s by the very people who called themselves Christian; but he refused to admit that such a betrayal could find permanence in France.

> I do not believe that it would be imprudent for me to claim that a self-styled Christianity which would no longer know of what spirit it is, which would connive with political state-worship or with Hitler's racism and would find its learned Doctors among the journalists of the totalitarian states, a self-styled Christianity which would found its unity on the hatred of a political enemy, which would despair of the soul of the people and the strength of the Gospels and would renounce all hope of penetrating the temporal life of nations, such a self-styled Christianity could not possibly make itself at home among us.[8]

In his lecture, Maritain outlined once again the "new humanism" of the age that was to follow la fin du temps. If there was a kind of resignation to the long night that must inevitably fall on Europe, there was just as much certainty of the dawn that would inevitably follow the night:

> In the evening twilight where we stand, a number of signs . . . already lead us to discern the uncertain glow of a new dawning. The spiritual reawakening, which has been taking place in our country for several years, now has great importance for the whole future of civilization. And so too has the

development and growing influence of the new parties of French young people, whose political and social concepts are founded on the value of the human person.[9]

The months that followed the outbreak of the *drôle de guerre* were filled with heartbreaking confusion. During the days of anxious waiting for the invasion which would follow upon Hitler's conquest of the Lowlands and Norway, Maritain refused to despair over the crumbling fortunes of France or of the survival of civilization. Paradoxically, in the midst of the despairing resignation to the imminent invasion of France, Maritain began to write of what must be done to assure a lasting peace after the defeat of Germany. During the first four months after the declaration of hostilites, he wrote a series of articles about the war which appeared in periodicals in Argentina, the United States and France. They were gathered together by Daniel-Rops and published in his collection "Présences," under the title *De la justice politique: Notes sur la guerre présente*. These six articles, printed in one volume, form a remarkable unity, for they are concerned with one point: the necessity of forming a federal Europe and a federal Germany after the war to ensure a lasting peace. Such a program was certainly not an expression of fatalistic resignation to the end of the world.

As a fundamental condition for the preservation of civilization, Maritain laid down the necessity of a moral renewal which would be specifically and radically applied, in particular, to national and international politics:

> The renewal toward which we are impelled to work here and now and which likewise implies a profound moral revolution, consists of finding in both thought and action the intrinsically ethical character of politics on the international as well as the national level. Without this neither an authentic sense of the common good, nor an authentic sense of the solidarity of all peoples can be re-established. In addition, I do not believe that those peoples, who at the present moment are engaged in a just war and who cling with an unshakable hope to the final outcome of their cause, can escape their responsibility of bringing this renewal to the world.[10]

But once the necessity of this moral renewal was recognized, said Maritain, the first and most necessary practical step toward a peaceful and stable world would be the founding of a federation of European states, one of which would be Germany, itself a federation of equal states. A lasting peace in Europe was an inconceivable ideal unless it were based on federal cooperation which turned the constructive energies of the divers peoples of Europe toward accomplishment of a common task. He foresaw the difficulties that such an organization would have to face. One condition for the success of such a venture would be that

> all the participating states admit simultaneously and on an equal basis to those diminutions of sovereignty required by an organic institutional cooperation. To arrive at such a stage, profound and awesome remouldings of social forms must take place; in these changes alone can there be any hope for Europe and for Western Civilization.[11]

Maritain called for England to abandon its principle of "political insularism" and for his own country to give special consideration to the organically international character of modern economy and to the international control that it requires.[12] He called on France to abandon its traditional nationalism, which dated back to Richelieu and Louis XIV. Such a political orientation, he said, was inconceivable today.[13]

A European federation was impossible, however, without the admission to that federation of a unified and stable Germany. What had to be avoided by all means was the kind of humiliation, vindictive constraint and punitive reprisals which vitiated the peace of 1918 and facilitated the rise of Hitler. An Allied victory, he wrote, while Hitler was marching from one conquest to another, should aim at four objectives:

> 1. to exclude, because it renders impossible any kind of normal international life, the National-Socialist Party, and force it to bear the responsibility for the evils it has let loose upon the world; 2. to wipe out any vestige whatever of Nazi nihilism, and to work without respite to help the new generations purge themselves of this spiritual poison; 3. to reduce completely the domination of Prussia and Prussianism, to establish a federal system in which all the German "nations" would find their home and be constituted as atonomous political units and to give back to Austria and to all those regions below the *limes*, whose civilization has been formed by the influences of Rome and Christianity, the political importance called for by their role in the formation of

Germanic Culture; 4. to put the German people, for whom a just peace must wish good, and not evil, in such conditions as would bring about the overriding influence of the peaceful elements among them, by providing for their lives and their work possibilities of normal expansion, turned, not toward the domination of others, but toward the common good.[14]

This preoccupation with a European federation gradually grew to include countries of the other continents as well. Since the concept of this new international society derived, he said, from the "temporal hope implicit in the Gospels" for all mankind, the role of establishing it fell particularly to Christians — to the members of the only truly and absolutely universal society, which transcends all human boundaries and all diversities, whether of race, of class, or of nationality.[15]

Maritain's indomitable hope would let him consider nothing but an eventual victory over Nazi Germany. He wrote and spoke repeatedly,[16] even during the darkest days between Dunkirk and the Allied invasion of North Africa, of how the French, more than any other people, would have to know at the same time how to conquer and to pardon; for France was the conscience of Europe.

France is the nerve center of the conscience of Europe, the promontory of Europe turned toward the Atlantic and the new world; her geographic position and political tradition make her a natural link between the East and the West in our civilization, between the Russian world and the world of the English language. Her historical mission and her strength in the period after the war, will be to determine and to stabilize the destiny of Europe in the cooperation between these two worlds, and to contribute to their mutual understanding by giving formal expression to the new ideas which are at present in a period of gestation in all the free hearts of oppressed Europe. The action and the responsibility of France will thus be of considerable importance in international organization after the war and in the reestablishment of that federation of nations which we all hope for.[17]

From Brazil, where he had exiled himself because of his refusal to face the coming decomposition of France, Bernanos too never ceased to call his country to its role as the "conscience of

Europe." However much he may have denounced France for stubbornly plodding to its degradation and destruction, he never ceased to hope against hope, with Maritain, that France would once again recognize its peculiar vocation and regain its honor. In 1953, André Rousseaux wrote of how Bernanos could speak of "France's surrender," even before the capitulation in 1940, and warn his countrymen in terrible terms of what was so infinitely serious in this eclipse of her mission. But Bernanos always admitted the possibility that the soul of France was only slumbering. He implored France to waken, and never lost his faith in her. She was, in fact, the only one to whom he called out, whom he loved in her sick body, despite and beyond the invectives. Bernanos' hope, said Rousseaux, was invincible.[18]

As in the case of Maritain, Bernanos' hope for a lasting peace and a stable Europe was conditioned on the conduct of the Allies after the war. Though he held up Clemenceau, time and again during the war years, as the hero Pétain should have been, because Clemenceau would have refused to capitulate and sign an armistice with the enemy, he nevertheless clearly recognized the injustices of the reprisals and revenge of Versailles. He spoke of "fatal Germany at once the victim and the executioner of the human race."[19] He looked forward, likewise, to an international society of nations and particularly to a federation of European states. Bernanos gave less consideration to the practical aspects of this supranational unity than did Maritain. The unity he looked forward to was inspired by the Christian unity of the Middle Ages:

> In the course of three centuries the politics of our two countries [France and England] have no longer been inspired by a common idea; we have let the Christian front fall apart; we have lost the sense of that European unity whose foundation had been assured by the genius of the thirteenth century; we have pursued the chimera of a balance based on empire in the hope of being the only beneficiaries of its instability.[20]

Bernanos opposed the Christian unity which was on the point of being realized in the thirteenth century to the modern disorder and rivalry among nations. When the Curé de Torcey spoke of the unity of Christendom in *Journal d'un curé de campagne* (1936), it was of a work that was interrupted, not of an accomplishment that was repudiated:

> Ah! if we had only let the men of the Church do their work.
> . . . We were in the process of founding an empire, beside
> which that of the Caesars was nothing but dung, a peace, a
> real *Pax Romana*.[21]

In his *Lettre aux Anglais* (1942), Bernanos alluded to that "Federation of Nations" which "in its spiritual unity" the thirteenth
century was about to realize.[22]

It would be naive to think that Bernanos looked simply for a
return to the past. The Christian order to which Bernanos aspired
came from a dream, an unattained and perhaps unattainable
ideal, not from a past reality. "What Bernanos demands is beyond
all reality," wrote Gaeton Picon; "dissatisfaction is his destiny."[23]
But nothing was further from the thought of Bernanos than that
the concept of world unity should be fixed in the immobility of
the past:

> I demand neither for you [America] nor for France a resto-
> ration of the past, which would be just as artificial as ret-
> rospective exposition.[24]

Conservative and reactionary immobility was unnatural to
France, he said, because the French are essentially a revolutionary people, that is, a people with many crimes on its conscience
but a people who can make reparation for these crimes only by
moving forward.[25]

For Bernanos, the forward movement would receive its driving force from a spiritual unity based on common religious beliefs
and aspirations. On this point Bernanos and Maritain differed.
Maritain was far more explicit on the relation of Christianity to
the new international political order than was Bernanos, whose
position was ambiguous. At times Bernanos seems to imply a direct relationship between Christianity and the new world order,
so that in spite of material differences in organization the formal
relationship between Church and State would remain identical in
the modern world to that of the Middle Ages.[26] At other times he
seems to be saying that a new principle of unity must be found,
having its foundation not in a common religious faith, whether
Catholic or Christian, but in a common recognition of basic values:

> When I speak of a restoration of Christian honor I do not
> mean a religious renewal, in the strict sense of the term. . . .
> Christian honor can revolt just as well in the heart of an

unbeliever as in that of a believer, because it has formed the consciences of both of them.[27]

This latter, pluralistic attitude toward international political organization is implicit in what Bernanos wrote after 1940, but his attachment to *l'Ancienne France* and to the monarchical form of government, and his lack of acquaintance with countries outside the Latin-Catholic tradition, prevented him from developing and clarifying this line of thought.

In Maritain's political writings the principle of pluralism played the central role as far back as his *Lettre sur l'indépendance* in 1935. In a broadcast to France on October 28, 1943, Maritain explicitly applied the principle of pluralism to the new international order that had to follow the war:

> There is only one temporal common good, that of political society, just as there is only one supernatural common good, that of the Kingdom of God, which is above politics. In the course of modern times political society has succeeded in becoming distinct in its own strictly temporal domain. To introduce into this domain a particular religion, and which would demand for them a privileged situation in the state, would be to introduce a principle of division into political society and by that fact to fall short of the temporal common good of all.[28]

The social and political organization of medieval Europe, in Maritain's opinion, was not simply inappropriate, but impossible in the world today. Given the diversity of religions in the West, consensus could not be found in religion itself, considered particularly as an institution. The consensus had to be found in the common ground of basic human values, such as the dignity and rights of the human person, the foundation of moral authority, the capacity to obligate in conscience (which is the property of just laws), the right to work and to have access to the goods of this life, the right of free association and assembly, the right of free speech, the law of brotherly love, and the sacredness of the natural law.[29] Maritain felt that these fundamental values were the result of Christian ferment in the world, "a manifestation of evangelical inspiration." Christianity, Maritain said, should furnish the best defense of these basic human values, and he was quick to add that this did not mean that such values could not be found among men of other confessions or that even, on frequent occasion, non-Christians were not far more active in the defense of these values than "the Children of Light."

It was not given to integrally faithful believers in Catholic dogma, it was given to Rationalists in France to proclaim the Rights of Man and of the Citizen, to Puritans to give the death-blow to slavery, and to atheistic communists to abolish the absolutism of private profit in Russia. This last operation would have been far less vitiated by the force of error and would have been far less costly in catastrophe, had it been carried out by Christians. The effort to free man and his work from the domination of money has its origin nevertheless in currents let loose on the world when the floodgates were opened by the preaching of the Gospels, just as was the case in the effort to abolish slavery and in the effort to bring about a recognition of the rights of the human person.[30]

On this point, as on almost every fundamental issue, Bernanos was of one mind with Maritain. In a tribute to the countless men who died in defense of human rights, with no external attachment to the institution of Christianity, Bernanos said:

You, oh! you who ask bitterly if you have not died in vain, — no one hears the sigh escaping from your bullet-ridden breasts, but this feeble breath is that of the Spirit. I am not using here the language of a pulpit orator or of a neo-Catholic poet; I am simply stating a truth as simple and as certain as two and two make four. A great number of you who are free men would be greatly surprised to learn that they are marching in the vanguard of Christianity, that God sends them ahead of Him to open the passage. And if I told them this to their faces, perhaps they would answer with blasphemy.[31]

This is exactly what Maritain said. Bernanos was basically a pluralist in his conception of the international organization of nations, without perhaps realizing it. The differences between him and Maritain arose from a confusion of words. Maritain took time to make careful distinctions; Bernanos did not. When Maritain spoke of the "spiritual unity" of the West, he was careful to point out that he had in mind a unity of the spirit, not an institutionally religious or confessional unity. Bernanos used the term ambiguously, sometimes appearing to refer to the confessional unity of medieval Europe as an ideal; sometimes hinting at a pluralistic interpretation.

On many questions this same superficial, apparent disagreement unnecessarily troubled the relations of these two men, who were in reality profoundly one in their attitudes. Maritain had written in 1925 that the worst conflicts often arise from a matter of simple lexical interference:

> What makes misinterpretation so easy is that the meaning of a word, well-determined in one context, has its harmonic echoes in entirely different contexts, and these are all the more numerous as the timber of the word is richer.[32]

This was especially the case for Bernanos and Maritain with the word "democracy."

The history of Maritain's thought on democracy is a gradual evolution. It is the story of a mind that was able to divest itself of early prejudices, broaden its perspective, deepen its understanding, and accept the changes which new knowledge and insights imposed on it. The early writings of Maritain, which were concerned with problems far removed from politics, nevertheless contain a number of ironical quips at the expense of democratic institutions (quips for which he later expressed regret).[33]

During the period of collaboration on *La Revue Universelle*, he distinguished three meanings that could be attributed to the word "democracy": (1) social justice, (2) the republican regime, and (3) the sovereignty of the people. He considered the first interpretation acceptable and necessary, admitted the possible legitimacy of the second, and rejected the third with short shrift. He admitted with regret, in 1943, to having discredited not only the idea of a democratic government, but also, though unintentionally, the efforts of sincere democrats toward social justice.[34] Henry Bars remarked that Maritain resigned himself only with difficulty during the thirties to adopt the word "democracy." Bars notes its first use in a favorable sense in *Du régime temporel et de la liberté* in 1933, and then only very prudently.[35] After attentive reflection, Maritain admitted that there might be something very profound and healthy and worthy of being safeguarded in the concept of democracy, provided it were purged of the myths of Rousseau's *Contrat social*.[36]

It was Maritain's visits to America before the war, and particularly his long stay during the war years and after, which most affected his attitude toward democracy. Near the end of his long sojourn in America, Maritain referred directly to this influence:

In actual fact, it is in America that I have had a real experience of concrete, existential democracy: not as a set of abstract slogans, or as a lofty ideal, but as an actual, human, working, perpetually tested and perpetually readjusted way of life. Here I met democracy as a living reality. Residing in this country, and observing with lively interest the everyday life of its people, as well as the functioning of its institutions, is a great and illuminating, an unforgetable lesson in political philosophy.[37]

In the lecture he gave in October 1938 at the Théâtre des Ambassadeurs, he used the term "Christian democracy." The expression had been coined by Pope Leo XIII and had occasioned many bitter disputes. It had been shelved in Catholic circles as promptly as the principles of social reform contained in the pope's encyclical *Rerum Novarum*. Maritain noted that Pope Leo's expression had been reestablished officially in the Catholic vocabulary by the American episcopate, and added: "I suppose that no one, because of this, will mistake the American Bishops for *Red Christians*," which was precisely the label tacked on Maritain by those with whom he had formerly shared a deep distrust of democracy.[38]

In 1943 Maritain published a short but very important study of the democratic philosophy of society, and the influence of his stay in America is evident. "The word democracy itself," he said, "has very different resonances in America and in Europe."[39] This little book, *Christianisme et démocratie*, marked a new stage in Maritain's thought. From this time on he was wholly committed to democracy as a political and social institution. Democracy had become for him a topic of intense study, which rapidly developed and clarified his thought, and produced *Scholasticism and Politics* (1940), *Les Droits de l'homme et la loi naturelle* (1942), *Christianisme et démocratie* (1943), *Principes d'une politique humaniste* (1944), *La Personne et le bien commun* (1947), and *Man and the State* (1951).

According to Henry Bars, Maritain overcame the last obstacle to his complete acceptance of democracy when he expressed *philosophically* what he had expressed affectively in the article "Exister avec le peuple" in 1937. It is a classical position of the right that the people, lacking education, maturity and responsibility, are incapable of governing themselves. Once Maritain had chosen to "exist with the people," not through a unity of benevolence but through a unity of love, he no longer had the right to consider the people as minors, since he had renounced forever his right to put himself above the people. Maritain's observation of the fidelity of the "little people" of France throughout the war showed him where confidence could most safely be placed for the preservation of human freedom. It was the "educated, mature and responsible" classes that for the most part, he claimed, capitulated and then collaborated with the enemy in the destruction of freedom in France.[40]

The central theme of Maritain's *Christianisme et démocratie* was that the principal reason for the failure of the modern democracies, particularly in Europe, was their inability to recognize, through a tragic prejudice and misunderstanding (caused for the most part by the negligence of Christians), that

> in its essential principle the form and the ideal of common life called democracy comes from the inspiration of the Gospels and cannot subsist without it. . . . The question is not to discover a new name for democracy, but to discover its true essence and to bring it to realization, to pass from bourgeois democracy, dried up because of its hypocrisy and because the sap of evangelical inspiration no longer runs in its stem, to an integrally human democracy; from a democracy that has failed to a real democracy.[41]

The term "democracy" is nothing, said Maritain, but the profane or secular name of the Christian ideal. The Christianity in question was not that of a religious credo or an ecclesiastical institution, but Christianity considered as a ferment in political and social life, as the bearer of the temporal hopes of men, and as an historical energy at work in the world.[42]

Maritain spelled out, in the chapter of *Christianisme et démocratie* titled "L'inspiration évangélique et la conscience profane," the particular elements in the concept of democracy which are derived from the Christian heritage. Among these elements are the sacredness and inviolability of the human person, the dignity and equality in rights of the common man, the distinction between the rights of God and the rights of Caesar, the impulse to ameliorate and emancipate all of human life, and the ideal of human brotherhood. All of these elements were more or less recognized, at least in theory, as deriving from Christianity or finding their support and defense in Christianity. To these, however, Maritain added another element which was not generally accepted as flowing from evangelical inspiration: the idea that political authority derives from the consent of the governed. Maritain wrote:

> By virtue of the unnoticed work of evangelical inspiration the profane conscience has come to understand that the authority of governments, by the very fact that it comes from the author of human nature, is addressed to free men who belong to no master and that it is exercised by virtue of the consent of the governed. . . . What has been acquired by the profane conscience, if it doesn't turn to barbarity, is the conviction that authority or the power to exercise it, is held by the governing bodies of the terrestrial community uniquely because that authority expresses in them the common consensus, and because they have received their charge from the people. This is the conviction that the normal condition to which all human societies should tend is a condition where the people act as adult persons in political life.[43]

After the war, in a series of lectures at the University of Chicago (which resulted in the book *Man and the State*), Maritain developed this idea further in treating the concept of sovereignty, and his thoughts ran as follows. Sovereignty, particularly as understood by Rousseau, was a deformation of a Christian concept. The idea of a power and independence supremely transcendent, separate, and above all that the sovereign governs is a concept attributable only to God. In the political order, he said, there is no such thing as absolute sovereignty. The idea of absolute sovereignty was devised in the sixteenth century by Jean Bodin to invest the king with separate and transcendent power and thus free him from responsibility to the people. Hobbes assured the solidity of the social contract in the seventeenth century by transferring sovereignty to the great Leviathan, and in the eighteenth century Rousseau took it from the king or the State and conferred it on the people under the guise of the General Will. In making all individual wills lose their independence in the indivisible, monadic General Will, which was always right, which made the deputies of the people mere instruments without responsibility, and which excluded the possibility of any autonomous societies within the State, Rousseau paved the way for the twentieth-century totalitarian State. It was Rousseau's spuriously democratic philosophy, claimed Maritain, that inspired the Jacobin revolution and the democracies which followed. Authority in a true democracy, according to the Christian tradition, said Maritain, resides in the elected representatives of the people, who are responsible to the people for the conduct of their office because it is from them that this authority derives. The people, in turn, are responsible to the natural law or to God, the ultimate source of all authority. The people are accountable too, Maritain remarked, in the sense that it is always the people who pay for the decisions made by the State in the name of their sovereignty. (One is reminded of his remark about the people in his 1937 essay "Exister avec le peuple": "They are always the same ones who get themselves killed.") In *Man and the State* he wrote:

> The woes of the people settle the accounts of the nonaccountable supreme persons or agencies, State, ministries, committees, boards, staffs, rulers, lawgivers, experts, advisers, — not to speak of the intelligentsia, writers, theorists, scientific utopians, *connoisseurs*, professors, and newspapermen.[44]

With *Man and the State*, wrote Henry Bars,

> Maritain has finished once and for all what he had begun to sketch out in rough form thirty years earlier in his reflections on Rousseau and Maurras; he has philosophically justified the notion of democracy by purifying it of the parasitic errors sucking at its life.[45]

Bernanos is quite often — and quite erroneously — considered to have been an enemy of democracy and hence ideologically opposed to Maritain. If one considers in isolation the innumerable sallies of Bernanos against democracy, often at the expense of Maritain (with his "effeminate day-dreams about democracy"), one could easily come to the conclusion that Bernanos considered democracy essentially vicious. No conclusion could be more removed from reality. In his book *Bernanos, His Political Thought and Prophecy*, Thomas Molnar took Gaeton Picon to task for suggesting that a man with Bernanos' generous soul and vision "ought to have accepted the democratic system." Molnar claimed that this mistaken notion arises from the fact that Picon "speaks of democracy in such vague and sentimental terms and equates it with such splendid virtues that these in themselves would be enough to repel the man they were supposed to persuade."[46] It is possible that Picon is vague and sentimental; nevertheless, there seems to be excellent grounds for Picon's statement that there is a noticeable evolution in the thought of Bernanos on democracy. His attitude in *La Grande Peur des bien-pensants* is certainly no longer the same in *Le Chemin de la Croix-des-Ames.*

Bernanos' change of attitude toward democracy, it seems to me, is closely related to his change in attitude toward Maritain. From the time when Maritain arrived at his philosophical acceptance of democracy and began to write incessantly in its defense, Bernanos ceased almost entirely what Henry Bars called his "unpleasant mockery" and began to refer to Maritain in most friendly and respectful terms, called him "my illustrious friend, Jacques Maritain."[47] The two men began to refer to and to quote each other in their writings during the war.

The fact that during these years Maritain and Bernanos were attacked continually by the same enemies and for the same reason, namely, their political position, would seem to indicate that these two men agreed on the fundamental principles of government. Bernanos often spoke of this fact. In his *Lettre aux Anglais* he wrote:

> Dear Mr. Roosevelt, in reading some of the pages of this book, many of your compatriots will doubtless take me for an anti-democrat. At least that's the accusation I expect from a certain number of American Catholics who in the past took up, against me and Mr. Maritain, the defense of the "good dictators" — Messrs Mussolini and Franco.[48]

These are the same enemies who

> After having treated me as a communist, as they also did Mr. Maritain, . . . today . . . treat me as a fascist.[49]

The same enemies who had harassed him and Maritain at the time of the Spanish Civil War, he said, were again sniffing out heresy in Maritain because of his part in drawing up and signing the *Manifeste des catholiques européens séjournant en Amérique* (May 1942), which contained much of Maritain's thought on national and international democracy and the principle of pluralism, particularly as concerns religious freedom.[50] Bernanos was confident that heresy hunters would find Maritain's position completely orthodox:

> Oh! such a document will cost many a sleepless night to certain heresy-hunters of the Holy Office, personal enemies of Mr. Jacques Maritain, and they will vainly turn over this

dialectical hedgehog in their expert hands. They will never succeed in finding the fold, the joint. They'll just uselessly prick their fingers.[51]

During the war years, Bernanos and Maritain represented for their mutual friends the true voice and the only hope of France. Mauriac wrote:

> Does Georges Bernanos realize what he represented for us during those four abominable years? How we longed for his return, and that of Maritain. . . . Before the Liberation, in the thickest darkness of that night where many in whom we believed wandered off, where the best perished, our hope turned toward a few writers across the sea, who would some day come back.[52]

On the eve of the Allied invasion of Normandy, Maritain, in his turn, quoted Bernanos and Mauriac in his moving essay "A travers la victoire" as representing the voice of hope for France.[53]

The defense of freedom by Maritain and Bernanos during the war years reestablished to a certain degree their friendship, which had suffered in the crisis of Action Française. In the early 1950s, not long after the appearance of Maritain's *Man and the State*, when Father Raymond Bruckberger, O.P., wanted to contact Bernanos to ask him to write the script for his film about sixteen Carmelites from Compiègne *(Dialogue des Carmélites)*, he went to Maritain to get an introduction to Bernanos. The friendship between Maritain and Bernanos became closer, and Bernanos ceased his criticism of Maritain's ideas on democracy precisely at the time when Maritain wholeheartedly took up the defense of democracy. This would seem to indicate that in the 1940s there was no serious political disagreement between the two men whose friendship had been broken off in 1927 because of a difference over the condemnation of Action Française.

Comparison of the criticism of what both men considered the parasitical errors attached to democracy seems to indicate even more strikingly that Bernanos, perhaps under the influence of Maritain's writings (he frequently shows himself quite familiar with what Maritain was publishing), was much less an enemy of democracy than he had always imagined himself to be. Bernanos was not a man of fine distinctions. For him, the word "democracy" meant one of two things: the Jacobin revolution or capitalism. These were the very "parasitic errors" from which

Maritain was struggling to free the notion of democracy. Both men agreed that the democracies of Europe, before the war, were in an unhealthy state. "Mr. Jacques Maritain told you so, and I tell you again, our democracies were sick," wrote Bernanos.[54]

Both Maritain and Bernanos considered modern democracies corrupted by their alliance with capitalism. Maritain wrote:

> In the end a coalition was established among the interests of the ruling classes, corrupted as they were by money, desperately clinging to their privileges, and thrown into panic by their blind fear of Communism. . . . The unresolvable antagonisms inherent in an economy based on the fecundity of money, the selfishness of the propertied classes, and the withdrawal of the proletariat, set up by Marx on the mystical principle of Revolution, have kept democratic affirmations from passing into social life; and the powerlessness of modern societies in the face of poverty and the dehumanization of work, their inability to overcome the exploitation of men by men, have been for them a bitter failure.[55]

Bernanos saw the same relationship. Recognizing that the coming of democracy was historically linked with the triumph of profit, he maintained that

> democracy is the political form of capitalism in the same sense that the soul, according to Aristotle, is the form of the body. . . . Capitalism as it began, as it grew, and as it evolved has little by little transformed democracy according to its own needs.[56]

Through this alliance with capitalism, Maritain and Bernanos saw that democracy became the government of the *bourgeoisie*, for whom "progress" meant the development of industry, the multiplication of machines, well-being and material comfort, and the security and immobility of the *status quo*. Both Maritain and Bernanos considered the bourgeois classes as having betrayed the cause of freedom and justice; therefore the world, after the war, would need a new *élite*. Maritain wrote:

> All depends on the new *élite*. The world needs them desperately. . . . The first question that must be answered tomorrow, not by theories, but by strong and wise action, is the

substitution of a new *élite* for the former ruling elements which have proved corrupt. It is the French people who will resolve this question. . . . If we let the old corrupt *élite* set themselves up once again on the nation like a layer of corpses, we will miss our historic chance. . . . Those who will wield power immediately after the liberation, during the transition period that will lead to the election of a Constituent Assembly, will not yet be able to claim to incarnate the new *élite*. Their role will be to banish the false and corrupt *élite*, to re-establish the vital, primordial functions and the liberties of our country, and thus to make possible the work of the new *élite* who exist already but have not yet come to the fore.[57]

Bernanos also laid the great responsibility for the decadence and the capitulation of French democracy at the feet of the *bourgeoisie*. It was in the common people, who had been betrayed by the bourgeois elite, that Bernanos too found fidelity to the principles of freedom:

I accuse the French *élite* of having betrayed [the people] by making them doubt themselves and what they loved. . . . The people had believed they were fighting for democracy. . . . The *élite* . . . no longer had enough humanity to try to understand what the people were trying to express by this word, and that the illusions of a great people are a precious and a fragile thing, that one cannot use the knife without the risk of cutting away, along with their illusions, the very root of their hope. . . . I call it betrayal because, up till the very last day, up to the day when all was surrendered, the *élite* continued to speak the language of honor, and now for cowardliness they use the words moderation, wisdom and prudence, as if cowardliness were not the only real risk, the only irreparable imprudence. . . . For the humblest bachelor of theology it would have been no more than a game to demonstrate to the people, with irreproachable syllogisms, that the interests of God, of the Church, of respectable people and of good principles demanded submission to the conqueror. But thank heaven that neither Joan nor our people are up to debating with the casuists. This is why one day or another the Saints of the fatherland end up whispering in their ears, in the silence of their hearts.[58]

Maritain and Bernanos both pointed to the pseudo-democratic principles of Rousseau as the original source of the sickness of the democracies before the war.[59] In the cult of the General Will, in which the individual person is lost in the Collectivity, Mass and Number, the way led directly to the hypertrophy and absolute primacy of the State. Referring to Rousseau's remarks about the origin of authority in the *Contrat social*, Maritain said:

> To declare that authority resides in the whole multitude as in its proper subject and without being able to emerge from it and to exist in such or such responsible men, — this is a trick permitting irresponsible mechanisms to exercise *power* over men, without having *authority* over them. . . . Such power tends to become infinite . . . democracies of the Rousseau type not only grant the State all the usurpations of power, but they tend toward these very usurpations. . . . Thus, through an inevitable dialectic, and so long as a new fundamental principle has not been found, democracies of the bourgeois liberal type tend to engender their contrary, the totalitarian State.[60]

In Bernanos' *Lettre aux Anglais* we find:

> I've had enough, dear Mr. Roosevelt, of hearing about the democracies being opposed to the dictatorships, even by Mr. Maritain. Democracy furnishes no defense whatever against dictatorship, and that's the truth.[61]

Maritain would probably have agreed with Bernanos completely, if the latter had not changed from *"les démocraties"* in one sentence to *"la démocratie"* in the next. But here, for Bernanos, the word "democracy" meant exclusively the Rousseau-inspired bourgeois liberal type. Nor could Bernanos' claim to have always been a monarchist, and his resolution to remain so, make him an enemy of the principles Maritain defended, for as Maritain wrote:

> This [democratic] philosophy and this state of mind do not exclude *a priori* any *"régime"* or "form of government" that the classical tradition has recognized as legitimate, that is to say, as compatible with human dignity. Thus a monarchical regime can be democratic, if it is in accord with this state of mind and the principles of this philosophy.[62]

Bernanos, although he claimed he had never been a democrat and never would be one, insisted just as forcefully: "We are neither democratic nor anti-democratic."[63] What is really significant is the fact that Bernanos had always defended, with as

much devotion and tenacity as Maritain, the fundamental principles of democracy: that government should be of the people, by
the people, and for the people. Bernanos acknowledged the
preeminence of the people's role in government when he spoke of
his ideal government as a *popular* monarchy, in which the king
was to be kept in power by the consent of the people to whom he
was responsible. Moreover, he considered the role of the king as
essentially one of disinterested service to the people. "There are
no privileges, only services to be rendered."[64]

Besides, Bernanos was a monarchist who subscribed to the
principles of the Revolution. He made use of the revolutionary
slogan *Liberté, Fraternité, Egalité* as often as did Maritain. He
could declare that no one was "more attached than I to the famous Declaration of Rights and understands better than I its
meaning, for the simple reason that it was men like me who drew
it up."[65] This was possible only because, like Maritain,[66] he distinguished between the revolution of 1789 and that of 1793:

> The men of '89 did not leave any real posterity; their work
> must be taken up again. But the men of '93, the inflexible
> men of the National Convention — of the type of
> Robespierre — have sons that they could not deny if they
> were living today; they are the heads of the totalitarian
> states and their accomplices. To express my thought in a
> way I would like to be more forceful: '89 is Péguy; '93 is
> Maurras or Lenin.[67]

Finally, Maritain and Bernanos placed identical confidence
in the people, whom Maritain called "the great reservoir of spontaneity and non-pharasaism" and whom Bernanos called "the
last reserve of humanity, of human substance, in a dehumanized
world." Both men defined the people in almost identical terms[68]
and both placed a limited but wholehearted confidence in this
people as the best hope for the future of the world. Maritain
wrote:

> Faithful people, the little people of God, royal people called
> to share the work of Christ; people as a community of the
> citizens of a country, united under just laws; people as a
> community of manual work and as the reservoir and re-
> source of humanity in those who labor and suffer close to
> nature. The people is not God, it is not infallibly right, it
> does not have faultless virtues; the will of the people or the

mind of the people is not the norm of what is just or unjust. But the people is the body, slowly prepared and formed of common humanity, the living patrimony of common gifts and common promises made to God's creature — more profound and more essential than all the added on privileges and social distinctions — with equal dignity and equal weakness in each one as a member of the human species.[69]

Bernanos wrote a year later:

Everything is miracle, everything is grace, I am myself a good enough Christian to know that; but there is the miracle and the instrument of the miracle, more or less conscious, more or less worthy, but always chosen — *vocatus* — called. There is the Deliverance of Orleans and there is Joan of Arc. There is the Marne and the people of France, that hardheaded people, with sensitive hearts and violent hands. . . . I am speaking of a Christian humanity, I mean a humanity formed by Christianity, that is to say, whose moral reactions are commanded by this millenary atavism. This is what some refuse to accept. The people no longer go to Mass or to sermons, they do not know their catechism; but the image they bear within themselves, in their deepest hearts, without their knowing it, is one of a society that has never existed, whose coming their ancestors waited for from century to century, that City of Harmony, under the sign of Fraternity. . . . If you took the trouble to listen for five minutes in a restaurant, in a cabaret, in a factory to the French workers that you take for communists, discussing what is just and what is not, you would say that the conscience of these people is difficult to satisfy in a way far different from that of a Greek or Roman freedman, or even of an ancient Jew. . . . And society, such as it is conceived by our bankers, our engineers, our economists, our moralists, will never satisfy them — never! They will say that it is because such a society does not give them enough money, that they have to work too much; you will accuse them of being insatiable. They will agree and even boast cynically of being so, but if they do not feel at ease in society, it is because they do not consider it just — without being able to sort out the reasons why — it does not work, that's all, they are not at home in it.[70]

At the end of the war, Bernanos turned his wrath successively against the war itself, the resistance, the liberation, victory, the peace, de Gaulle and the MRP. Thomas Molnar cites this fact as evidence that Bernanos had begun to turn his allegiance once again to the far right. But Mr. Molnar does not seem to take sufficiently into consideration that Bernanos was a complete and incurable idealist whose destiny was *l'insatisfaction*, a prophet who had to denounce the inevitably human infidelities to the ideal he loved. The ideals he loved were the ideals of democracy, and his violent criticisms of democracies and democrats after the war arose from the fact that they were proving unfaithful to these ideals.

Whether it was Maritain's influence which caused the change in Bernanos' attitude toward democracy is perhaps debatable. What seems to be undebatable is that there was a gradual evolution in his attitude toward democracy and that his writings show that, whether he would admit it openly or not, he was always defending with vigor and passion the basic principles of democracy.

In Maritain's thought about democracy there is likewise a long and gradual evolution. As in the case of Bernanos, this evolution was the result of a remarkable intellectual honesty. It was evidence of an intellect that was always moving forward, that rectified itself with no attempt to excuse or justify itself, that had no fear of change or novelty which was intellectually justified, that knew how to criticize its own prejudices and finally dissolve them.

The question of Vichy posed difficult problems for all Frenchmen. In June 1940 the almost simultaneous appeal by de Gaulle from London for continued resistance to Nazi Germany and the capitulation of Pétain forced upon every Frenchman a tragic but inevitable choice. To continue the struggle seemed suicidal. The hopes of an Allied victory were crushed and an Axis-dominated Europe, for decades to come, seemed unavoidable. An officially unsubmissive and resisting France could expect the most horrible reprisals from its conqueror. One had to go on living, yet to capitulate and submit to the directives of Hitler would mean a complete loss of national honor, with no assurance that conditions under capitulation would be any less humiliating and destructive than those involved in a refusal to capitulate. As Maritain was to claim, there was no really favorable choice.

When France fell in June 1940, Maritain was in America. He

had gone there in January for a series of courses at the Pontifical Institute of Mediaeval Studies in Toronto, which he had been giving annually since 1933, and for a lecture tour at American universities. In the months that followed, Maritain wrestled with the problems of capitulation and resistance. He wrote down his reflections, collected them for publication in December of that year, and they appeared as a brochure entitled *A travers le désastre* early in 1941 (Editions de la Maison Française). It was soon smuggled into France and published clandestinely by Frères Ribaud at Gap in the same year and by Editions de Minuit in 1943.

A choice between de Gaulle and Pétain was inevitable, and Maritain's instinctive reaction was in favor of the former. Maritain criticized the Pétain regime for having based its political decisions on purely military reasons. A military defeat was inevitable, the argument went, and to continue the struggle in France would have meant the butchery of the French army, with no chance of redressing the situation. Purely military solutions, said Maritain, have all the possibilities of being very bad political solutions. Besides, he claimed, the men who made the decision to capitulate were suffering from a rightist complex, with all the prejudices, pessimism, illusions and resentments that disposed them to appeal not to the supreme resources of the country to continue the struggle at any cost, but to maintaining order within the country.[71]

Maritain's first concern was for the true and lasting welfare of France. His anguish over her terrible humiliation and sufferings led him to suggest that there might be a kind of division of labor between de Gaulle in England and France's overseas empire, on the one hand, and Pétain's regime at home on the other. Vichy was, after all, the *de facto* government, and France was under the conqueror's heel. France had to be kept alive. Maritain made it clear, however, that this "division of labor" was possible only if the Pétain government would make no further moral concessions to the enemy and take no positive steps to implement the moral capitulations it had already made in the armistice pact (for example, the agreement to hand over to the Gestapo the refugees who had counted on French hospitality for asylum). Maritain had some misgivings about the possibility of Pétain's following a course of nonviolent but morally responsible and heroic resistance to Nazi demands.

Marshal Pétain's experience, linked to the heavy responsibilities he has assumed, and to the hopes that he knows rest on him, in the last few months since he has become the *de facto* head of the nation, is an experience that would tend to raise a man's sentiments. Will he be able to avoid the new moral capitulations that Germany will exact and dominate the contradictory components that make up the policy in which he has involved the country? In order not to surrender the fleet or let them lay a hand on the empire, will he be reduced one day to some supremely heroic decision? Or on the other hand will we witness in a new phase of France's misfortune that unheard-of contradiction of an official policy dominated more and more by the desire to collaborate with the conqueror?[72]

Maritain's worst fears were confirmed, of course, and hardly had *A travers le désastre* appeared in print in 1941 than Maritain felt obliged to write:

> I would prefer not to have to speak of those who are governing France at present. What they must be reproached with above all is to have lacked faith in their people. . . . In a man who prefers anything to the acceptance of what is abominable, there is at least a secret natural confidence in the principles of being, even if he does not know its name, and the source of justice. But to be resigned, for self-styled reasons of political realism, to the enslavement of a country, is to lead this country to the great cemeteries of history because there is no longer any faith in the force of life which gives that country its existence.[73]

Two months later, speaking before a meeting of the French Relief Committee, he said:

> To trust the people of France does not mean to trust the leaders who at present rule France. I am one of those who consider that the armistice and the *coup d'état* of June 1940 have been, despite the intentions of their authors, a tragic trap into which France has been thrown and in which she is now caught, and that the unholy things we are witnessing at present are but the sequel of this first abandonment of the spirit and vocation of France. I think that the French soldiers who continue to fight side by side with England do not represent only their own will, their own honor and their own calculable power, but also the will, the honor and the latent power of the French people as a whole.[74]

As the weeks passed and Vichy's "necessary and inevitable" armistice turned to more and more active collaboration with the policies of Hitler, Maritain began to speak and write more and more against the Vichy government. In New York, Maritain became a kind of ambassador of France without portfolio, who enjoyed far greater influence and prestige than the Vichy ambassador in Washington. After the war, Gustave Cohen wrote of Maritain upon the latter's appointment as ambassador to the Vatican:

> Having lived and worked intimately at his side during two and a half years of exile in the United States, I wish simply to bear witness to what he was there, — already — as an ambassador of France.
>
> An unofficial messenger, but whose spiritual authority was ever so much more radiant than that of the official ambassador who held his post unduly in Washington. Our ambassador had, from the very beginning, opted for the Voice from London, in which, as we all did, he recognized in the call of June 18, the Voice of France.[75]

In Brazil, Bernanos took the same uncompromising stand as did Maritain, against Vichy and in favor of de Gaulle, much to the embarrassment of the official French ambassador at Rio de Janeiro, who realized that Brazilians were turning more to Bernanos than to him as the real representative of France in Brazil.[76]

Three weeks after the British-American landing in North Africa in 1942, Antoine de Saint-Exupéry published in the November 30 edition of *Le Canada* of Montreal an open letter to Frenchmen, calling on them to put aside their differences over Vichy and unite in the common struggle against the Nazi oppressor. It was an eloquent appeal. The article had appeared in English the day before, in the *New York Times Magazine,* and it was this version which Maritain read and to which he found it necessary to take exception. Maritain's criticism of Saint-Exupéry's letter appeared in the November 19 edition of *Pour la Victoire* under the title "Il faut parfois juger." An English version, called "An Open Letter to Frenchmen," appeared in the April 1943 issue of the *Atlantic Monthly.*

Maritain admitted that the honor of Saint-Exupéry's intentions was beyond question, as was the generosity of his appeal. He felt, however, that Saint-Exupéry had touched on certain very vital problems in such a way as to cause a number of serious misunderstandings. These misunderstandings had to be cleared up, Maritain believed, particularly since Saint-Exupéry enjoyed such prestige in both America and France.

The central theme of Saint-Exupéry's letter was summed up in the text of the telegram he urged each Frenchman to send to Cordell Hull, the American secretary of state, to assure the United States of France's complete and unified cooperation. The text is as follows:

> We request the honor of serving under any form whatever. We wish the military mobilization of all Frenchmen in the United States. We accept in advance whatever structure will be judged suitable, but hating any spirit of division among Frenchmen, we want it to be completely separate from politics.[77]

Maritain considered a unity "purely exterior to politics" impossible. Saint-Exupéry's contention that the only duty of Frenchmen in 1942 was to obey their military leaders, without regard to political considerations, struck Maritain as a thoughtless resignation to the same kind of irresponsibility that had caused the disaster of 1940. Political considerations necessarily had to enter in; for if at the moment those who had accepted Hitler as the savior of Western civilization and cooperated in his crimes of oppression were now, in the face of the crumbling fortunes of the Third Reich, turning their coats to save their hides, they were not, by that fact, washed clean of their political crimes. They were responsible to the French people, as every government must be responsible to the people in whose name it acts. Ignoring responsibility for political crimes was no way of surmounting political disunity. Vichy was not dead, as Saint-Exupéry had claimed it was, because those who had perpetuated the crimes of Vichy were not dead.

Maritain agreed with Saint-Exupéry that the government of Vichy was forced to submit to many of the demands of Germany under the most horrible conditions of blackmail. But Maritain insisted that

> many of these things were agreed to fully or even actively willed by the leaders of Vichy, when such things contributed to their interior political programs. He [Saint-Exupéry] forgets that the effort to disorganize the French people morally, to throw them into the cult of defeat and of an unhealthy self-accusation, to impose on them the myth of a

wavering leader who was the incarnation of France, and to make them accept the abject ideology of the enemy, was the specific program of the Pétain regime.[78]

Such men, turning to the side of the Allies and of *La France Combattante*, might redeem themselves on the field of battle; they could not do so in the field of politics.

In spite of the fact that she owed complete cooperation, confidence, and friendship to the Allies and had a strict obligation of devotion to the common military effort, France could not abdicate its right to rule itself and accept, "in advance," "any form whatever" of some "provisionary structure." The *"structure provisoire"* could never be a pseudo government of the Vichy type, even if demanded by the Allies.

> Until the moment when the French people can make its will known, and do so freely, on the new constitution of its republic, there can be no French government having the legitimate power to commit France definitively in any one particular political direction, whether interior or international. And it is just as necessary, at the moment we are speaking of, that the people of France be truly in a condition of freely deciding its future, and not be subject to the pressure and violence of some equivocal pseudo-government, installed in some part of its territory and claiming unscrupulously the right to impose itself on them according to its whim. . . .
>
>   . . . Let no one ask us . . . to transform our union in the struggle against the enemy into submission to a pseudo-government of the type of Vichy. . . . If the misfortune of our torn and betrayed country has caused the French army to be divided under two different commands, nevertheless it is essential that both sides fight with the Allies against the common enemy. The map of the war and of the world is vast enough for that.[79]

Maritain sent a copy of his critique to Saint-Exupéry before it appeared in print, and Saint-Exupéry published a reply to Maritain. He admitted that certain of Maritain's criticisms cast a new light on reactions he had not expected from his readers. He explained that the Frenchmen he wished to call to unity were the Frenchmen who were living outside of France, who were sharply divided over the question of Vichy. Saint-Exupéry's explanation did not alter the fact that these men too had to make a judgment. It may be that the mistranslation of the words *"structure provisoire"* by *"government"* and *"commander"* by *"govern"* may have caused misinterpretations. However, his statement:

> I have noted, when I compared the English translation with the original version of the text (which Mr. Maritain has not seen) that a number of abridgments of the text, once they were translated, made possible certain misinterpretations[80]

seems a kind of camouflage, for a careful comparison of the texts shows that the *New York Times* version is a sentence-by-sentence translation of the original text. There were no omissions of any significance.

Near the end of 1943, Maritain seems to have felt constrained to warn in advance against the wholesale purges of collaborators that would take place during the liberation of France. He warned the people that retribution must be meted out by legal tribunals, not by individuals:

> In order to spare our country the plague of a rash of private vengeance, justice is necessary, and generosity too. It will be a question of the health and safety of our country *to know how at one and the same time,* according to the words of a famous author, *to conquer and to pardon. . . .*
> Human justice goes awry if it lays claim to the absolute rigor of Divine Justice, from which nothing can escape. All things being equal, it is preferable that a guilty person escape than that an innocent person be condemned. The essential thing is that those responsible in high places be brought to justice without respect of persons.[81]

The following week he told his audience in France:

> Let us leave aside the very clear-cut question of the traitors, the agents of the enemy and the profiteers of infamy. They are the responsibility of the courts and pose no particular problem. The political problem is involved with the work of illusion and moral disintegration brought about by Vichy, and which constrains or leads a certain number of Frenchmen to serve in some degree or other, sometimes in appear-

ance only, at other times in reality, a policy that France will condemn tomorrow and indeed condemns already today. What equity demands is a clear definition of what we call "the men of Vichy" and that this name be applied to those who assumed a position of leadership and responsibility in the capitulation, the laws, the policies, and the persecutions of the *régime* of defeat, and to those who instead of understanding that they were led down a false path, will continue to fight for the ideology of the *"Révolution Nationale."*

And what honor and political morality demand is that not a single one of these men be permitted to govern the nation or exercise any political authority whatever.[82]

During the years of his wartime exile in the United States, Maritain lived in an apartment in Greenwich Village, and this apartment became "a veritable island of French land" in the heart of New York City.[83] Like his home at Meudon, it became a meeting place for the French intellectuals and artists in exile in the New York area, many of whom Maritain had helped escape to the United States. After the fall of France, Maritain realized the danger under Vichy, as well as in the occupied sector of France, which menaced French intellectuals, scholars and those who had fled to France as refugees, who were known for their struggle against fascism and for their love of liberty. This was particularly the case for those of Jewish ancestry. During the terrible days following the capitulation, he searched frantically in all directions, "with death in his soul," for affidavits and visas for his menaced friends.[84] His efforts to cut through the bureaucratic red tape of the American Immigration Service seemed hopeless, until he enlisted the aid of Dr. Alvin Johnson of the New School of Social Research and of Dr. Frank Kingdon of the Emergency Rescue Committee and the International Rescue and Relief Committee. They furnished him with the proper contacts and themselves worked with Maritain to bring to the United States scholars whose lives or careers were endangered in Europe.

Maritain became known as the man to see to have someone brought across the Atlantic to safety. Scholars from various American universities, whose professional friends were in danger in France, came to him to ask for his help. Gustave Cohen is an example of such a case. Deprived of his post at the Sorbonne and sent to Aix-en-Provence, where he was again deprived of his chair, he sent a note to his friend and former student, Professor Seznec at Harvard, who relayed the information to Henri Grégoire and Henri Peyre. These two men went immediately to Maritain. Henri Peyre, head of the French Department of Yale, offered Cohen a position of visiting professor if Maritain could procure the necessary documents and money to bring him to America. Cohen was brought to America and was deeply grateful for what Maritain had done for him. In the chapter on Maritain, from his book *Ceux que j'ai connus*, he wrote:

> The blow that fell most violently on this Christian, in all the policies of Vichy, was its unconstrained adherence to Hitler's racism, the persecution of the Jews, the anathema hurled at an entire race, whose crime was to have given birth to the Man-God. He had many friends among the Jews: Jean Wahl, Jankelevitch, Meyerson, philosophers like himself and whom he dreamt of bringing to the United States to save them. He did not know me, but immediately upon learning that I had been dispossessed of my chair at the Sorbonne and then at Aix, which had at first been offered in compensation, he acceded to the requests of Henri Grégoire and Henri Peyre to bring me to the United States.
>
> One of the first visits I made in New York was to his apartment at 30 Fifth Avenue, which will remain famous as a place of asylum where there was a continual procession of the persecuted, welcomed by him, by his wife Raïssa, a poet and essayist, and by her sister Vera.[85]

In the months that followed his arrival in America, Cohen saw Maritain frequently and became a very close friend. In September 1941 he told Maritain of his dream of a University of Free France which would gather together all the French and Belgian professors in the United States who refused to see the light of independent French thought extinguished. Maritain's reaction to the suggestion was one of sympathetic but amused skepticism, because the project seemed audacious but chimerical. His greatest misgivings arose from the publicity which such a project would inevitably attract, which could hamper his efforts to save Jewish friends who were still in Europe. Cohen persisted, and little by little Maritain let himself be convinced. "In one of his customary flashes of wit," wrote Cohen, "one day Maritain said: 'The University, nobody wanted it; Cohen wanted it and there it was.' "[86]

Maritain delivered the inaugural address of the Ecole Libre des Hautes Etudes at Hunter College on February 14, 1942. In the Ecole Libre, Maritain was able to realize one of the ideas to which in the following years he would devote a number of essays and lectures: the possibility of intellectual cooperation for the common good among men of divergent philosophical positions and religious beliefs. In his address he said:

> In the Ecole Libre there are men of philosophic and religious convictions as diverse as the traditions which run together in the history of our land. In this diversity, at the very heart of a common undertaking, can be seen a witness to the fact that French traditions, in particular those of the faith of the Cathedrals and those of the Declaration of Rights, as long as they remain faithful to what is best in them, are also faithful to freedom. All of us have cause to examine ourselves, to reject the ancient prejudices and misunderstandings, to raise our thinking to the level of the new things that are in preparation and which will certainly be newer than we think. In the cruel conflicts through which French thought has passed, one thing at least is common to all our great thinkers: the preoccupation with knowing man, with penetrating the mystery of his grandeur and his misery, of his nature and his destiny, and at the same time the preoccupation with the analysis and the rationalization of the conditions of political life. The age into which we have entered, if it escapes from barbarity and chaos, will be an age of the rediscovery of man and of his true image, of his true situation in the cosmos and of the roots of his dignity, and an age wherein we will see in human society the incarnation of that friendship and civic brotherhood, which presupposes an indispensable justice, but which, even more so than justice, is the soul of community life.[87]

Through his friend, Dr. Alvin Johnson, Maritain obtained the use of the facilities of the New School of Social Research for the Ecole Libre. Henri Focillon, professor of the history of art and a close friend of Maritain's, was elected first president of the institution, but as his health began to fail seriously almost immediately after his election, Maritain, the vice president, had to assume the burden of running the university from the very beginning. He succeeded to the presidency on the death of Focillon, and at the expiration of that term he was elected to the office by unanimous vote. Cohen recalls the heroic first days of this enormous undertaking and compares the enthusiasm evoked by Maritain's lectures to that aroused by the lectures of Bergson many years before at the Sorbonne:

> How I remember those heroic days of the Ecole's beginning, those public courses whose formula was introduced by us, professors without pay in a country where everything has its price. In the auditorium of the New School of Social Research, where the venerable Alvin Johnson gave us the protection of American law, students sat the the foot of his podium, and on the steps of the auditorium, just as in the old days at the Collège de France for the courses of Bergson.[88]

Gustave Cohen, as dean of the university, read a list of the faculty at the inauguration of the university. This list covered three pages in his book *Lettre aux Américains*. It was broadcast to France the next day, with the news of the founding of the university, and was so prestigious and imposing that it compelled even the minister of education of the Vichy government to accept the diplomas of the Ecole Libre.[89]

After the first two years of the school's existence, Maritain was able to report, at the second anniversary celebration, a prodigious amount of intellectual activity: over 1,000 students attended 2,200 lectures and conferences given by 91 professors. Such activity was not missed by de Gaulle, who sent a representative, M. Hoppettot, to the celebration to represent the Comité de la Libération Nationale.[90] During the years of the war, the Ecole Libre des Hautes Etudes was an outstanding witness of the glory of that French civilization which consists, in the words of Maritain, "of producing a honey with a flavor unique in the world from the nectar of all the flowers of the world."[91]

These were probably the busiest years of Maritain's life. Although he was turning sixty, he spent himself in the time-consuming work of rescuing victims of Nazi persecution, in the organization and direction of the Ecole Libre, in weekly broadcasts to the French people, in numberless lectures on the problems of war and peace — and all this without prejudice to his courses and lectures in philosophy at Columbia, Harvard, Princeton, Yale, Chicago, Notre Dame, Marquette, the Pontifical Institute of Mediaeval Studies, the University of Pennsylvania and Brooklyn Institute, or to his numerous contributions to scholarly journals, seven books of his own and prefaces to books by others.

As much as he could during these years, by correspondence and through messages delivered by refugees, he kept in contact with his friends in France, many of whom played an active part in the resistance, but contact became more and more difficult. Pierre Emmanuel wrote from France (Sept. 27, 1941):

> Dear Friend, For a long time now I have wanted to write you, but the distance and the absurd delays make letters seem so abstract, that the very idea that you would receive them only after three months, or perhaps never, makes them very difficult to write. On the other hand, I have no trouble finding you again in my thoughts, whether at your house in Meudon, or as you left your courses at the Institut Catholique. I know what your thoughts must be at this time, and how ardently watchful you are, in spite of the confusion of voices that rise on all sides to lead us astray. It is good for us to reimmerse ourselves in friendship and in the thought of those who are our masters, and you are certainly one for us. I am sure you are acquainted with the great movements that are taking form in France: some were familiar to you before the war, others born yesterday, or that have taken form since yesterday, are rich with hope and promise. . . . In the youth movements, whose leaders are among our friends, there is the same spirit of enthusiasm in discipline and hope in the future. L'Ecole des Cadres d'Uriage [under the direction of Emmanuel Mounier] is forming true men, in whom the feeling for spiritual reality is not stifled, but rather exalted, because it is considered in its relation to the most ordinary and everyday realities of political and social life. It is not on today's results that our youth must be judged, but on the future that they are preparing, for the most part in silence and obscurity. I do not have to tell you that the best among them have not repudiated the old humanism — I use this expression in its universal, catholic sense — and that they judge men and events in relation to it. . . . I am working very hard and am sending you — but by ordinary mail — my new book *Tombeau d'Orphée*.[92]

Stanislas Fumet's *Temps Présent*, after several suspensions, was finally suppressed, as was Emmanuel Mounier's *Esprit*, by order of Admiral Darlan, "because of its general tendencies."

Fumet began another publication, *Temps Nouveau,* which was in turn suppressed. Through certain contacts which Maritain had in the French underground, copies of *Cahiers du Témoignage Chrétien,* edited by many of his friends, were smuggled out of France, copied photostatically, and distributed in America. When Paul Vignaux collected these texts for publication under the title of one of them, *France, prends garde de perdre ton âme* (Editions de la Maison Française, 1943), Maritain supplied the preface.

Many people (Julien Green, for example) came to Maritain for information about what was happening in the French underground.[93] Several of Maritain's books and many of his articles and braodcasts were published clandestinely and distributed in France by such presses as *Editions de Minuit* and *Cahiers du Témoignage Chrétien.* On his first visit to France after the war, he was surprised that his *A travers le désastre,* which was the first book published clandestinely by the underground, had been circulated so widely and had had such a profound influence. He wrote to Yves Simon, a former student of his at the Institut Catholique who at the time was a close friend and colleague in the United States:

> It has been a wonderful thing for me to learn of the influence exerted in France by *A travers le désastre,* so much more profound than I had imagined. This was the first book published clandestinely. At first it was typed out almost everywhere in "Free" France. Then there were four editions, the last from *Editions de Minuit.*[94]

He also published and supplied the preface to a manuscript sent him by a young director of Catholic Action in France, entitled *Témoignage de la situation actuelle en France* (1941).

From London, Ecole Libre received the warm approval of Charles de Gaulle, who recognized it as the only "Free French university in existence," proclaimed the national validity of the degrees it conferred, and sent a modest grant from the Free French treasury. Henri Bonnet, the unofficial ambassador of Free France in the United States, was instructed to give its founders what help he could.

In late 1942 General de Gaulle invited Maritain and the poet Alexis St. Léger (St. John Perse) to serve on his National Committee of Free France. Maritain respectfully declined, perhaps because of the uncertainty of the times (Britain recognized de Gaulle as the leader of Free France; the United States gave its recognition to General Giraud) or perhaps because, having taken on so many obligations, he did not feel he could leave the United States. Then, too, he found it difficult to imagine himself in any role other than philosopher and teacher.[95] In the fall of 1944 Maritain received another call from the Free French government, strongly urging him to come back to France in his own interest and in the national interest. Since his mother had died in the previous fall and there were pressing family affairs to be settled, he felt he could take care of these personal matters as well as be of help to his country; so he decided to accept the invitation. On November 10 he received an *ordre de mission* and left for Paris on an American military plane.

In Paris, Maritain worked for several weeks in the Foreign Ministry under his friend Georges Bidault, General de Gaulle's minister of foreign affairs. Both men urged Maritain to accept the post of ambassador to the Vatican to replace Léon Berard, the Vichy ambassador, who had been removed. Maritain declined vigorously, for the same reasons that he had previously refused to serve on the Committee of Free France, but de Gaulle and Bidault were determined to have him in Rome. They insisted so forcefully on his duty to serve his country, which was still at war, and on the great help he could afford the Church in France that Maritain finally succumbed to their requests. He spent the rest of his stay in Paris briefing himself on the complicated problems he would face as ambassador to the Vatican.

During his seven-week stay in France, Maritain had little rest. Besides briefing himself on the problems he would confront as ambassador, he saw almost 300 people, a great number of whom were Jewish friends and acquaintances and families of friends involved in politics who counted among their relatives numerous victims of racial and political deportations, "who have no idea where they are, who have no possible way of helping them, and live in a maddening nightmare."

> It has been a long time [he wrote to Yves Simon] since such a heavy sadness has weighed on my soul. . . . I am saturated with their anguish, for it is especially among them that I have lived, since, thanks to Eveline [Maritain's niece], I have been lodged in the homes of people involved in the Resistance.[96]

Maritain received firsthand information from his niece Eveline Garnier, whom he admired for her participation in the resistance and for her work after the liberation. At the time of his visit, she was working at the ministry, handling the problems of deportees and visiting execution and burial sites to gather information on the executed and the deported, then notifying the families. What Maritain learned from her did not lighten the heavy burden of his sadness, and he was appalled to find to what extent torture had been used during the occupation:

> There is another atrocious wound which has pierced the very depths of the soul and from which human history will take a long time to recover. It is the re-introduction of torture into the lives of men. The spiritual significance of this phenomenon is far, far greater than its physical horror.[97]

Politically, he found that things were not going "too badly." The gravest dangers had been avoided. The French people, he wrote, had shown admirable qualities of reasonable restraint and sought national unity before all else — "but not without a certain amount of disillusionment and resentment. The revolution has been put off till later."

Eveline was also involved in the efforts to purge all levels of governmental administration of all who had collaborated in the crimes of the Nazis and Vichy, but Maritain was disappointed at the incompleteness (and sometimes at the misdirection) with which the purgation was carried out.

> It was conceived on a juridical basis totally inapplicable to the reality of the situation, instead of on a basis of political justice and according to specially adapted laws and with the measures necessary to expedite the matter. The *bourgeoisie* is more self-satisfied than ever, in the name of competence, and with that hideous sense of personal security which comes from the refusal to examine itself. The Resistance is disconcerted, hindered by the sudden influx of the new faces who proclaim themselves members of the Resistance after the Liberation, and it is at pains to find its place in the political life of the country. The government offers little help in this regard; as always in France, they don't know how to seek out and find the men they need. The communists insist on unity but create problems in every direction by their machinations, and thus distort many situations. There is a very real fifth column which continues to cherish Pétain and creates a *milieu* favorable to acts of violence. And since the

communists spend all their time denouncing it, many people (ministers included) minimize the existence and the danger of this fifth column. They regard it as a matter of communist propaganda. Nevertheless the attempted acts of violence are very real, in spite of what is done to hide them. The straightening out of our ideas, our spirit, our ideology is falling far behind the immediate effort that has brought about the Liberation. I have seen the General; he told me: Everything must be re-done.[98]

With a few exceptions, he found the public press in a pitiful state:

Fumet is admirable; *Temps Présent* is going very well. I saw Father Chaillet, S.J., who edits with great courage the *Cahiers du Témoignage Chrétien*. The daily press is in a deplorable state. The best daily is *Combat*, edited by Camus. Camus and Sartre are the protagonists of a philosophy of the absurd and of nothingness which, alas, is extremely popular with the young. Mounier is doing well and publishing *Esprit* once again; but he is still the same. I find people older, but scarcely renewed.[99]

After returning to New York on New Year's Day 1945, Maritain spent three months fulfilling his commitments in America and preparing for his departure. At a banquet in his honor by the French-American Club, he pronounced his farewell address and two weeks later left for France, accompanied by his future secretary Jean Cattaui de Menasce, a French priest who had spent the war years working in a New York parish because he was of Jewish extraction. Maritain left for Rome on April 20, and three days after the end of the war in Europe, on May 10, he presented his credentials at the Vatican.

CHAPTER 7

Ambassador to the Vatican and Professor at Princeton

THE POST OF FRENCH ambassador to the Vatican entailed a complete change of life style for Maritain, and indeed a sacrifice as well. Many aspects of the new position were uncongenial. The time he could devote to the study of philosophy and to the books he felt obliged to publish in the years left to him was extremely limited. He had always prized the company of his friends and his home had always been open, both to those who were sympathetic to his ideas and to those who came to challenge them. Now he was separated from his friends in France and the United States, and at the Palazzo Taverna he was obliged to receive all comers, some of whom were most unsympathetic to all he stood for or had no ideas at all. He felt himself unsuited to the kind of entertaining expected of him and to the delicate diplomatic negotiating required by his post. Also, the Roman Curia was rife with bitter enemies who could never forgive him for his support of the condemnation of Action Française, for his position on the Spanish Civil War, for his opposition to the Vichy *régime*, and for the liberal tendencies of his political and social writings.

Maritain had no illusions about the reason he was chosen for the post. He wrote to Yves Simon: "What the General has in mind is not so much the success of this or that diplomatic transaction. It is the gesture itself of choosing me to represent France at the Vatican and which he considers significant in itself."[1]

As soon as the provisional government had been installed, General de Gaulle demanded that all diplomats formerly accredited to the Vichy government be replaced immediately, and the papal nuncio, Msgr. Valerio Valeri, who by international convention was head of the diplomatic corps, was no exception. The Vatican filed no formal protest to his dismissal and replaced him by

Archbishop Angelo Roncalli, the future Pope John XXIII. It was with this papal nuncio that Maritain had to work out solutions to such Church – State problems as subsidies to private schools, the rebuilding of destroyed and damaged churches, and the status of Alsace, where a prewar concordat with Germany was still in effect.

One of the most delicate and difficult problems Maritain had to confront was collaborationist bishops in France. De Gaulle's provisional government had demanded the resignation of thirty-three bishops and archibishops. Since, of course, not a single one resigned, an investigation was undertaken to establish grounds for their removal. Eventually, only three were removed, and Maritain had to handle the delicate negotiations with the Vatican involved in their removal.

One problem, internal to the French church, with which Maritain had to grapple at the Vatican was the French priest-workers, whom the Vatican had always regarded with an uneasy eye. Julie Kernan notes that Maritain and Roncalli seem to have protected the movement from the wrath of the Curia.[2] No action was taken against the movement as long as either was at his post, but in 1954, after Maritain had returned to the United States and immediately after Roncalli had been elevated to the patriarchate of Venice, the movement was suspended by the Vatican. Kernan suggests that Maritain and Roncalli saw eye to eye on this and many other religious and social problems, and she finds "traces of Maritain's thinking . . . in John XXIII's important encyclical *Mater et Magistra* (1961), which goes far beyond the social and economic thinking of his predecessors."[3]

Many considered de Gaulle's choice of Maritain for ambassador to the Vatican a "lesson" to the politically conservative Pius XII, but Vladmir d'Ormesson of the Académie Française, who succeeded Maritain at the Vatican, insists that nothing could be further from the truth.[4] No one, he says, could have been more welcome in the higher circles of the Vatican. A letter which Maritain sent to Yves Simon (Mar. 24, 1946) seems to confirm d'Ormesson's opinion and to hint that Maritain and Roncalli were not as close on all points as Kernan seems to suggest:

It is not professional secrecy, but a lack of time that keeps me from telling you of my non-philosophical activities. It would take too long to tell of them. In short my mission seems to have given satisfaction both here and in Paris (about my qualities as an ambassador things have been said in Paris that modesty forbids me to repeat). You can well imagine that the nomination to the Cardinalate of Msgr. Saliège and of his two other colleagues is an act (accomplished despite the papal nuncio and many French bishops) for which the French Ambassador owes a very special and personal gratitude to the Holy Father.

In some circles, Maritain's appointment to the Vatican was treated as a joke, but Vladmir d'Ormesson points out that during the "joke" of his ambassadorship, Maritain, though little seen in public, was extremely active and exercised enormous influence in Rome. He points in particular to the creation of the Cultural Center at St. Louis des Français, the French seminary in Rome. There were more than fifty national seminaries in the Holy City and the young clerics who were sent to them for their training were the most promising in their dioceses and were destined to hold positions of leadership in their countries of origin. Maritain, who saw at once the importance of this audience for the spread of French Catholic thought, accordingly set up a series of lectures and conferences for them at the Cultural Center and furnished them the possibility of many enriching contacts. The success of the conferences was such that eventually the hall proved too small for the crowds that pressed in to hear the many eminent speakers, one of whom, of course, was Maritain himself. A much larger hall was found by Maritain's successor and the popularity of the center continued long after Maritain's departure from Rome.[5]

Maritain's influence at Rome was not limited to student circles. D'Ormesson remarks that Pius XII and Msgr. Giovanni Battista Montini, the Vatican undersecretary of state and the future Pope Paul VI, took inspiration from his teachings. Msgr. Montini, who as a young priest had translated Maritain's *Three Reformers* (a book which Maritain would admit was not one of his best), often referred to Maritain as his "teacher," and later, as pope, used Maritain's social and political thought as the foundation for his social encyclicals, in which he quoted his "master" directly.

In spite of such acceptance in high places, Maritain did not lack enemies in Rome. A considerable number of the clergy at the Vatican, even those who held positions of authority in the Roman Curia, were openly hostile. The presence of such enemies was no surprise. Even before his arrival in Rome, Yves Simon had warned that the attacks that Maritain had suffered in the past would be

> trifles compared to what you will have to endure: the Franquists, the Pétainists, etc. of the entire world, mumbling stories about ambition finally satisfied, etc. especially if you are, as I hope you are, the man who will have carried out the purgation of the French hierarchy. The muck of their mudslinging will fall like rain. But after all, this is quite in the order of things. It is part of the grandeur of that vocation which is yours.[6]

When a calumnious attack on Maritain appeared in 1945 in a book (*De Lamennais à Maritain*) by an archconservative Argentine priest, Julio Mienvielle, copies were widely circulated among the Vatican conservatives. Father Garrigou-Lagrange, who had defended Maritain on doctrinal grounds in Rome during the Spanish Civil War, in spite of their radical differences on political and social issues, wrote to Mienvielle to defend Maritain against the grossest absurdities of this attack, but in the same letters made such generous concessions to Mienvielle that the latter published his correspondence with Garrigou-Lagrange as a confirmation of his position.[7] Maritain was indignant that his former mentor seemed to be bringing aid and comfort to his enemies. He wrote several letters of protest and self-defense to Garrigou-Lagrange and complained to Yves Simon about the need "to have to defend oneself by slopping about in the mud wallows of these South American calumniators."[8] He expressed regret that the book which Yves Simon intended to write in his defense had not yet appeared. Somehow, Maritain's letters to Garrigou-Lagrange came into the hands of Mienvielle, for he published his own reply to two of them.[9]

Such attacks continued in Rome long after Maritain's departure from the Vatican. Vladmir d'Ormesson speaks of such an attack in an article published in a "famous periodical"[10] and tells of a speech by a highly placed personality which filled him with such disgust that he rose and left before it was finished.[11] He was glad to notice that in these two cases his emotion was shared "at the top" (*en haut lieu*).

The three years at the Vatican were very busy for Maritain. In addition to fulfilling his onerous, time-consuming obligations as ambassador, he found time to resume the lectures he had given in the years before the war at the Angelicum, the Dominican house of studies in Rome; to publish numerous articles in European and American periodicals; to furnish prefaces and introductions to books written by his friends; and to produce two books of his own. One was a revised and expanded French version of *La Personne et le bien commun;* the other was a metaphysical treatise, *Court traité de l'existence et l'existant,* written as an answer to the existentialism of Heidegger and Sartre, which was enjoying great popularity in postwar France.

One of the prefaces Maritain supplied during this period for books by his friends was for a republication of Julien Green's *Pamphlet contre les catholiques de France.* It was shortly after the first appearance of the pamphlet, in 1925, that Stanislas Fumet presented Green to Maritain. Fumet wanted Maritain to meet the promising young author of a short novel, *La Traversée inutile,* to be published in their collection *Le Roseau d'Or.* This was the beginning of one of the most beautiful friendships in literary history.[12] During the war, Green was in the United States and saw Maritain frequently. When he returned to Paris with his sister after the war, Maritain offered them use of his mother's apartment, vacant since her death, until they could find a permanent lodging of their own.

Maritain, who had expressed reservations when Green spoke to him of the new edition of his *Pamphlet,* decided to write a preface to clear up some misunderstandings that might follow upon its publication. After reading this preface, Green wrote:

> How can I tell you what I feel about these pages. They delighted me as much as they saddened me, for I could never have dreamed of a more intelligent introduction which does more honor to my little book. Furnished with such a passport, the pamphlet should easily cross the frontier which separates it from those for whom it is destined, that is those Catholics who are a little too satisfied with their Catholicism, whom I would like to shake up a bit in 1946 as I did in 1924. But don't think I have forgotten what you told me the last time I saw you. As far as republishing this book with an introduction by the author is concerned, I would not even have thought of it had not Albert Béguin and Father Carré insisted that I do so. Father Couturier says he will re-read the pamphlet and tell me what he thinks. I will have to re-read it myself, for many years have gone by since I last read it. . . . What bothers me a little is that this re-edition

has been presented to me as a kind of duty, and I certainly wouldn't want it to be a mistake. In any case, if I write the introduction, I'll have you read it and if you think it could dissipate the misunderstandings the pamphlet might cause, I will consider republishing it. You know, this pamphlet is very far from me today, but if it could do some good, even to just one or two people, I think it would be worth republishing.[13]

Green had sent Maritain a copy of the third volume of his *Journal* (*Devant la porte sombre*), which Maritain read with great relish before answering the letter about the *Pamphlet:*

I put off writing to you in the midst of all the bothersome tasks that fall on me like rain, until I had finished reading your *Journal*. For all its admirable restraint it is an extraordinarily moving book, which I found particularly touching because it made me relive those years in America where our anguish was perpetual and where nevertheless our hearts became strangely attached to that country and its people. I was happy to catch again the echo of some of your conversations with Raïssa and me. There are many profound things in your book, and that marvelous love of Paris, and that image of your soul which shines through, as if in spite of yourself, with so much mystery and truth. Thank you, dear Julien, for having sent us this beautiful book. . . .

What you write me about my preface to your pamphlet gives me the joy of knowing that you like those pages, and reawakens my perplexity about their publication. . . . If you decide not to republish the pamphlet, the scruples I mentioned to you will have full satisfaction. But if you do decide to bring out an edition with a new introduction by the author, the so affectionate and touching manner in which you spoke of my preface makes me think that it would be better for it to appear along with your introduction. If there is a new edition, I would be too full of regret if it did not appear. Write me, dear Julien, to tell me what decision you have made.[14]

When the pamphlet appeared, Green respected Maritain's wishes and included both the introduction and the preface.

In 1947 a Mr. d'Angelo came to Maritain in Rome, seeking an introduction to Green, with the intention of persuading the author of *Minuit* to adapt his novel to a film production. Green welcomed d'Angelo, on Maritain's recommendation, but the film was never produced.

While Maritain was ambassador at Rome, his influence in the field of social justice and world peace extended far beyond the Vatican, and indeed far beyond the Catholic Church. In 1947 he was happy to remark to Yves Simon the impact he had on the social thought of the new French hierarchy:

> Have you noticed that in his Lenten Pastoral Letter, to which all our friends in France attach an enormous importance, Cardinal Suhard has taken general positions which are our own? They say that the editors of the letter took their inspiration from *Humanisme intégrale.*[15]

Maritain's prestige was no less outside religious circles. In October 1947 the ambassador to the Vatican was invited to head the French delegation to the second general conference of UNESCO, to be held in Mexico City that November. Maritain at first refused the honor, for the same reasons that he had at first refused the ambassadorship, but Minister Georges Bidault insisted so strongly that he felt obliged to accept, though *"à contrecoeur."* When he arrived in Mexico City, he was elected president of the conference and delivered the opening address, "The Possibilities for Cooperation in a Divided World."

While he was returning from Mexico City, Dr. Harold Willis Dodds, president of Princeton University, came to New York to seek him out, during a stopover in New York for a change of planes, to offer him ("with that American generosity and courtesy which we know so well," he wrote to Yves Simon)[16] the post of resident professor at the university whenever he should decide to leave his post at the Vatican. The appointment required that each year in the philosophy department Maritain give a graduate course in Ethics, "based on the spirit and principles of Thomas Aquinas." For the rest, his time would be his own, for writing and research. His resident obligations would cease after the end of April to enable him to return to France each summer.

This was an offer he could hardly refuse. The three years he had promised de Gaulle and Bidault at the Vatican ambassadorship were drawing to a close and he was anxious to return to the intellectual and meditative life of a philosopher. He still had many important books he wanted to publish in the few years left to him, and he had spoken to Bidault of his resignation as early as August 1947. On February 9, 1948, he wrote to Yves Simon:

For my part, I too am about to change my life once more. Though the newspapers have already spoken of it, I ask you to keep this information most confidential until my departure from Rome is officially made public (I am obligated to an extreme discretion *vis-à-vis* the French government). Last August I asked Mister Bidault to set me free; it is high time for me to return to my vocation as a philosopher. (I am 65 years old, Yves. There can be no retirement. I need fifteen more years of service. From the point of view of teaching, the age limit is drawing near. As of the next academic year I must return to teaching.) Bidault strongly insisted that I remain at my post, but in the end he sympathized with my reasons, and on my last trip to Paris, in January, he gave me his definitive word.

There were press leaks, as Maritain suggested, and the news spread like wildfire. "Official or not, the news of your return to academic life and to the United States has run across France, Canada and the United States," wrote Yves Simon.[17] At the University of Chicago, where Thomism was much in vogue at the time, under Robert M. Hutchins and Mortimer Adler, John U. Nef wanted Maritain as a member of his distinguished Committee on Social Thought. Yves Simon said Nef was "heart-broken":

> He wanted you at Chicago, not at Princeton; he has been working at that for fifteen years now! Zut! I hadn't thought of that, undoubtedly because to be your colleague at Chicago, to see you every week, that would be too good to be true.[18]

Maritain's resignation became official on May 10, exactly three years after he presented his credentials at the Vatican. Two weeks later he left for Princeton, where he would live and teach until Raïssa's death twelve years later.

The Princeton years were extremely fruitful. Maritain was everywhere in demand as a lecturer and as a visiting professor. Though at times the honorarium was ridiculously small, and occasionally nil, he rarely refused such invitations. They came from great universities and small, and when he accepted, the enthusiastic anticipation seemed to know no bounds. Learning that he had agreed to speak at the University of Chicago only a few months after his return to the United States, Yves Simon wrote to him: "This whole enormous city is in a state of intense excitement because of your visit."[19] In 1950, when Maritain accepted the invitation of Florence Roll to speak to the Newman Club of Brooklyn College on "The Problem of World Government," Miss Roll wrote:

> At the committee meeting today at Brooklyn College there was a feeling not only of jubilation, but indeed, of exaltation as your name was spoken and plans got under way for the event of your lecture.[20]

Some of Maritain's most famous works, later published in book form or as articles, were the result of such lectures. *Man and the State* was the result of six lectures given at the University of Chicago. *On the Philosophy of History* was the expanded version of a series of conferences at the University of Notre Dame. *The Responsibility of the Artist* came from a series of lectures at Princeton. Another series, at Chicago, resulted in *Reflections on America*. The Mellon Lectures in the Fine Arts, which Maritain delivered at the National Gallery in Washington, became *Creative Intuition in Art and Poetry*.

Maritain's appointment at Princeton left him free to return to France early each spring to pass the summer renewing his contacts in French intellectual circles and visiting his friends. This contact was very important for him, since his long absence from France during the war years and his ambassadorship had made such contact difficult.

During the summer of 1949 he opened the annual Semaine des Intellectuels Catholiques at Paris with an address entitled "Les Chemins de la foi," after which Robert Barrat published an interview with him in *Témoignage Chrétien*. He gave a conference at the Insitut Catholique de Paris on "La Signification de l'athéisme contemporain" and another at Eau Vive, a Dominican house of studies. Maritain looked forward to a long series of such summers, part of which would always be spent with his good friends, the Grunelius family, in Kolbsheim, but circumstances made this impossible. In 1950 he had to remain at Princeton, due to Raïssa's illness, and in 1954 he had a heart attack. The 1955 visit to France was complicated by Raïssa's accident: she was knocked down by a motorcycle in Paris. This was the last summer visit to France; the following year Vera, Raïssa's sister, fell gravely ill, first with heart trouble and then with cancer, and needed constant care. During this period his contact with French Catholic intellectuals was considerably reduced. His work on his publications and his care of Vera and Raïssa too, whose health was failing, precluded visits to France and reduced his correspondence even with such close friends as Julien Green. Vera died on New Year's Eve, 1959.

Besides bearing up under a heavy burden of sorrow, Maritain now had to support Raïssa, whose fragile health had broken under the long strain of Vera's suffering. She recovered sufficiently, however, to return with him to France the summer of 1960. Scarcely had they arrived in Paris than Raïssa was felled by a cerebral thrombosis. Maritain was in despair. When Antoinette Grunelius learned of their plight, she rushed to Paris, put an apartment at their disposal, and obtained nursing help.

One of the effects of Raïssa's stroke was aphasia, which lasted several months. Whenever Jacques was in her presence, Raïssa made such exhausting efforts to speak to him, and became so agitated by her frustrations, that the doctors advised him to visit her as seldom as possible. To be cut off suddenly from communicating, even by a look or gesture, with someone next to whom he had passed his whole married life in the closest communication of thoughts, sentiments and words was almost more than he could bear. He shut himself up in an adjoining room, trying to lose himself in his writing and in correcting the proofs of his books, but he listened with anguish to every sound that passed through the wall. Raïssa died on November 4, 1960, and was laid to rest in the little cemetery at Kolbsheim, near the home of the Grunelius family.

Deprived of her whom he called (in the dedication of one of his books) *"dimidium animae"* — who truly was the very half of his soul — and physically exhausted from his heart ailment, he set about planning the years that were left to him. He wanted to live in retirement and contemplation, working on the books he had not yet been able to write, and accepted an invitation to live in the community of the Little Brothers of Jesus, at their study house in Toulouse, as a lay advisor to the brothers who were students of philosophy.

Maritain turned over his home in Meudon to the artist Gino Severini, who had been using it as a studio. With Madame Grunelius' help, he sold most of his furniture; the rest, along with his books and papers, he sent to the guest rooms of the Grunelius residence at Kolbsheim, where they would always be available to him. Returning briefly to Princeton to dispose of his possessions there, he turned over his New Jersey house to a close friend, the musician Arthur Lourié, and his wife Ella for as long as they should live, after which it was deeded to the University of Notre Dame, where a Maritain Center had been founded in 1958. To return to a house filled with so many memories, in the very palpable absence of her who was the source of these memories, was difficult beyond description. He wrote to Julien Green:

> You must certainly have obeyed an inspiration from heaven in sending me that letter which moved me so deeply. It arrived only Friday (December 2) because of a delay in the distribution of my mail. But even that was providential, for what I felt before I received it showed me how true it was.
>
> I wept quite a bit on the plane (not as much as at Paris) before passing my first night at Princeton at the home of Sir Hugh Taylor and I was very much afraid of entering our empty house on December 1. But no, it wasn't empty; *it was as if Raïssa welcomed me to her home.* It must have been she who guided the dear ladies, Jane, the seamstress, and Julia, the cook, and Nini Borjerhoff [Maritain's secretary and the wife of a colleague], who had arranged everything in the room with such marvelously delicate care so that everything should be as it had been. (It was only into Raïssa's room that I found it painful to enter.) At any rate, in the very heart of my sorrow I had the impression that Raïssa was waiting for me in the living room filled with flowers; her atmosphere and her spirit were there with that grace, that gay yet grave sweetness, that elegant and pure valiance that emanated from her. I firmly believe, as you do, that Raïssa is happy and that she wants me to be courageous. Happy, Julien? How could I be happy? I have lost the presence of her whom I loved more than myself; I have witnessed the slow and implacable destruction of her poor body. (In one of her poems she said to God: "You want my destruction and my death.") But it is true that she is with me ceaselessly and that she watches over me. And in my sadness I feel a kind of joy (the English word "elation" is perhaps more exact). May I never make myself unworthy of this grace.[21]

On returning to France, after spending a few days in Kolbsheim, he went to Toulouse to live in the tiny hermitage which the Little Brothers of Jesus had prepared for him.

CHAPTER 8

Peasant of the Garonne
and Little Brother of Jesus

IN HIS HERMITAGE AT Toulouse, where in his last years he hoped to find a refuge from political and social turmoil and devote himself to philosophical reflection, prayer and contemplation, one of the first tasks to which Maritain set himself was the preparation (for posthumous publication) of Raïssa's *Notes sur le Pater*. By the end of May 1961 he had finished the task, which he enjoyed so much and which helped relieve the burden of loneliness. When the little book appeared, he sent copies to his and Raïssa's friends. Along with another book on art, Maritain sent a copy of *Notes sur le Pater* to François Mauriac, who wrote in return:

> I must send a double "thank you" for this book on art which I intend to read with all the attention of someone who himself has never been able to find the answer to the question posed by his vocation as a novelist. As far as Raïssa's *Pater* is concerned, it will help me to pray. . . . I thank you for counting me among those who love you. You are not mistaken about my wondering what your life must be like in the midst of the Little Brothers. I envy you. In my old days I harbor a certain phobia (it has been noticed on several occasions) for Reverend Fathers, Jesuit or Dominican. And I could give you some very precise reasons for this.
>
> The Little Brothers alone correspond to my idea of what an apostle should be in these times, in these Latter Days.
>
> Dear Jacques, pray for me and believe in my affection for you.[1]

Mauriac also suggested that he visit Maritain the next time he went to Malagar. This was the beginning of a warm renewal of

217

their old friendship (which lasted till Mauriac's death). A few years later, in his *Nouveaux Mémoires intérieurs*, Mauriac wrote:

> Jacques Maritain has never ceased to watch over me with an uneasy and even anxious eye. But he never tried to interfere directly. He responded publicly to any call for help that came from me. I had the certitude that he was listening in on my life.

Further on in the book he wrote:

> In those days I leaned on others. . . . I used to speak with Du Bos, with Maritain. And even if I did not see them very often, I knew that they were working and praying somewhere in the world. I was not alone.[2]

To Julien Green, whom he saw each summer on his way to and from Kolbsheim, Maritain likewise sent a copy. It was customary for these two friends to exchange what books they had written, to read them with devoted care, and to exchange reflections. In his *Journal*, Green wrote:

> I remember that between Jacques and me there existed no familiarity whatsoever, but rather a tenderness. We never felt the need to exchange useless banalities. He would question me on my work, wanted to see everything I wrote. I sent him the texts. Three or four days later an admirable letter would arrive, carefully written and thought out, after a very attentive reading.[3]

Green did the same with whatever Maritain sent him. After reading *Notes sur le Pater*, he wrote:

> This book of Raïssa's is a work of light which I thank you for having given me in her name. We found her in all her fullness in these pages, with her piety, her feeling for the divine and her great intuitive insights. I would be at a loss to tell you what struck me most in her meditations, for I would have to copy out long and numerous passages. But more than any other doubtless the passage where she speaks of the soul in the state of grace, which is really a heaven where God makes his home, and also her remarks on God's pardon which extends also to those whom we pardon. There is such great beauty in all this. It makes us love God.[4]

In June of that year Etienne Gilson, the famous Thomist philosopher and friend of Maritain, who had first invited him to come to the New World to give a course at the Institute of Mediaeval Studies at Toronto in 1932 and who now was a member of the Académie Française, proposed the name of his friend for the Grand Prix de Littérature de l'Académie Française, and Maritain was subsequently chosen for the prize. When Julien Green wrote to congratulate him, Maritain expressed an uneasy embarrassment with the honor. He wrote from Kolbsheim:

> Thank you for writing me, my very dear Julien. It does me some good that you are happy about this prize, for to tell the truth, my feelings about it are somewhat mixed. This kind of award unsettles me enormously. Then too, with the exception of Gilson, who they tell me took the initiative in this decision, the other members of the Académie certainly haven't read a single one of my books:[5] it's more like a longevity prize they are awarding me. But you are right; it would have given pleasure to Raïssa. I think she is happy about it (for this is all that matters) and that she is a bit amused at my embarrassment.[6]

One day that summer, during his stay at Kolbsheim, after he had returned from the grave of Raïssa (where he spent some moments each day in meditation), Madame Grunelius presented him with two huge bundles of notebooks and papers which Raïssa had left in her keeping. One was marked "To keep, perhaps"; the other "For Jacques to look over." They contained her journals, notes, outlines, essays, memoranda and jottings. Maritain was so moved by the flood of memories they evoked that he decided to organize the material and publish it privately as *Journal de Raïssa*. He had 250 copies printed privately and distributed among their friends, who, after reading it, insisted that he prepare an edition for the public.

Just before the public edition came out, in 1962, Maritain was awarded the Grand Prix National des Lettres, and as a result of the notoriety associated with the prize, the first printing of *Journal de Raïssa* sold out immediately. Maritain was deeply disturbed by this because the most intimate reflections of Raïssa and certain aspects of her spiritual life would be exposed before a public that would have no way of appreciating them, in some cases might even hold them up to ridicule. When Julien Green wrote of his appreciation of the *Journal*, which was like a "great trail of light in the world where we live," Maritain replied:

> All that you write to me of the *Journal de Raïssa* is infinitely dear to my heart. You, my beloved Julien, who were so near

to her up to the end, in those months of agony. I believe as
you do that the decision to publish these notes was inspired
by her — if you only knew how much she helped me in this
work. I think she wants her witness to be spread among
men. For she has many things to teach us.

And I too must learn to let myself be led like a blind
man. My God, I had it all planned that this publication
should be as discreet as possible, convinced that the book
would make its way alone among souls. I had even persuaded the editor to give it no publicity. . . . And then just at
the moment when the book appeared, there was all this
exasperating fanfare about me! Even here Raïssa protected
me, sending me a little attack of the flu which made it possible for me to hide from all the journalists and photo-
graphers who invaded the quarters of the Little Brothers.
And now I am submerged under a pile of aberrant letters
from people who have read nothing I have written. And then
there is the fact that all the publicity I feared has come
about indirectly because of me and my prize. The first printing of the *Journal* is already sold out. At first I reacted to all
this with considerable bitterness. But now I say to myself
that Providence moves in ironical ways, and that among all
those people who bought the *Journal,* most of them without
knowing what they were getting, it is sufficient that there be
turn toward God. . . . I am also touched by all that Mauriac
has said about the *Journal* and about Raïssa in his Bloc-
notes.[7]

During these years, Maritain continued to work at his books.
In 1963, from three seminars he had conducted for the Little
Brothers, he published *Dieu et la permission du mal,* which, along
with *Court traité de l'existence et de l'existent,* he considered his
most important contribution to Thomistic thought. In 1965 he
published his own diaries as *Carnet de notes,* which received an
enthusiastic reception. From Paris, Mauriac wrote:

My gratitude extends especially to those *Carnets* which I
have received and which I have already devoured. What a
time that was, those days at Meudon and what remorse I
feel for having made such poor use of them.[8]

Julien Green was even more enthusiastic about *Carnet:*

Those were marvelous hours that I just passed with you, for
you have never sent me a book that has touched me more

deeply than did this *Carnet de notes,* where once again I find you and Raïssa and Vera as I have known and loved you, known all of you as one knows the beings he loves, by intuition. In fact you have taught me many precious things about the three of you that I did not know and which bring you still closer to me, within my heart. I regret only that I learned all this so late; but it could not have been otherwise. In this book there are treasures, yes, I dare to say it, treasures of grace. From the very first pages, I was overwhelmed by the tone of your words, for God made use of you long before your conversion, in order to get to us, to us who owe you so much. I know you well enough to recognize that you don't put much stock in admiration. Let me tell you at least that I admire God in you. You have finally opened to us the grand avenues of your soul and I see there nothing but light.[9]

Maritain was profoundly touched by Green's letter, which came when he was passing through a period of depression occasioned by the untoward and, what he considered, the vulgar publicity that his book was subject to. Also, he was becoming more conscious of the ravages of age and the profound changes that come with the passage of time, changes which seemed to pass him by and leave him a stranger at the side of the road. It was the changes in the Church that disturbed him most deeply.

May you be blessed, my very dear Julien [he wrote], for that letter so filled with marvelous charity. It touches me all the more deeply since I find myself at the moment in a very thick night, and since I cannot see what you loved in the book. . . . But I believe you, Julien, and for me that is infinitely sweet. You cannot know how much I needed that encouragement, which seems to come to me from heaven, as do many things that come to me through you.

In fact during all the time I was working on that book, I thought only of my friends, of those to whom it was addressed. The idea of the public never occurred to me. And then, when I saw the book printed, I felt a shock that disconcerted me enormously. To hand such things over to the public, to readers who had never known or loved Raïssa and Vera, are you mad, I said to myself. You reassure me as you alone know how, and I had a terrible need of that. Thank you for telling me that I did well "to publish this book now"; this dissipates my doubts and puts me back in my place before God.

At my age you feel bizarre sensations. You are a
stranger everywhere. You are not in eternity and everything
seems to chase you out of time, to deny you your poor little
place, your poor little instant in which you existed in the
past, and all the while the present instant means nothing at
all. (There was still an oasis of peace for me in daily mass.
Now even that is finished, with this invasion of ugliness and
vulgarity.)[10]

For a long time Maritain had been disturbed by what he saw
happening in the Church and he shared his concerns with his
friends. He was disturbed by the continued, vociferous, and retrograde influence of the *"intégristes,"* who had attacked him,
persistently and violently, during his days at the Vatican — and
had continued to do so during his years at Princeton. On the other
hand, he had long been disturbed by the *"progressistes,"* who, in
justified reaction to the *intégristes,* seemed, without realizing
what they were doing, to rush precipitously toward any change
whatever, with little regard for historical or theological justification.

While he was still at the Vatican, he had written to Yves
Simon in America (Mar. 10, 1946):

The thought of the work that you are doing in America
brings me great consolation, — both for America and for
France, whose intelligentsia is going through a bad period
right now. I was in Paris in January and I could see that no
poison has yet been eliminated. The people are good, but the
intellectuals are feeble and intoxicated; all the old poisons,
and new ones too, have gone to their heads. Some Catholics
have become *"intégristes"* (out of resentment at or compen-
sation for the crumbling of Action Française, whose spiritual
influence has not disappeared). Others, clergy and laity
alike, have no other thought than to eliminate St. Thomas,
who is decidedly too difficult and too demanding, in order to
"conquer souls" by contracting their diseases and following
the fashions of the times.

At the end of 1946, in a letter he wrote to Father Garrigou-
Lagrange concerning the latter's support of the attacks on Mari-
tain from South America and the implication by Garrigou-
Lagrange that Maritain might be guilty of doctrinal "deviation,"
Maritain stated, in no uncertain terms, what he considered to be

one of the principal causes for the general rejection of systematic theology among the younger clergy and laity, and especially of any theology associated with the word "Thomism":

> Now you answer me that in your mind the *deviation* in question concerned General Franco and my preface to Mendizabal's book. Ah! you reassure me, Reverend Father. . . . For a long time now I have been afraid that "I believe in the justice of the revolt of the Spanish Generals against their government in the year of grace 1936" has been added to our Catholic Credo, by a very strange phenomenon in the development of dogma. . . .
>
> . . . Whatever our political differences may be, you had no right whatsoever in this regard to cast the slightest suspicion on my doctrine. When you took the side of Marshal Pétain, to the point of declaring that to support de Gaulle was a mortal sin, I felt that your political prejudices blinded you in a matter that was very serious for our country, but it did not even cross my mind to suspect your theology or to accuse you of deviation in matters of doctrine.
>
> I might add that I was very sorry about the way you compromised Thomism through your political positions that were justifiably odious to those who were struggling for the liberation of our country. If there is at the present moment a crisis of Thomism in France, if many young minds seek their intellectual nourishment in new theologies, you can be sure that one of the causes of this disaffection is the fact that since the quarrels of the Ralliement, the roadblocks set up against any progress in the practical acceptance of the social teachings of Leo XIII, and above all the prestige of Action Française, we have seen defenders of Sacred Doctrine let themselves be taken in completely by outrageous illusions in the domain of national politics. Not everyone makes the distinction between substance and accident.[11]

For Maritain to speak so strongly to a man whom he had always revered, and would continue to revere, shows how deeply he felt about this matter.

As early as 1948, shortly after Maritain's return to the United States from Rome, Olivier Lacombe wrote him of a project that had been discussed by the friends of Maritain at a summer reunion at Kolbsheim. Lacombe had proposed a manifesto, similar to the *Manifeste pour le bien commun* of 1934, but in an entirely different domain, taking a position equally distant from both integrism and religious liberalism. Its purpose would be to call attention to the "present theological disarray of the Church in France." Signed by a long list of prominent French Catholic intellectuals, it would have an impact similar to Maritain's *Lettre sur l'indépendence* and the manifesto of 1934. This project, which was to be carried out only with the approbation of Maritain and with his careful consideration of each detail of the text.[12] The text of the manifesto, whose final draft was composed by Olivier Lacombe in 1949, shows the concern of Maritain and his friends over a situation which, in their opinion, was growing to crisis proportions. In 1964 Julien Green wrote of his dismay about changes in what he considered doctrines that were "beyond discussion":

> It is strange, this young Church, the Church of the seminaries. One senses in it a will to break with the past, with all that is static and paralyzing in the past, and up to a certain point I understand, and I agree; but I'm afraid they are going too far. . . . I would like to have spoken of all this with you, for there have been moments, especially before John XXIII, when I was very uneasy, seeing the turn that things were taking in the ecclesiastical *milieux* as well as among laymen, this great confusion of ideas, to say nothing of the beliefs we used to think were beyond discussion. Without being in the least *"intégriste,"* I have often asked myself if the essential elements of the Faith were not in danger. I have heard some truly stupefying things said by priests. It is probable that around 1900 some very strange opinions were also put forth, but the groundswell of modernism did not carry off the Church. It is trials like that which prove it is built upon a rock.[13]

In the letter he wrote in reply, it is easy to recognize the tone and the subject matter of his next book, *Le Paysan de la Garonne*, already present in the mind of Maritain:

> I agree with you completely, Julien, on the situation of the young Church, the Church of the seminaries (and to tell the truth, the entire present situation of the Church). We are at the heart of an extraordinary mystery. That kind of throwing the reins on the horse's back by John XXIII was absolutely necessary, but with what risks at the same time. Poor

Paul VI. All that is *professionally* intellectual (professors, universities, seminaries) seems to me either spoiled or in a very dangerous position. A certain exegesis has gone mad and stupid. There is a new modernism full of pride and obstreperousness that seems to me more dangerous than that of Pius X. (It was after all a rather strange spectacle to see all the bishops of the Council — the Teaching Church — each one flanked by his experts, professors, scholars, and pedants of the Taught Church, of whom a good number were off their intellectual rails, and of whom almost none has any *wisdom*.) So, it is in the middle of all this hubbub that the work of the Holy Spirit is carried out.

In my opinion the attitude of the young clergy is very understandable, because we are face to face with a *general mentality* which has been taking form since the Middle Ages and the Baroque period, but which is completely formless and untamed, as violently uncontrolled as a tidal wave, and which instead of having found its normal forms of intellectual expression, hurls itself against a sea wall raised up by a *theology* that is faithful, but has not known how to renew itself (the intelligence is always too late). For many years now I have been shouting that we have to ask St. Thomas to open doors, not to close them. But the theologians continue to close them (unless they are modernists, although to tell the truth there are no longer any modernist theologians, but only historians, exegetes and other rabid specialists who want nothing more to do with theology), and the general mentality that I speak of wants nothing more to do with St. Thomas (who alone could save the situation, if they understood him as he should be understood). . . . [14]

It was in this letter, too, that Maritain expressed his deep disappointment that Pope Paul VI, on the occasion of his visit to the Holy Land, did not place the six candles at the memorial to the six million massacred Jews, but had Cardinal Tisserant place them there in his stead. Maritain was equally disappointed with the second version of the council's schema on the Jews, which had been watered down because of pressure from the bishops of the Arab states and the political forces behind them.

In 1965 Mauriac wrote to Maritain, asking if he might come over to Toulouse from Malagar, where he would be spending a month, to speak with him about the present crisis and what, in his opinion, must be said and what must be kept quiet.[15]

Later that year, on December 8, in the simple gray suit of the Little Brothers of Jesus, Jacques Maritain was present on the great dais before St. Peter's Basilica, amid all the spendor of the council's closing ceremonies. The presence of this simply-dressed, frail old man among all the ecclesiastical dignitaries, clad in their splendid vestments, seemed anomalous. He had been invited by the pope to receive the council's message to the intellectuals of the world, which stressed the intrinsic compatibility and mutual understanding possible between secular knowledge and faith as servants of one another. It was read by Cardinal Liénart of Lille, after which Pope Paul VI, with deep emotion, placed the text in the hands of his friend Jacques Maritain.

What went through the old philosopher's mind at this moment? He was certainly enthusiastic about the work of the council, and shortly afterward wrote to Julien Green of "the admirable things the Council had accomplished."[16] On the other hand, he was disappointed with the wording of certain declarations of the council. For example, did he publish in the same year as the closing of the council his *Mystère d'Israël*, a collection of his most important writings on the Jewish problem, because he felt that the wording of the council's declaration on the Jews did not go far enough, and left the door open to continued anti-Semitism among Catholics? He was even more disturbed by the atmosphere of enthusiasm for novelty, for any change at all, and by the apparent determination to cut loose from any attachment to the past which seemed to permeate the Catholic world after Vatican II. He was not the only one to sense danger, and many looked to him for guidance in the confusion and turmoil. In his "Bloc-notes" Mauriac wrote: "Caught up in the slip-stream of Vatican II, how many times have I asked myself, What does Maritain think of it all?"

At any rate, a little more than a month after his return from the council closing Maritain announced to Julien Green that

> as a result of circumstances that I shall tell you about later, I have imprudently undertaken something way beyond my strength, — a little book that I will probably never finish but in which I would like to try to say certain things that only a *very* old man can say (if he has the strength). We are in a very serious modernist crisis.[17]

This "little book" was *Le Paysan de la Garonne*, and the welcome accorded it surprised everyone — the author most of all, then his friends, who were the first to salute its appearance. But it also surprised his enemies, both from the right and the left, who at first preferred to remain silent but were eventually forced to take a position by the enormous success of the book.

Le Paysan made the number one spot on the nonfiction list of best sellers for January 1967. Seventy thousand copies were sold and seven printings were exhausted in four months — a phenomenal record for a 400-page theological essay. Evidently, from the aging philosopher who had retired from the public forum to devote his declining years to the contemplation and serenity denied him during the busy days of his active career, Maritain's public had come to expect a "final testament" of calm and dispassionate judgment on the philosophical and religious movements that were troubling the world of the Second Vatican Council; but his testament proved to be far from dispassionate and serene. What was particularly surprising was the ferocity of the attacks from the left. Henry Bars suggests that this was so because "there was question of a book that proved quite embarrassing for certain currents of thought; perhaps because it expressed a position counter to an intellectual policy that was accepted in high places without ever being avowed openly."[18] Even in the Catholic press, discussion of the book was slow to get started. The book had appeared at the beginning of November, but it was not until mid-December that the controversy over it really began; then it took off like wildfire.

At a meeting of the Académie Française in 1966, when Jean Guitton asked François Mauriac if he had received his prepublication copy of *Le Paysan*, he replied: "I drank in that book like milk." "So did I," said Guitton. Both published very complimentary reviews: Guitton in *Le Figaro* and Mauriac in several of his "Bloc-notes" in *Le Figaro Littéraire;* and the next time Maritain passed through Paris, Mauriac rushed to see him. On December 1 he wrote:

> Your letter — rather your two letters have brought me joy for several days — indeed for always, it seems to me. Julien Green told me you will be coming back to Paris. All he had to do was mention it to me. This time it is I who will go to see you. It seems to me that your book has been understood even by those who seem to be farthest from it, and that it makes the mad a little less mad.[19]

From Paris, Julien Green wrote:

> This is a book of yours that I have been awaiting for years
> without knowing what form it might take. I was certain it
> would be something important, but you have exceeded all
> my hopes. I could not, however, tell you that each time I
> receive another one of your books, the last seems more
> beautiful than all the others. I would really end up selling
> short the books that preceded it, but this last one is some-
> thing special! I believe this is due to the fact that you have
> attained such a great interior freedom, which permits you to
> say all you wish with a simplicity that does not recognize
> obstacles, and you say what must be said at the moment
> when it seems indispensable that someone raise his voice. If
> someone has defended the faith at a time when, in spite of
> certain appearances, it is so bitterly attacked, it certainly is
> you, my dear Jacques, just as you are, just as we love you,
> and just as you appear in this book. Those who know you
> well, as Anne and I do, will not be astonished by that smile
> which appears from time to time, lighting up pages that are
> in danger of seeming severe, but I think you will only be
> loved all the more for it. Your irony has an element of sur-
> prise and enchantment — and it is not without some useful-
> ness in a country where good humor still counts. I will have
> many things to say to you, when I have the joy of seeing you
> again, about this work which in my opinion is of capital im-
> portance and whose echo will be great throughout the
> Catholic world.[20]

Louis Chaigne welcomed *Le Paysan* as a much-needed cry of
alarm, to recall to the Catholic world the forgotten warning of
John XXIII, whose *aggiornamento* was often used to justify the
unthinking rush toward seductive novelties — a warning he had
given as papal nuncio at Paris when he inaugurated the UNESCO
conference there. He had warned of the dangers of "creating
something new, something modern, even something bizarre, in
any way and at any price." Maritain tells us, Chaigne said, that
the indispensable and necessary *aggiornamento* does not mean an
attack on essential structures. Chaigne concluded his praise of *Le
Paysan* by saying that

> far from being a work of negative and polemic character,
> this generous book, by freeing the intelligence, establishes
> the unshakable foundations of modern thought which is in

search at one and the same time of progress and of stability, of penetration and of balance. It will permit us to live the postconciliar period in all its fullness.[21]

The public controversy over the book did not get under way until mid-December, almost a month and a half after its appearance. Indeed, it seems that the editorial board of the well-known French Jesuit Catholic review *Etudes* debated long and hard over whether it should even speak of *Le Paysan*. Henry Bars feels that this attitude was common in the Catholic press and that, when the attacks finally got under way, they seemed, from both the right and the left, (apart from a few cases of individual initiative), to be the result of concerted strategies.[22] The "affair" of *Le Paysan de la Garonne* began to take on the aspect of a war, *"la belle guerre des chrétiens,"* as Fabre-Luce said. Few reviewers of either the right or the left seemed capable of looking at the book from an objective distance, and this was perhaps due in some measure to a certain tone in the book itself. Most reviewers became partisanly and emotionally involved in the controversy because they seemed to feel themselves attacked, even denigrated personally, for positions they took as phenomenologists, religious integralists, Teilhardists, traditional Thomists or "new theologians." The result was a flood of reviews filled with invective from the right, which Maritain nicknamed *"les Ruminants de la Sainte Alliance"* (cud chewers of the Holy Alliance), and especially from the left, which he dubbed *"les Moutons de Panurge"* (sheep of Panurge).

The first reaction of the right was one of joy — Maritain was attacking the left — and the initial impulse was to annex this peasant of the Garonne, as had been done in the days of *La Revue Universelle*. But the old peasant would have none of it. At the very beginning of the book he placed himself above the partisan quarrels of the right and the left, as he had done years before in his *Lettre sur l'indépendance* and continued to do throughout his career. Though a number of positions taken by Maritain against certain changes in the Church's traditional philosophical and theological orientation and in its liturgical, spiritual and internal disciplinary traditions delighted the "cud chewers of the Holy Alliance," they could not show their delight too openly, for Maritain had clearly set forth, in the beginning of his book, a list of the inestimable accomplishments of the council: its declarations on religious liberty and the rights of the individual conscience, on cooperation with non-Catholics and non-Christians in a divided world, on democracy and the relations between Church and State, on the goodness, value and beauty of the world as God's creation and the temporal mission of the Christian in this world, on the eminent dignity of the lay state, on the anti-Christian aberration of racism and especially anti-Semitism.

All the liberating words he had written on these subjects during his long career, which made him one of the principal artisans of the openness of the Second Vatican Council, made it impossible for the right, for his old enemies from Action Française, to expropriate this old, inveterate "laic," as they had tried to do years before. They felt themselves the target of his straightforward criticism of religious integralism and rigid, traditional Thomism. Reversing the old adage, "If you can't lick 'em, join 'em," they decided on the only tactic open to them: "If we can't annex him, we'll destroy him"; and that is what they tried to do. It was the same tactic that Massis and Maurras had chosen after the condemnation of Action Française. Maritain must be discredited. If he could be pictured once again as a turncoat; if the structure of his thought could be made to appear without solid foundation, without consistent direction; if the old, radical firebrand could be portrayed as terrified by the fires he had set; if the old colossus could be shown to have crumbling feet of clay, so that, with his resounding fall in this "last testament," the whole edifice of his thought would come tumbling down — then the credibility of the positions he took in 1927 could again be called into question.

More than any other publication, the review *Itinéraires* — in spite of the editor's protestations of giving his collaborateurs complete liberty to say exactly what they thought — showed how well orchestrated was the tactical strategy of the right in a series of articles on *Le Paysan*. But such a reaction was to be expected. What came as a complete surprise to many was the violence of the concerted attacks from the left. One famous religious went so far as to claim that the old philosopher, who had never really converted from the ultraconservatism of his young years, was now, in his senility, "returning to his vomit." For another, "St. Thomas muzzles the old anarchist in him." A Dominican parish priest maintained that Maritain showed "profound and culpable ignorance" of the contemporary pastoral problems confronting the Church, such as penance, sexuality and the role of the priest in the modern world (*Signes du temps;* Feb. 1967). An editor of the Belgian periodical *La Revue Nouvelle* excoriated Maritain's "closed and ratiocinating Thomism," which inspired his *"jeremiades"* against Hegel and every school of philosophy since Descartes, in particular the phenomenologists. In regard to the latter, claimed the reviewer, Maritain's "myopic" Thomism rendered him incapable of distinguishing between "what is method and what is system." Such a radical Thomism, he said, completely alienates the man of today, whose mind has been formed in the language and method of positive science, evolution, psychology, and existential philosophy and who will not be convinced by "summary anathemas." Others accused him of sowing confusion in the ranks of those who were working for renewal.

Henry Bars found that the same kind of "group dynamics" which united the right against Maritain did the same for the left, particularly among the clergy:

> The position taken by *Témoignage Chrétien* has been most revealing in this regard. When interviewed a bit later on the radio, the editor, Georges Montaron, replied with some embarrassment that his collaborators were free to hold their own opinions. But who will believe that the choice of his collaborators at the time was not the result of a concerted design? "Has the Church betrayed the Church?" This title in huge red letters, by which Maritain's book was announced on the first page, defines very precisely the tone it was intended to give. And I can well understand that the editorial board of the magazine felt itself particularly under fire from *Le Paysan: Témoignage Chrétien* has a very noble origin, though a bit weighted toward the negative political position it has chosen, as it is toward the theological orientation it supports.[23]

The same kind of orientation that had caused problems between Mounier and Maritain was at work here. Too bad, said Henry Bars, that instead of examining their position the "sheep of Panurge" were content to bleat.

François Biot accused Maritain of dishonesty and injustice for his attacks on the "new theology" and for his contention that the new generation of Christians was on its knees before the world (*Témoignage Chrétien;* Dec. 15, 1966). In the same issue, Henri Fesquet found unbearable Maritain's "involuntary fatuity" and his "exclusive" love of St. Thomas Aquinas, as well as his strange tendency to defend his leftist positions with the "mentality of a Right-wing extremist."

Though his last expression is a gross exaggeration and shows woeful ignorance of Maritain and his mentality, Fesquet comes close to the heart of the problem of the critics of the left. The younger generation of the new Catholic left had grown up in an intellectual atmosphere where Maritain's presence and influence were no longer felt. He had been in America or Rome; so they had lost the habit of his presence. They had lost, or never had, the habit of discussing him and his liberal positions, which so often corresponded to theirs, but for different reasons. They had not heard his repeated insistence that however just a political or moral choice may be at a given moment, if it does not have a solid philosophical or theological foundation, it would eventually go astray. They did not really know Maritain, they knew his legend; for there was a legendary Maritain just as there had been a lengendary Mounier, who had established the tone of this new Catholic left. They did not realize that Maritain and Mounier had been continually at odds over this very question. They missed a very essential point about Maritain: his metaphysics was the in-dispensable foundation of his political and social humanism; and without the former, the latter would disappear. Henry Bars re-marks that to establish his definitive political philosophy, it was necessary that Maritain, during an extended period of his life, turn entirely away from politics.[24]

The philosophy that shored up the whole structure of Mari-tain's political and social thought was Thomism. But "Thomism" meant only one thing for them: that rigid, closed and sterile brand of Thomistic thought that had been imposed on every cleric who had passed through a Catholic seminary. It was this brand of Thomism with which opponents had tried to silence Maritain so often in the course of his career and of which he complained so bitterly in the letter (quoted above) he wrote many years before to Garrigou-Lagrange ("that sacred monster of Thomism," according to Mauriac). The very word stirred an im-mediate "gut reaction" and raised the hackles of the new Catholic left. In many cases, what they set out to attack was not the real Maritain but a Thomistic straw man, which they proceeded to beat lustily with their phenomenological, existential, and Marxist cudgels, raising thick clouds of dust and straw, most of which got in their own eyes.

But prejudice and misunderstanding about Maritain's Thomism are not sufficient to explain completely the widespread adverse reaction of the new Catholic left. If Julien Green could write to Maritain: "I hear you spoken of everywhere with as much admiration as affection. One would say that your *Paysan* has brought you nearer to all of us,"[25] he must have been moving in a very limited circle. Even a good number of Maritain's friends and admirers expressed a very serious reservation about the book. If prejudice on the part of many readers kept them from hearing what Maritain was saying, there was something about the tone of the book that tended to close the eyes and ears of many readers. A good number of his most sympathetic readers deplored, on the one hand, a certain negativism and, on the other, a bitterness of sarcasm atypical of him who had come to be known as *"le gentil Jacques,"* *"le bon Jacques."*

The Jesuit Bruno Ribes spoke with great admiration of the "witness" Maritain gave to fundamental truths about man, society and the Church, but he feared that *Le Paysan*, through a certain negativism concerning contemporary philosophical and theological efforts to cope with actual problems, might not be exploited by those "denigrators who fraternize with strangers and are themselves strangers to their own brothers," so that "the very success of the book could end up as a formidable counter-witness":

> I have dwelt a bit — perhaps too long — on this savage attack against philosophers, with the single intention of pointing out the partiality of this book. If I had pointed out the excess of a certain denigrating criticism that present Christian research receives, I would be suspected of belonging to one faction or another.
>
> For his part, Maritain claims to put himself above parties. . . . If he is taken at his word, all the energy mobilized at present by our contemporaries is nothing but futility and imposture.[26]

The Dominican Yves Congar, one of the *periti* of Vatican II and a longtime friend and admirer of Maritain, published a review in *Le Monde* (Dec. 28, 1966) entitled "Une certaine peine." He found a certain negativism also, not only in what Maritain said but, in particular, in what he did *not* say. Father Congar agreed wholeheartedly with Maritain that, through ignorance of certain fundamental distinctions — for example, between the Kingdom of God and the world — through an uncritical conformism to certain contemporary philosophical and theological currents, and through a kind of unreflecting adulation of everything modern, there was a very grave risk of rushing headlong down the wrong path, of forgetting that the world does not become the Kingdom of God through its own impulses and initiatives, that evil is present and active in the world, as well as good, and that zeal for the community must not trample on the rights of the person. He praised Maritain's "admirable sense of the transcendence of God and his grace, which he expresses with moving sincerity." He shared with Maritain the conviction (though not, he adds, with the same exclusiveness) that St. Thomas is for the Catholic today, and should remain tomorrow, a master thinker and an incomparable guide — that St. Thomas represents realism and openness and patient attention to truth.

However, that "certain sorrow" which Father Congar felt in reading *Le Paysan* — not only the first time but the second time as well — came from what he felt was Maritain's failure to recognize that the theological excesses and aberrations that he denounced in the book came from sincere attempts to solve very pressing problems and to cope with very real difficulties. He felt that Maritain's almost exclusively negative approach and his sweeping generalizations led the reader to believe that the great majority of contemporary theologians are seriously tainted with neo-Modernism. While exalting the theological breakthroughs of the council, to which he gave not only his adhesion but also his admiration, Maritain gave the impression (by his silence, claims Congar, with considerable justification) that the theologians who were responsible for these breakthroughs either do not exist or are in connivance with error. In fact, the only theologians to whom he accorded any credit were a few of his personal friends, such as the deceased Father Clérissac or the venerable Cardinal Journet. Maritain substantiated his generalizations about contemporary theologians with only one specific example, the unfortunate attempt of Father Schoonenberg to cope with the mystery of original sin, and one veiled, snide allusion to Father Marc Oraison.

From across the sea came a similar reaction. At the beginning of a long, perceptive and very sympathetic article on *Le Paysan*, in which he recognized that "Maritain is on full target with his questions," James Collins spoke of the reaction of Maritain's many friends in America:

At least some of them will be repelled, as I am, by the savage mocking style and the mood of isolation pervading the book.

The atmosphere in which Maritain carries on his reflections is often too contentious and too contemptuous to permit serious discussion of the problems and a recognition of the worth of the contributions made elsewhere than in his own tradition.

... In treating those other subjects Maritain managed to hold his satire and outrage in check to permit his readers to concentrate upon the intellectual issues involved. Unfortunately, the proportion is reversed in the present work: the reader must struggle mightily to attain even a minimal reflective attitude toward the questions themselves, which constantly get submerged in the emotive spray.[27]

In these remarks Collins notes not only the negativism of Maritain's approach but the bitter, sarcastic tone that makes it difficult "for anyone now to approach [the book] with an unprejudiced mind." He found that Maritain "wielded the knife of sarcasm none too gently." Bruno Ribes found his sarcasm "repugnant." The lack of serenity in the first chapters of the book, Ribes said, evokes a kind of "muffled resentment," and if it can be said that this "acrimony hides a secret tenderness," "it hides it only too well." This scorn and satire, which are almost brutal at times, were completely out of character and they surprised and disheartened many readers. Why did Maritain, who spoke so eloquently of the need for and the possibility of cooperation among all men of good will in a divided world, seem to refuse the presumption of good will to so many of his contemporaries? Why should he refuse the presumption of good will to a man like Marc Oraison, and dismiss him with an *ad hominem* aside about a "much-admired moralist" in whom he finds "nothing attractive except his name, what a lovely name."[28]

Louis Chaigne found nothing either negative or polemic in the book and felt that Maritain "reconciled his humor with his dignity as a philosopher," but he did not find much company. Maritain, who knew he was going to make some very unpalatable statements, perhaps chose a "humorous" style to make the intended bluntness of his remarks less unpalatable. The "Chinese proverb" he invented for the title page, "Never take stupidity too seriously," seems to prepare the reader for the sardonic tone. Maritain, very conscious of what he was doing, admits to certain "humorous remarks made in poor taste" *(mauvaises plaisanteries)* and excuses himself for "unintended insolence" *(involontaire in-*

solence). Whatever his intention, he alienated in great numbers the very souls he hoped to convince, and he realized the fact. He must have regretted it, too, for he soon decided that *Le Paysan* could not be his "last book."

In the seven years between the appearance of this controversial book and his death in 1973, Maritain published three more books which took up many of the problems he had dwelt upon in *Le Paysan* or which were being carefully, even heatedly, discussed by theologians. The first of these books was *De la grâce et de l'humanité de Jésus,* which was the development of a series of personal views he had presented in what he called "small research meetings" in 1964. It appeared one year after *Le Paysan.* In the foreword to the book, Maritain admitted that he had hoped *Le Paysan* would be his last book; nevertheless, he decided to publish a work that had been written three years before (except for a few revisions). This reinterpretation of a Christological thesis of St. Thomas was "valuable in itself," he said, and "of central importance." Then he added:

> It may be that a misunderstanding may be occasioned by a few allusions which I have been led to make, very incidently, two or three times in my recent additions, to currents of thought which had no place in my concerns when I was preparing the two *seminars* in question. I insist on noting that of all the confused uproar of those who claim to call into question every aspect of the traditional teaching (an uproar which holds center stage at present), or of all the voices of those who (some attached to truth alone, others to immobilism as well) protest against the mad arbitrariness thus set in motion — absolutely nothing is at the origin of the reinterpretation I propose here, and on which I have meditated for many years. The idea came to Raïssa and me in happier days, when we were living in serene indifference to the swirling eddies (less violent then, it is true) of the Catholic Intelligentsia.

All this may be so, but it is hard to imagine that the violently swirling backwash caused by the passage of *Le Paysan* through the already troubled waters of Christendom did not occasion the decision to publish as a book in 1967 what he had written three years before and already published as two articles in *Nova et Vetera.* In 1970 he published *De l'Eglise du Christ,* in which he tried to explain the Church in the light of the council. The writing of this book cost him dearly, for his health was weakening. He wrote to Julien Green (whom he would not see that summer because his doctor had forbidden him to stop in Paris on his way to Kolbsheim):

> I am filled with remorse when I think of you; I would so much have liked to write you at length about the two volumes of your Journal! To tell the truth I absolutely could not do so, because of this book on the Church which devours all my time and the last drops of my strength, and which has put me in a veritable agony of fatigue. I have just finished the manuscript.[29]

Green replied:

> I won't say anything to you about what is going on in the Church at the moment but there are things that really break my heart. Some priests have simply lost their faith. That you are here is a grace and a comfort for many.[30]

The proofs for the third book, *Approches sans entraves*, a collection of conferences he gave for the Little Brothers of Jesus in Toulouse and which had been published separately in the course of these years in *Nova et Vetera* and *La Revue Thomiste*, were on their way to Maritain when he died.

Whether Maritain would have published these writings, after the book which he had called his last, if *Le Paysan* had not stirred up such a violent controversy is a matter of speculation. One can hardly imagine Maritain, whose mind remained clear and active to the end, not addressing himself to the problems that confronted his world and not seeking to deepen his understanding of those questions in which he had so passionate an interest. What is certain is that in none of these works, which dealt with the same topics, can one find the mordant satire that was so anomalously present in *Le Paysan de la Garonne*.

After the death of Raïssa, Maritain spent his last twelve years among the Little Brothers of Jesus at Toulouse (except for the summers he regularly passed at Kolbsheim). They were years devoted to study and to that contemplation which he had longed for ardently, which, in the rare moments he could find, he had shared with Raïssa before she died and of which he spoke so eloquently in the last chapter of *Le Paysan*. But the serenity of these last years was not easily maintained. There were, of course, the difficult months of the controversy over *Le Paysan* and the publicity that followed, as well as the publicity connected with the two literary prizes he received. There was no end to the importunities of the curious, the interview seekers, or those who simply wanted to add another name to the list of celebrities they had met. The Little Brothers protected him as much as they could, and the letterhead at the top of his stationery (which he used with all but his closest friends) read: "I am an old hermit, come to the end of his life, but who still has work to do. To my great regret, I am forced to give up all correspondence." However, this printed note would often be followed by a long and very personal handwritten letter.

In addition, his health was failing rapidly. He was under the continual care of doctors, who tried to limit his activities. When he adamantly insisted on going to Kolbsheim each summer (all his books and notes were there and — perhaps even more important — all the momentos of Raïssa: her furniture, her paintings, her books, the little things she used, etc.), they demanded that he lessen the fatigue of the journey by limiting his business in Paris; later, by not stopping there at all; and in the last years by making the trip stretched out on a mattress in the rear of a station wagon.

In spite of his fatigue and the immense amount of work he set himself, he never failed to find the time and the strength for anyone who wrote to him or who came to him with a sincere question, a call for help, a need for affection. He was an accomplished listener who radiated welcome, sympathy, and understanding, inspiring in his correspondents or his listeners the sense that, however humble their station, they deserved — because they were what they were — his complete attention and concern. For example, in 1964, just before he left for Kolbsheim, he wrote to Julien Green:

> I cannot write you any more than this. For two months now my health has been declining at an alarming rate, and I know now what it is to feel fatigue *usque ad mortem*. In spite of it all I intend to leave soon for Kolbsheim (by automobile, on a mattress) and pass through Paris. Alas, my doctor will permit only a very short passage and I have some indispensable business to transact. . . . I would so much like to see you, both you and Anne, even if for only a few minutes. Will I be able to? I'm not sure of anything. In any case I will try

to get the Little Brother (Brother Joel) who is driving to telephone you.[31]

Not long after he arrived exhausted at Kolbsheim, he received from a young, unknown girl a letter filled with despair and a cry for help. In spite of the fatigue of his journey, he replied immediately, and a copy of this letter was recently found in his correspondence.[32]

> Your letter, after having gone to Toulouse, has finally caught up with me in Alsace (where I am spending my summer vacation). I am answering you at once, for I would be distressed if any undue delay should make you think that I am guilty of the least indifference.
>
> You are seventeen and I am going on eighty-two; it seems to me we should be able to understand one another. Let me tell you two things right off. 1. I think you are really a poet at heart (that is evident from the very start because of a certain tone). 2. I do not think you have lost God. You would not feel so furious with Him if He did not appear to you as someone who had betrayed you, and who makes you indignant because you love Him. Yes, you are "in quest of Beauty, of the absolute, of a God who is not one of hate." And how right you are! Your revolt is healthy because it is a revolt against a God who is not the true God.
>
> The Christianity you were taught is a child's religion. At seventeen your eyes have begun to open on the world as it really is. You are asked to realize that Christianity is a terrible mystery of love, and that the Cross is not a pleasant and comfortable figure of speech protecting those joys over which popular preachers wax so eloquent, but actually a gallows of horror on which God was hanged for love of us — because all the abomination of this world comes not from Him, but from man's freedom, which is the *prime cause* of evil. And God restores all things — invisibly by His love, and the love of His saints who lay down their lives for their friends. Perhaps what I am writing you here seems to make no sense, but I am writing it all the same because it is the truth, and someday you will see that it is.
>
> I am not telling you to wait. I am telling you rather to take advantage of the fact that you are completely broken and beaten to the ground in order to set yourself to a real search for truth — putting your childhood behind you.

He then suggested a number of books for her to read, including Raïssa's *Les Grandes Amitiés* and Léon Bloy's *La Femme pauvre*. He also offered to send her a book of his own:

> And since, if I am not mistaken, next year will be your year of philosophy, you could at that time, if you are not afraid of tackling difficult problems, read a little book I published recently, *Dieu et la permission du mal*, and I would be most happy to send it to you.
>
> Cocteau came to see us because he felt, by his poetic intuition, that the very evil that shocks and scandalizes us makes us cry out to the innocence of God and that if we have to suffer the intolerable and the inadmissible, it is because on the other side of the tapestry, hidden from our view, there is a love infinitely more true than all the misery through which we must drag ourselves.
>
> All those chapels that he decorated in honor of the Blessed Virgin, how could your unfortunate *directrice* understand what they meant? He never lost his faith. I have the greatest hope for him (as I have for Reverdy). Bloy said to me one day: "In hell there are no sinners because sinners are the friends of Jesus. There are only the malicious." In Jean there was never even a shadow of malice!
>
> I am not telling you to wait — but I am telling you to *pray* as best you can, blaspheming perhaps, groping and stammering. Tell Him, "If you exist, make yourself known to me." And ask Jean Cocteau too, and his friends in heaven to help you.
>
> Your letter moved me deeply, and I had to overcome great fatigue to write you. If my letter is awkward or clumsy in any way, please forgive me. With all my heart I want to do something for you. On this poor earth I am praying for you. And in the Light of God Raïssa too is praying for you.

In 1970 this eighty-eight-year-old "inveterate layman" asked permission to make his religious profession as a Little Brother of Jesus. An exception was readily made for his advanced age, and in the autumn of that year he took the habit of the Little Brothers, among whom he had lived and studied and prayed for ten years. Because of his weakened condition, he was permitted to pass his year as a novice at Toulouse instead of in the regular novitiate, which was situated in a harsh, desertlike region near Saragossa, Spain. During this year of undisturbed contemplation he produced a personal translation of the Canticle of Canticles. In the autumn of 1971 he pronounced his vows of religion.

As he grew weaker, he was given a room near the chapel and close to the rooms of several brothers, so that he could be more readily under their continual and watchful care. Sensing, perhaps, that he was nearing the end, instead of waiting for the summer to make his annual trip to Kolbsheim he decided in January of 1973 to visit his friends there for the last time and to sit once more at the grave of his beloved Raïssa.

After his return to Toulouse, he fell several times during the month of March. Though the brothers procured him a wheel chair, he could no longer attend Mass after April 8. After the eleventh, his doctor confined him to bed, but he continued to work, and a special table was rented to hold his books and papers. After April 14, the doctor came to examine him daily. On the nineteenth, the Last Sacraments were administered. He attended Mass for the last time on Easter Sunday. Two days later he suffered another fall, which left a serious bruise near his left eye. At about seven o'clock on the morning of April 28, he rose as usual, with the help of one of the brothers, but shortly afterward he collapsed from heart failure. A few moments later he died peacefully in the presence of four Little Brothers — and in the twinkling of an eye the last veil was drawn aside that hid from him the fullness and splendor of that Truth which he had sought unfailingly during the ninety-one years of his long and fruitful life.

A few days later, in a simple wooden coffin, he was laid to rest next to Raïssa in the little cemetery at Kolbsheim. On the small, unpretentious tombstone, under the name RAISSA MARITAIN — but according to a strict prescription of his will, which he refused to change in spite of the arguments of his friends — in much smaller letters at the bottom right-hand corner, low enough to be hidden (he thought), by the flowers that are carefully planted each year upon the grave, were inscribed the words *"et Jacques."*

But visitors know he is there. He forgot to proscribe the low-growing flowers which his friends now lovingly plant there.

Notes

1. Action Française: Maurras, Massis, Maritain

1. Jacques and Raïssa Maritain met while he was collecting signatures of prominent people in behalf of a student committee he had formed to protest the violent suppression of Russian socialist student riots by the czarist police. See Raïssa Maritain, *Les Grandes Amitiés* (Paris: Desclée de Brouwer, 1949), p. 52.

2. Adolphe Tanquerey, *The Spiritual Life, a Treatise on Ascetical and Mystical Theology* (Tournai: Desclée de Brouwer, 1923). See also Auguste Poulain, *Des Grâces d'oraison, traité de théologie mystique* (Paris: Victor Retaux, 1906), pp. 487ff., and Réginald Garrigou-Lagrange, *Les Trois Ages de la vie intérieure* (Paris: Editions du Cerf, 1938), pp. 200ff. The eminent theologian Garrigou-Lagrange was a very close friend and advisor of Maritain's. He conducted the annual retreats for the Cercle Thomiste at Meudon.

3. Henry Bars, *Maritain en notre temps* (Paris: Grasset, 1959), p. 370. See also R. Maritain, *Les Grandes Amitiés*, pp. 180 – 85.

4. R. Maritain, *Les Grandes Amitiés*, p. 400.

5. See the pages from the journal of Maritain, cited by his wife, in *Les Grandes Amitiés*, pp. 404 – 6.

6. The Syllabus of Errors was the name given to two series of propositions containing modern religious errors condemned respectively by Pius IX (1864; 80 propositions) and Pius X (1907; 60 propositions). The general heresy condemned by these two syllabi was false Liberalism or "Modernism," which proclaimed man's absolute autonomy in the intellectual, moral and social orders. Modernism tended to deny, at least from a practical point of view, God and supernatural religion by putting a deified mankind in the place of God. The condemned propositions referred particularly to the relations between religion and science, between Church and State, and the extent and binding power of the Church's authority. Unfortunately, each heretical proposition was condemned by its contradictory proposition or by a universal negative introduced by the words "It is not true that. . . ." Because universal negatives leave themselves open to multiple interpretations, there was a long controversy over the infallibility and binding power of these propositions, and it is generally held today that the Syllabus is not of *de fide* definition.

For a long time there was a tendency to interpret the universal negatives absolutely and to equate any religious Liberalism whatever, of any degree or form, whether political, religious or social, with the pernicious Liberalism which the Syllabus condemned.

7. Raïssa Maritain states that Father Clérissac administered the anti-modernist oath of Pius X as part of the ceremony of Psichari's baptism (*Les Grandes Amitiés*, p. 369). This oath, usually required at the ordination of priests, the consecration of bishops and the installation of superiors of religious communities, and sometimes included in the ceremony of adult baptism, consisted of a formal renunciation of the errors condemned in the Syllabus.

8. Henri Massis, *Maurras et notre temps* (Paris: La Palatine, 1951), 1:168f.

9. R. Maritain, *Les Grandes Amitiés*, p. 398.

10. Massis, *Maurras et notre temps*, 1:160.

11. Ibid., pp. 160–61; see also Adrien Dansette, "L'Eglise et l'Action Française," *Esprit*, 19 (Sept. 1951): 284.

12. Eugen Weber, *Action Française, Royalism and Reaction in Twentieth Century France* (Stanford: Stanford University Press, 1962), p. 222.

13. Massis, *Maurras et notre temps*, 1:160.

14. Dansette, "L'Eglise et l'Action Française," p. 285.

15. R. Maritain, *Les Grandes Amitiés*, p. 400.

16. Weber has two excellent chapters (12 and 13) in his *Action Française* describing the role of the clergy in the growth and activity of the movement, even after the condemnation in 1926.

17. Weber, *Action Française*, p. 220.

18. Maritain, *Carnet de notes* (Paris: Desclée de Brouwer, 1965), p. 103.

19. See esp. R. Maritain, *Les Grandes Amitiés*, pp. 401–11 passim, and Massis, *Maurras et notre temps*, 1:166–69 passim.

20. From unpublished letters, dated Nov. 16, 1914, and Aug. 26, 1918, in the Maritain Archives at Kolbsheim, France.

21. Maritain, *Carnet de notes*, p. 178.

22. Unpublished letter in Maritain Archives, Kolbsheim.

23. Maritain, *Art et scolastique* (Paris: Librairie de l'art catholique, 1920), p. 61.

24. Maritain, *Théonas* (Paris: La Nouvelle Librairie nationale, 1921), pp. 159–61.

25. R. Maritain, *Les Grandes Amitiés*, p. 400.

26. Henry Bars, *Maritain en notre temps*, p. 119.

27. Maritain, *Carnet de notes*, p. 180.

28. Henri Massis, *De l'homme à Dieu* (Paris: Nouvelles Editions latines, 1959), p. 226.

29. R. Maritain, *Journal de Raïssa* (Paris: Desclée de Brouwer, 1963), p. 103.

30. Quoted by Raïssa Maritain in *Les Grandes Amitiés*, pp. 402–3.

Valois was Maurras' economic theorist. The break between Maurras and Valois, after Maritain's acceptance of a position with *La Revue Universelle*, began with Valois's unorthodox pronouncements on the nature and role of industrialism in society, and it became definitive with Valois's denunciation of Mussolini's invasion of Ethiopia. Cf. Weber, *Action Française*, pp. 205–12.

31. R. Maritain, *Journal de Raïssa*, p. 107.

32. Maritain, *Carnet de notes*, p. 180.

33. R. Maritain, *Les Grandes Amitiés*, p. 405.

34. Maritain, "A propos de la question juive," *La Vie Spirituelle*, 4 (July 1921): 305–10. See also his *Réponse à Jean Cocteau* (Paris: Stock, 1926), pp. 46f.

35. Maritain, *Réponse à Jean Cocteau*, p. 48; see also his *Théonas*, pp. 159–61, and *Antimoderne* (Paris: Editions de la Revue des Jeunes, 1922), pp. 192 and 199.

36. Massis, *De l'homme à Dieu*, p. 227.

37. Lefèvre published these interviews regularly in the series called *Une Heure avec* . . . (Gallimard). The interview with Massis and Maritain is in the second series (1924), pp. 43ff.

38. Jacques Rivière, "Notes," *La Nouvelle Revue Française*, 13 (Sept. 1919): 617.

39. Massis, *De l'homme à Dieu*, p. 226.

40. R. Maritain, *Les Grandes Amitiés*, p. 391.

41. Massis, *Maurras et notre temps*, 1:208.

42. R. Maritain, *Journal de Raïssa*, p. 167.

43. Nicolas Berdyaev, *Dream and Reality, an Essay in Autobiography* (New York: Macmillan, 1951), pp. 259ff.

44. Massis began writing *Défense de l'occident* in 1919. It was published in 1929. It is interesting to note that these galley proofs figured in an exposition of the works of Massis in 1960 at the Lardanchet Bookstore in Paris (Place Beauvau). In a report on the exposition for *France Catholique* (Feb. 12, 1960), Gilbert Ganna quoted this animadversion of Maritain's: "Communism will never take over China. Not even the propagandists maintain this." Henry Bars wrote to a friend (in an unpublished letter): "It took a very careful choice to see to it that the document should present to the eyes of the public the single palpable error of the philosopher." The campaign to discredit Maritain and justify himself which Massis began with his friends after Maritain supported the condemnation of Action Française has still not ended.

45. Unpublished letter, Mar. 4, (?), in Maritain Archives, Kolbsheim.

46. Unpublished letter, Oct. 1, 1925, in Maritain Archives, Kolbsheim.

47. Massis, *De l'homme à Dieu*, p. 462.

48. Unpublished letter, Sept. 6, 1926, in Maritain Archives, Kolbsheim.

49. Unpublished letter, in Maritain Archives, Kolbsheim.

50. Dansette, "L'Eglise et l'Action Française," p. 289.

51. Maritain, *Une Opinion sur Charles Maurras et les devoirs des catholiques* (Paris: Plon, 1926), p. 33.

52. Ibid., pp. 47f.

53. Ibid., p. 62.

54. Ibid., p. 72.

55. Ibid., p. 70.

56. Ibid., pp. 62f.

57. Maritain, *Carnet de notes,* p. 217.

58. Unpublished letter, Dec. 21, 1926, in Maritain Archives, Kolbsheim.

59. See Maritain, *Carnet de notes,* p. 217; Dansette, "L'Eglise et l'Action Française," p. 450; Massis, *Maurras et notre temps,* 1:172.

60. Weber, *Action Française,* p. 235.

61. Unpublished letter, in Maritain Archives, Kolbsheim.

62. See R. Maritain, *Les Grandes Amitiés,* p. 395, and Stanislas Fumet, "Amour de la sagesse et amitiés des hommes," *Recherches et Débats,* 19 (July 1957), p. 29.

63. Unpublished letter, in Maritain Archives, Kolbsheim.

64. Unpublished letter, Aug. 10, 1927, in Maritain Archives, Kolbsheim.

65. Unpublished letter, Mar. 19, 1928, in Maritain Archives, Kolbsheim.

66. Unpublished letter, Oct. 25, 1928, in Maritain Archives, Kolbsheim.

67. Unpublished letter, June 5, 1931, in Maritain Archives, Kolbsheim.

68. Unpublished letter, July 24, 1931, in Maritain Archives, Kolbsheim.

69. Unpublished letter, in Maritain Archives, Kolbsheim.

70. Michel Mourre, *Charles Maurras* (Paris: Editions Universitaires, 1958), p. 142.

71. Donald and Idella Gallagher, *The Achievement of Jacques and Raïssa Maritain* (New York: Doubleday, 1962), p. 41.

72. Massis, *Maurras et notre temps,* 1:175.

73. Later in the same book in which he speaks of Maritain's solitude, we find: "One cannot save oneself through error. . . . At the twilight of his life M. Georges Duhamel passes his days regretting that he tried to do so and covering his head with ashes" (p. 278). In another place: "The lonely man, all alone in the world, this is what Bernanos was" (p. 224). And again: "As for Mauriac, he pouted in his corner" (p. 276). In his *Mémoires intérieurs* (Paris: Flammarion, 1959), Mauriac painted a rather pitiful picture of Massis, but certainly an interesting one, particularly in the light of Massis' remarks about the loneliness of others. "But then in the end, after all these somber years, the battle has moved to other

places, and Massis, I see him standing immobile at the same spot on the battlefield, now almost completely deserted in the gathering gloom, erect near the tomb of his vanquished master" (p. 200).

2. Action Française: Bernanos, Massis, Maritain

1. Unpublished letter, Feb. 7, 1945, in Maritain Archives, Kolbsheim.
2. Georges Bernanos, *La France contre les robots* (Paris: Robert Lafont, 1947), p. 112.
3. Albert Béguin, ed., *Georges Bernanos, essais et témoignages* (Paris: Editions du Seuil, 1949), p. 40.
4. Massis, *Maurras et notre temps*, 1:193.
5. Lefèvre, *Une Heure avec* . . . (2nd series, 1927), p. 172.
6. Thomas Molnar, *Bernanos, His Political Thought and Prophecy* (New York: Sheed & Ward, 1960), p. 55.
7. Quoted in *Documentation Catholique*, No. 355 (Nov. 13, 1926), p. 881.
8. R. Maritain, *Les Grandes Amitiés*, p. 402.
9. Georges Bernanos, *Nous autres Français* (Paris: Gallimard, 1939), p. 64.
10. *Documentation Catholique*, loc. cit.
11. Massis, *Maurras et notre temps*, 1:194.
12. *Documentation Catholique*, loc. cit.
13. Molnar, *Bernanos*, pp. 61f.
14. Ibid., p. 196. See also Frank O'Malley, "The Evangelism of Georges Bernanos," *Review of Politics*, 6 (Oct. 1944): 403 – 19, and Gaeton Picon, *Bernanos* (Paris: Robert Marin, 1948), pp. 121 – 29.
15. Charles Plisnier, "Unité de Georges Bernanos," in *Georges Bernanos*, ed. Albert Béguin, p. 306.
16. *Figaro*, June 23, 1946, and François Mauriac, *Journal* (Paris: Grasset, 1934–), 5:57f.
17. Plisnier, "Unité de Georges Bernanos," p. 306.
18. Maurras, Daudet, Maritain, Claudel, Massis, Mauriac.
19. Mauriac, *Mémoires intérieurs*, p. 189.
20. Weber, *Action Française*, p. 254.
21. In "Une Vie" in Béguin's collection *Georges Bernanos*, François le Grix calls this period an "armed peace" (p. 289). See Molnar's account (in *Bernanos*) of the debate over Bernanos' association with François Coty (pp. 66ff).
22. Upon his death (Feb. 10, 1939) Pope Pius XI was succeeded by Cardinal Pacelli, who as Pius XII proved a very conservative pope in political matters. One of the first acts of the new pope's secretariat of state was to arrange a very easy submission for Maurras. Maurras seized the opportunity and the ban on Action Française was lifted. Pius XII

seems to have felt that, with the rise of communism throughout the world, a new *rapprochement* with the right would be to the benefit of the Church.

23. Bernanos, *Nous autres Français*, pp. 65f.

24. Massis, *Maurras et notre temps*, 1:214. These lines come from two separate letters (Oct. 25, 1928, and Nov. 1, 1928), but Massis quotes them as coming from one letter.

25. Bernanos, *Nous autres Français*, p. 68.

26. Georges Bernanos, *La Liberté pourquoi faire?* (Paris: Gallimard, 1953), p. 269.

27. Massis, *Maurras et notre temps*, 1:212.

28. Ibid., p. 214.

29. Molnar, *Bernanos*, p. 82. John Hellman, *Emmanuel Mounier and the New Catholic Left, 1930–50* (Toronto: University of Toronto Press, 1981), p. 269. n. 80.

30. Massis, *Maurras et notre temps*, 1:211.

31. Ibid., p. 213.

32. Albert Béguin, "Henri Massis, historien," *Esprit*, 19 (Sept. 1931): 392.

33. Ibid.

34. Ibid., p. 393

35. In his article (p. 391), Béguin notes a similar remark by André Gide in his *Journal* (entry for June 30, 1931): "It's curious, this impossibility of Massis to quote a text exactly or to do so without falsifying its meaning."

36. Bernanos, *Nous autres Français*, p. 63.

37. Béguin, "Henri Massis, historien," p. 395.

38. Georges Bernanos, *Combat pour la vérité, correspondance inéditée, 1904–34*, ed. Albert Béguin and Jean Murray (Paris: Plon, 1971), p. 277.

39. Ibid., p. 279.

40. Ibid., pp. 321f.

41. Unpublished letter, in Maritain Archives, Kolbsheim.

42. Bernanos, *Combat pour la vérité*, pp. 321f.

43. Ibid., p. 323.

44. Ibid., p. 366.

45. Georges Bernanos, *Les Grands Cimetières sous la lune* (Paris: Plon, 1938), p. 109.

46. See, for example, Bernanos, *Nous autres Français*, 61–62, 72.

47. Bernanos, *Combat pour la vérité*, pp. 267–68.

48. P. 63.

49. Plisnier, "Unité de Georges Bernanos," p. 306.

50. Molnar, *Bernanos*, p. 74.

3. The Decade of Manifestos

1. Maritain, *Lettre sur l'indépendance* (Paris: Desclée de Brouwer, 1935), pp. 5f.

2. Ibid., p. 91.

3. Maurice de Gandhillac, "Jacques Maritain et l'humanisme," *Recherches et débats* (July 1957), p. 35.

4. Etienne Borne, "Mounier: la courbe d'un destin," *France Forum*, no. 187 – 88 (Apr. – May 1981), p. 33.

5. Ibid.

6. *Maritain/Mounier, 1929 – 39, les grandes correspondances*, ed. Jacques Petit (Paris: Desclée de Brouwer, 1973), pp. 94f.

7. Ibid., pp. 75f.

8. Hellman, *Emmanuel Mounier and the New Catholic Left*, p. 30.

9. Bars, *Maritain en notre temps*, p. 380.

10. Borne, "Mounier: la courbe d'un destin," p. 36.

11. Hellman, *Mounier and the New Catholic Left*, p. 59.

12. *Maritain/Mounier*, pp. 56f.

13. Ibid., p. 60.

14. Ibid., p. 67.

15. Ibid., pp. 78 – 80.

16. Ibid., p. 82.

17. Ibid., p. 95.

18. Helen Iswolsky, *Light before Dusk* (New York: Longmans, 1942), p. 189.

19. Molnar, *Bernanos*, p. 91.

20. Henri Massis, *Débats* (Paris: Plon, 1932), 1:129.

21. The greater part of the text of this manifesto is found in *Les Catholiques, le communisme et les crises, 1929 – 39*, by René Rémond (Paris: Armand Colin, 1960), pp. 108 – 10.

22. Yves Simon, *La Campagne d'Ethiopie et la pensée politique française* (Paris: Desclée de Brouwer, 1936), pp. 99f.

23. Molnar, *Bernanos*, p. 95.

24. Aline Coutrot, *Un Courant de la pensée catholique, l'hebdomadaire Sept* (Paris: Edition du Cerf, 1961), p. 175.

25. *Esprit*, 4 (Nov. 1935): 308.

26. Cited by Coutrot, *Un Courant de la pensée catholique*, p. 175.

27. For more details about the suppression of *Sept*, see chap. 4 below.

28. Coutrot, *Un Courant de la pensée catholique*, p. 26.

29. Claudel's commitments in the diplomatic service made it impossible for him to attend regularly, but he appeared from time to time in the early days of the Cercle Thomiste. See *Journal de Raïssa* (Sept. 10, 1925), p. 184.

30. Coutrot, *Un Courant de la pensée catholique*, p. 61.

31. Ibid., p. 35.

32. *Sept,* June 16, 1934.
33. Ibid.
34. Coutrot, *Un Courant de la pensée catholique,* p. 15.
35. This article from the Apr. 12 and 26 issues of *Sept* was later published as an appendix to *Humanisme intégral* (pp. 299 and 302ff).
36. Coutrot, *Un Courant de la pensée catholique,* p. 85.
37. *Sept,* Oct.– Nov. 1936.
38. *Sept,* Apr.– May 1936.
39. Coutrot, *Un Courant de la pensée catholique,* p. 99; see pp. 89– 99 for a detailed account of this controversy.
40. Maritain, *Du régime temporel et de la liberté* (Paris: Desclée de Brouwer, 1933), pp. 172ff.
41. Maritain, *Humanisme intégral* (Paris: Aubier, 1936), pp. 310f.
42. M. Scherer, "Lettre ouverte à J. Maritain," *La Vie Intellectuelle,* (Jan. 10, 1936), pp. 11 – 23, and E. Mounier, "Lettre sur l'indépendance," *Esprit,* vol. 4, no. 1 (Jan. 1936): 598 – 603.
43. Maritain, *Lettre sur l'indépendance,* p. 27.
44. Dominique Auvergne, *Regards catholiques sur le monde* (Paris: Desclée de Brouwer, 1938), p. 79.
45. See Maritain, *Raison et raisons* (Fribourg: Egloff, 1947), pp. 247f.

4. The Spanish Civil War

1. Some of the prominent Catholic intellectuals in this group were Paul Claudel, Henri Bordeaux, Henri Massis, Gaeton Bernoville, Jean Guiraud, Général de Castelnau, Robert Brasillach, Pierre Gaxotte, Jacques Bainville, Vice Admiral Joubert, Thierry Maulnier and J.-P. Maxence.
2. Ramon Sugranyes de Franch speaks of this leadership: "so courageous and perhaps so lonely, yet so perfectly coherent with the ensemble of his teachings," ("Jacques Maritain et la guerre civile d'Espagne," *Notes et documents* [Oct.-Dec. 1979]).
3. *Temps Présent,* 2 (May 13, 1938): 1.
4. *Commonweal,* 28 (Sept. 2, 1938): 460 – 71.
5. Rayner Heppenstall, *The Double Image* (London: Secker and Warburg, 1947), p. 15.
6. Gabriel Jackson, *The Spanish Republic and the Civil War,* (Princeton: Princeton University Press, 1965), p. 385; Hugh Thomas, *The Spanish Civil War* (New York: Harper, 1961), p. 449; Richard Patee, *This Is Spain* (Milwaukee: Bruce, 1951), pp.193 – 95.
7. Iswolsky, *Light before Dusk,* p. 195.
8. Maritain, *Carnet de notes,* p. 233.

9. Ibid., p. 232.

10. See, for example, Reginald Dingle, "French Catholics and Politics," *The Month*, 171 (Feb. 1938): 140.

11. See G. Bernoville, "Le Pays basque à la dérive," *La France Catholique* (July 31, 1937).

12. Confederación Española de Derechas Autonomas was a federation of small, strongly Catholic and rightist parties under the leadership of Gil Robles.

13. Joseph Desclausais published in *La Revue Universelle* (June 15 and July 1, 1936) and then in book form (Paris: Plon, 1936) his *Primauté de l'être: Religion et politique*. Louis Salleron reviewed *Humanisme intégral* in *La Revue Hebdomadaire* (Aug. 22, 1936) with the subtitle "M. Jacques Maritain, marxiste-chrétien." Etienne Borne came to Maritain's defense against these attacks in *La Vie Intellectuelle* (Sept. 25, 1936) with an article "De quelques procédés nouveaux de polémique philosophique."

14. J. Lassaigne, "L'Espagne sera-t-elle fasciste!" *Sept*, Apr. 21, 1934.

15. J. Monréal, "Révolution en Espagne," *Sept*, Oct. 12, 1934.

16. Scrutator, *Sept*, Oct. 19, 1934.

17. See the letters of Nov. 2, 1935 and Jan. 18, 1937, in the correspondence of Bernanos, published by Béguin in *Bernanos, essais et témoignage*, pp. 46 and 48, and Molnar, *Bernanos*, pp. 101f., 113 (n. 29), for a discussion of Bernanos' sudden change of attitude regarding the Spanish Civil War.

18. Consult the letter of Jan. 18, 1937 (mentioned in the preceding footnote).

19. Bernanos, *Les Grands Cimetières*, p. 91.

20. Ibid.

21. Iswolsky, *Light before Dusk*, p. 195.

22. Bernanos, *Nous autres Français*, p. 137.

23. Bars, *Maritain en notre temps*, p. 137.

24. Bernanos, *Nous autres Français*, p. 68.

25. Heppenstall, *The Double Image*, p. 35.

26. Mauriac, "La Pierre d'achoppement," *La Table ronde* (Apr. 1948), p. 332.

27. See Maritain, *Art et scolastique* (nouvelle édition revue et augmentée, 1927) n. 154, pp. 327ff.; Mauriac, "La Littérature et le péché," *Figaro*, Mar. 12, 1938.

28. *Journal de Raïssa* (Nov. 22, 1931), p. 203.

29. It was Charles Du Bos who introduced Mauriac to the meetings at Meudon. See the entry for Apr. 2, 1928, in the *Journal* of Charles Du Bos (Paris: Corréa, 1946 – 59), 4:73.

30. *Journal de Raïssa*, p. 211.

31. See Mauriac, *Dieu et Mammon* (Paris: Editions du siècle, 1935), pp. 158, 169, 203f.; Maritain, *The Responsibility of the Artist* (New York: Scribner, 1960), pp. 61 – 64; R. J. North, *Le Catholicisme dans l'oeuvre de François Mauriac* (Paris: Editions du Conquistador, 1950), pp. 71ff.

32. Du Bos, *Journal* (Apr. 10, 1933), 8:45; (Nov. 9, 1933), 8:152, and (Nov. 14, 1937), 9:168.

33. Mauriac, *Paroles catholiques* (Paris: Plon, 1954), p. 32.

34. Du Bos, *Journal* (Nov. 22, 1929), 5:234.

35. *Figaro*, May 26, 1966.

36. In 1929 Maritain, Mauriac and Du Bos collaborated to found the periodical *Vigile* (Du Bos, *Journal* [Nov. 26, 1929], 5:235. In 1939 Mauriac, with Du Bos and Gabriel Marcel, became an enthusiastic supporter of the committee organized by the Maritains to promote the music of Arthur Lourié. Mauriac, in fact, became president of the committee (*Journal de Raïssa* [Apr. 10, 1934], p. 220). They all took the same position on the Ethiopian invasion.

37. July 25, 1936.

38. *Figaro*, June 30, 1938.

39. *Sept*, Jan. 21, 1927.

40. *Figaro*, Aug. 18, 1936.

41. Iswolsky, *Light before Dusk*, p. 194.

42. Among those who signed were François Mauriac, Charles Du Bos, Stanislas Fumet, Helen Iswolsky, Olivier Lacombe, Jacques Madaule, Gabriel Marcel, Jacques Maritain, Emmanuel Mounier, Boris de Schloezer, Pierre van der Meer de Walcheren, Maurice Merleau-Ponty, Claude Bourdet, Paul Vignaux, Pierre-Henri Simon, Etienne Borne, Elie Beaussart and Luigi Sturzo.

43. *La Croix*, May 8, 1937; *Sept*, May 14, 1937; *Esprit*, June 1, 1937.

44. See Iswolsky, *Light before Dusk*, pp. 194f.; Mounier, *Esprit*, 5 (July 1, 1937): 461, 643 and 648.

45. "Guernica ou la technique de mensonge," *Esprit*, 5 (June 1, 1937): 449 – 73.

46. *Sept*, May 28, 1937.

47. From a letter sent to *La Nouvelle Revue Française* and published in the issue of July 1, 1937; see 49:177.

48. See *Figaro*, June 17, 1937.

49. *Esprit*, 5 (July 1, 1937): 648.

50. "An Interview with Jacques Maritain," *Commonweal*, Feb. 3, 1939, p. 400.

51. Maritain stated in a footnote to one of the three articles he wrote directly on the war in Spain that the article in question, "Exister avec le peuple," as well as another, "D'un nouvel humanisme ou d'un humanisme intégral" (Bulletin de l'union pour la vérité, 44 [June-July 1937]: 359 – 418), made perfectly clear his personal position regarding the civil war in Spain, even though these two articles were meant to treat in a more general fashion, and according to eventualities that might take

place in other countries of Europe, the problems that the current crisis of civilization posed for the individual conscience. Both of these articles were published in the Spanish periodical *Sur*. See Maritain, "De la guerre sainte," *La Nouvelle Revue Française*, 49 (July 1, 1937): 34, n. 2.

52. *Esprit*, 5 (Mar. 1, 1937): 953f.

53. Claudel's poem was originally published as a preface to an anonymous account of the persecution of the Church in Spain: *La Persécution religieuse en Espagne*, poème-préface de P. Claudel (Paris: Plon, 1937).

54. Coutrot, *Un Courant de la pensée catholique*, p. 210.

55. Quoted by Rémond, *Les Catholiques*, p. 202.

56. This article also appeared as the preface to a book by Maritain's close friend Alfred Mendizabal, *Aux origines d'une tragédie: La Politique espagnole de 1923 à 1936*.

57. See the contributions of Bernanos to *Sept* which later made up the first part of *Les Grands Cimetières*. The "billets" of Mauriac to *Sept* and his articles in *Figaro*, the editorials of *Sept* (e.g. Jan. 8, 1937), or the articles "La Question d'Espagne inconnue" by J. M. de Semprun Gurrea and "Double refus" by A. M. V. (Mendizabal), published in *Esprit* (Nov. 1, 1926).

58. Maritain, "De la guerre sainte," *La Nouvelle Revue Française*, 49 (July 1, 1937): 23.

59. Ibid., pp. 22, 30, 32.

60. Ibid., p. 25.

61. Ibid., pp. 25f.

62. Ibid., pp. 26f.

63. Ibid., p. 29.

64. Mounier, "Espoir au peuple basque," *Esprit*, 5 (July 1, 1937): 645.

65. The letter did not express the unanimous opinion of the Spanish hierarchy. "The absence of two episcopal signatures was noticed immediately: the Cardinal-Archbishop of Tarragona, in Catalonia, Francesc Vidal y Barraquer, and the Bishop of Vitoria, in the Basque country, Msgr. Mateo Mugica, both of them in exile because of the persecution by the Reds, and hence free to make their own decisions, refused to sign." Cf. Ramon Sugranyes de Franch, "Jacques Maritain et la guerre civile d'Espagne," *Notes et documents*, 5, no. 17 (Oct.-Dec. 1979): 5.

66. Claudel, *Contacts et circonstances* (Paris: Gallimard, 1947), p. 102.

67. Ibid., p. 105.

68. Ibid., p. 106.

69. Ibid., p. 107.

70. Joubert, *La Guerre d'Espagne et le catholicisme* (Paris: S.G.I.E., 1937), pp. 7 and 45.

71. Lawrence Doyle, "Communications," *Commonweal* (Apr. 22, 1938), p. 722.

72. The complete statement, which served as the constitution of the committee, was published in *Esprit*, 5 (July 1, 1937): 651. The board of directors of the French committee consisted of Msgr. Beaupin, Georges Duhamel, Dr. de Fresquet, Daniel Halévy, Louis le Fur, Jacques Madaule, Gabriel Marcel, Jacques Maritain, Louis Massignon, François Mauriac, Emmanuel Mounier, Paul Vignaux and Claude Bourdet, secretary.

73. "An Interview with Jacques Maritain," *Commonweal*, Feb. 3, 1939, p. 400.

74. Ibid., p. 399.

75. *Sept*, May 28, 1937.

76. Bernanos, *Nous autres Français*, p. 247.

77. Coutrot, *Un Courant de la pensée catholique*, pp. 287–95.

78. F. Charles-Roux, *Huit Ans au Vatican* (Paris: Flammarion, 1947), p. 41.

79. Ibid., p. 181.

80. Ibid., p. 91.

81. Coutrot, *Un Courant de la pensée catholique*, pp. 292–95.

82. It may be apropos to recall that Catholics were forbidden by the Vatican, under penalty of being refused the sacraments, to read or to contribute to the newspaper *Action Française*.

83. Molnar, *Bernanos*, p. 110.

84. Ibid., pp. 106 and 113.

85. North, *Le Catholicisme dans l'oeuvre de François Mauriac*, p. 65.

86. Massis, *Maurras et notre temps*, 2:109.

87. Pattee, *This Is Spain*, p. 195, and Sugranyes de Franch, "Maritain et la guerre civile d'Espagne," p. 5.

88. Dingle, "French Catholics in Politics," p. 141.

89. Maritain, *Carnet de notes*, p. 232.

90. Ibid., p. 233.

91. Ibid., p. 231.

92. Dec. 31, 1937. Ramon Sugranyes de Franch makes the following remark about this article: "These three questions are the core of a whole system of political morality and . . . the response that one gives to them, positive or negative, depends essentially on one's acceptance or rejection of the new 'order' that the Nazis, the Fascists and the Communists proposed at that time to an anaemic Europe." "Maritain et la guerre civile d'Espagne," p. 6.

93. Dingle, "French Catholics in Politics," p. 140.

94. Mauriac, "Mise au point," *Figaro*, June 30, 1938.

95. *Temps Présent*, Mar. 11, 1938.

96. *Humanisme intégral*, p. 158.

97. See n. 51, above.

98. *Scholasticism and Politics*, p. 28.

99. *Figaro*, June 24, 1939.

100. Ibid., July 8, 1939.

101. Ibid.

102. How closely related many Spaniards considered this exchange between Maritain and Claudel to their own situation, even though the word "Spain" had not occurred, can be judged by an article of Augusto José Durelli, "Los cristianos et el repose," *Sur*, 9 (Sept. 1939): 74 – 80.

103. Claude Mauriac, *Conversations avec André Gide* (Paris: Albin Michel, 1951), p. 114.

104. Ibid., p. 117.

105. Ibid.

5. The Jewish Question

1. The pages listed under "anti-Semitism" in the index of Weber's *Action Française* furnish an excellent account of anti-Semitism in France from the Dreyfus Affair to the liberation of France from the Nazis in 1943. See also Louis Chaigne, *Les Lettres contemporaines* (Paris: del Duca, 1964), pp. 146 – 49; R. Bierman, "Racism in France," *Commonweal*, Apr. 12, 1938, pp. 402f., and Jeannine Roy, "Reveil de l'anti-sémitisme," *Esprit*, 4 (July 1936): 612f.

2. See Weber, *Action Française*, pp. 33 – 35 and 220. French-Catholic anti-Semitism had repercussions in American anti-Semitism. For example, the anti-Semitic information used by Father Charles Coughlin in one of his Sunday afternoon addresses came from an English periodical *The Patriot*, which in turn got its information from the quasi-official French-Catholic publication *Documentation Catholique*. Consult John A. Ryan, "Anti-Semitism in the Air," *Commonweal*, Dec. 30, 1938, pp. 260 – 62.

3. Maurice Reclus, *Le Péguy que j'ai connu* (Paris: Hachette, 1951), p. 11.

4. R. Maritain, *Les Grandes Amitiés*, p. 68.

5. Reclus, *Le Péguy*, p. 20.

6. Ibid., p. 136.

7. Edouard Drumont, "La Jeanne d'Arc d'un ancien dreyfusard," *La Libre Parole*, Mar. 10, 1910. See also Béguin, "L'Accueil fait au premier 'Mystère' de Péguy," *Mercure de France*, 328 (Nov. 1956): 426f.

8. Charles Péguy, *Oeuvres en prose, 1909 – 1914* (Paris: Editions de la Pléiade, 1959), p. 645.

9. From Péguy's "Louis de Gonzague," *Oeuvres en prose, 1889 – 1908* (Paris: Editions de la Pléiade, 1959), p. 938.

10. Péguy, *Oeuvres en prose, 1909 – 1914*, p. 549f.

11. R. Maritain, *Les Grandes Amitiés*, pp. 83 – 89, and J. Maritain, *Quelques Pages sur Léon Bloy* (Paris: Cahiers de la Quinzaine, 1927), p. 47.

12. Robert Rouquette, "Filleuls de Léon Bloy," *Etudes*, 209 (Feb. 1949): 201.

13. R. Maritain, "Concerning Henri Bergson," *Commonweal*, Mar. 17, 1941, p. 494.

14. P. 48f.

15. See the entries in Maritain's *Carnet de notes* for Oct. 15, 1908, Sept. 8, 10 and 11, 1909, and Mar. 30, Apr. 20 and July 15, 1911.

16. Ibid., p. 263.

17. From the preface to *Carnet de notes*, p. 11.

18. Maritain, *Quelques Pages sur Léon Bloy*, p. 39.

19. R. Maritain, *Les Grandes Amitiés*, p. 146.

20. Maritain, *Quelques Pages sur Léon Bloy*, p. 42. *Le Salut par les Juifs* is a series of essays in which Bloy tried to show that the Jewish Question is fundamentally a religious problem and not a social one.

21. *Quelques Pages sur Léon Bloy*, p. 42.

22. *Carnet de notes*, entry for June 11, 1908, p. 71.

23. Ibid. See, for example, the entries for Aug. 6, 1910, p. 92, and Apr. 20, 1911, p. 100.

24. Maritain, *Quelques Pages sur Léon Bloy*, p. 14.

25. Léon Bloy, *Oeuvres complètes* (Paris: François Bernouard, 1947), 1:22 – 26.

26. Ibid., chap. 33, pp. 94ff.

27. R. Maritain, *Les Grandes Amitiés*, p. 136.

28. *Oeuvres complètes*, preface to *Le Salut par les Juifs*, 1:6 and 7.

29. Maritain, *Quelques Pages sur Léon Bloy*, pp. 43f.

30. Ibid.

31. Ibid.

32. Ibid., p. 45.

33. In chapters 6 and 8 of *Les Degrés du savoir* (Paris: Desclée de Brouwer, 1958) Maritain holds that knowledge by mystical experience is superior to knowledge by ratiocination.

34. Msgr. Journet's book *Destinées d'Israël* (Paris: Egloff, 1945) was one of the most extensive and perceptive treatments of the Jewish Question by a Catholic theologian up to the time of its publication. He, too, attributed to Bloy the original insight into St. Paul's revelation on the Jews in chapters 9 and 11 of his Epistle to the Romans. The subtitle of this long and learned treatise is "A propos du *Salut par les Juifs*." Msgr. Journet was one of Maritain's closest friends and his debt to Maritain is evident in the fact that he quotes his friend almost as much as he does Bloy himself, whose ideas on the Jews are the central theme of his book. Almost all that Maritain wrote on the Jews had already been published when Msgr. Journet's book appeared in 1945. Albert Béguin, an admirer of Maritain's, studied the manuscript of Journet's book carefully in preparation for writing his own book, *Léon Bloy, l'impatient* (1944).

35. Journet, *Destinées d'Israël*, p. 433.

36. *Pages de Léon Bloy, choisies par Raïssa Maritain et présentées par Jacques Maritain* (Paris: Mercure de France, 1951), pp. 300f.

37. Journet, *Destinées d'Israël*, p. 430.

38. Published in *La Vie Spirituelle*, 4 (July 1921): 305 – 310, and republished in *Documentation Catholique*, 3, tome 6 (July 30-Aug. 6, 1921): 80 – 82.

39. Ibid., p. 305.

40. *Textes choisis de Léon Bloy*, published by Albert Béguin (Fribourg, L.U.F., 1943), p. 98.

41. *Pages de Léon Bloy*, pp. 299f.

42. Maritain, *Questions de conscience* (Paris: Desclée de Brouwer, 1938), pp. 55f. The original title of this essay, published in the collection *Les Juifs* (Paris: Plon, 1937), was "L'Impossible antisémitisme." When the English version of this essay appeared in *Ransoming the Times* (New York: Scribner, 1941), it bore the title "Mystère d'Israël," a title far more expressive of its central theme.

43. Ibid., p. 57. The final italics are mine.

44. Maritain, *Raison et raisons* (Fribourg: Egloff, 1947), p. 208.

45. *Questions de conscience*, p. 57.

46. Ibid., p. 79.

47. Ibid.

48. Ibid., p. 58.

49. Péguy's *Notre Jeunesse* was a tribute to his friend Bernard Lazare. The greater part of Péguy's book is taken up with the portrait of Lazare: "un des plus grands noms du temps moderne." Maritain was familiar with Lazare's book *Antisémitisme*.

50. "A propos de la question juive," *La Vie Intellectuelle*, 4 (July 1921): 305f.

51. (Paris, 1921), pp. 330–52,

52. Ibid., pp. 346f.

53. Ibid., pp. 347 and 213, n. 1.

54. Maritain, *Pour la justice* (New York: Editions de la Maison française, 1945), pp. 253–55.

55. "A propos de la question juive," *La Vie Intellectuelle*, 4 (July 1921): 307.

56. From the preface Maritain wrote for the book by Henry Bars, *La Politique selon Jacques Maritain* (Paris: Plon, 1961), p. 9.

57. Maritain, *Réponse à J. Cocteau* pp. 46f.

58. Friends of Maritain who also contributed to his collection were René Schwob, Georges Cattaui and Denis de Rougemont. Claudel was another contributor.

59. *Questions de conscience*, p. 59.

60. Ibid., p. 86.

61. Ibid., p. 65.

62. Claudel, *Le Père humilié* (Paris: Gallimard, 1920), act 1, scene 3, pp. 63–67.

63. Chapter 4.

64. See Pilate's remark in Claudel's *Figures et paraboles* (Paris: Gallimard, 1936), p. 50: "A man cannot be innocent if he is against the Public Order."

65. Claudel, "Trois Lettres sur Israël," *Les Juifs* (Paris: Plon, 1937), p. vii. For "prurient" readers, let me furnish an English translation of the text that Claudel's delicate modesty forbade him to reproduce in the ver-

nacular: "They that were brought up in scarlet have embraced the dung" (from Lamentations 4:5).

66. Maritain, *Le Philosophe dans la cité* (Paris: Alsatia, 1960), p. 67.

67. Ibid.

68. Gide, "Les Juifs, Céline et Maritain," *La Nouvelle Revue Française*, 55 (Apr. 1938): 634.

69. Ibid.

70. Ibid., p. 635.

71. Maritain, "Les Juifs parmi les nations," *La Vie Intellectuelle*, 55 (Feb. 25, 1938): 9 – 53.

72. Maritain, "Réponse à André Gide sur les Juifs," *La Nouvelle Revue Française*, 55 (June 1, 1938): 1020.

73. Ibid., p. 1201.

74. *Le Philosophe dans la cité*, p. 80.

75. *Questions de conscience*, pp. 79f.

76. Ibid., pp. 92f.

77. Ibid., p. 84 – 90.

78. "Les Juifs parmi les nations," pp. 26f.

79. "Réponse à André Gide sur les Juifs," p. 1022.

80. Lacouture, *François Mauriac* (Paris: Seuil, 1980), pp. 334f.

81. *Nous autres Français*, p. 68.

82. Picon, *Georges Bernanos* (Paris: Robert Marin, 1948), p. 171.

83. *Nous autres Français*, p. 68.

84. Bernanos, *Oeuvres* (Paris: Grasset, 1947), vol. 3: *La Grande Peur des bien-pensants*, p. 109.

85. Ibid., p. 154f.

86. Ibid., p. 157.

87. Maritain, *Crépuscule de la civilisation* (Montréal: Editions de l'Arbre, 1941), pp. 64 – 66.

88. *Nous autres Français*, p. 140.

89. Ibid., p. 168.

90. Maritain, *Messages* (New York: Editions de la Maison française, 1945), pp. 120f.

91. Ibid., pp. 123ff.

92. Bernanos, *Le Chemin de la Croix-des-Ames* (Paris: Gallimard, 1948), p. 422.

93. Ibid., pp. 313 – 16.

94. Ibid., p. 423.

95. *Pour la justice*, p. 324.

96. Ibid., p. 325.

97. Estang, *Présence de Bernanos* (Paris: Plon, 1947), p. xviii.

98. *Humanisme intégral*, pp. 244 – 49.

99. *Pour la justice*, pp. 238 and 242.

100. See pp. 35 – 39, 92 – 96, 174 – 76 and 298 – 301 of *Pour la justice*.

101. There was another anti-Semitic element to the prayer for the Jews on Good Friday. At the end of each of a series of prayers for various

groups of people throughout the world, the deacon invited the congregation to kneel for a few moments in silent prayer. After the prayer for the Jews, however, no genuflection was made — as if the Jews, unlike other men, were unworthy of such a liturgical gesture.

102. See Madaule, *Les Juifs et le monde actuel* (Paris: Flammarion, 1963), esp. pp. 4–6 and 213–17.

103. The editors publicly acknowledged their debt to Maritain in the Dec. 1942 (vol. 2, no. 2) issue of *La Nouvelle Relève*, which was a special edition of "hommages à Maritain." See pp. 65 and 70f.

104. Published in pamphlet form by *Our Sunday Visitor*, Huntington, Indiana, 1965.

105. *Gaceta Regional de Salamanca*, June 21, 1938, (cited by Auguste-J. Durelli in "L'Exemple humain de J. Maritain," *La Nouvelle Relève*, 2 (Dec. 1942): 80.

106. This attack on Maritain appeared in the May 16 issue of *Le Devoir* and was criticized by Jean le Moyne in the June 1943 (vol. 2) issue of *La Nouvelle Relève*, pp. 385–90.

107. "Billet de Christianus," *La Vie Intellectuelle*, 55 (Feb. 25, 1938): 6–8. "Christianus," and sometimes "Civis," were pen names used either by individual editors of *La Vie Intellectuelle* (Etienne Borne, for example) or by a group of editors.

108. Maritain, *Le Mystère d'Israël* (Paris: Desclée de Brouwer, 1965), p. 36 n.

109. *Questions de conscience*, pp. 90–92.

110. *Le Philosophe dans la cité*, pp. 110f.

111. Chaigne, *Les Lettres contemporaines*, p. 148, n. 5.

112. Gallagher, *The Achievement of Jacques and Raïssa Maritain*, p. 21.

6. The Second World War and the Defense of Democracy

1. Massis, *Maurras et notre temps*, 2:74f.

2. This is so even for the entry which Massis cites. See Julien Green's *Journal* (Paris: Plon, 1961), Oct. 1, 1931. See also entries for June 16, 1933, Jan. 23, 1941, May 8, 1941 and Aug. 28, 1942.

3. Maritain, *Humanisme intégral*, pp. 246–48.

4. Maritain, *Carnet de notes*, p. 232.

5. Ibid., p. 234.

6. It was Maritain's defense of democracy in this lecture and his expression of hope in the future of democracy which elicited a barb from Bernanos in *Nous autres Français*, p. 68.

7. Maritain, *Crépuscule de la civilisation*, p. 88.

8. Ibid., p. 70.

9. Ibid., p. 88.

10. Maritain, *De la justice politique* (Paris: Plon, 1940), p. 45.

11. Ibid., p. 102.

12. Ibid., p. 77.

13. Ibid., p. 100.

14. Ibid., pp. 103f.

15. Maritain, *Messages*, p. 74.

16. In 1945 the messages which Maritain had broadcast to occupied France between 1941 and 1944 over BBC, WRUL (Boston) and the Voice of America were collected in one volume entitled *Messages*. Preoccupation with the necessity of an international society for peace was everywhere. After the invasion of North Africa, when an Allied landing in Europe and the liberation of France began to seem possible, Maritain felt it all the more incumbent on him to remind the future victors of their duties as peacemakers. All seven messages (for example) which Maritain delivered between Feb. 16 and Mar. 29, 1943, were concerned with a European federation and international organizations to be established after the war.

17. *Messages*, p. 149.

18. From an article, "Le Désespoir de Drieu la Rochelle," in the July 1953 issue of *Le Figaro Littéraire*.

19. Bernanos, *Lettre aux Anglais* (Rio de Janeiro: Atlantica Editora, 1943), p. 56.

20. Ibid., p. 57.

21. Bernanos, *Journal d'un curé de campagne* (Paris: Plon, 1936), p. 22.

22. P. 236.

23. Picon, *Georges Bernanos*, p. 177.

24. Bernanos, *Lettre aux Anglais*, p. 255.

25. Ibid., p. 33.

26. Consult *Lettre aux Anglais*, pp. 56 – 58, 232 – 41, 248.

27. *Lettre aux Anglais*, pp. 244f.; see also, p. 212.

28. Maritain, *Messages*, p. 86.

29. Maritain, *A travers la victoire* (Fribourg: Egloff, 1945), p. 63.

30. Maritain, *Messages*, p. 90.

31. Bernanos, *Lettre aux Anglais*, p. 316.

32. Maritain, *Théonas* (Paris: La Nouvelle Librairie nationale, 1921), p. 85.

33. R. Maritain, *Les Grandes Amitiés*, pp. 405 – 6.

34. Maritain, *Christianisme et démocratie* (New York, Editions de la Maison française, 1943), pp. 35f.

35. Bars, *Maritain en notre temps*, p. 124.

36. Maritain, *Humanisme intégral*, pp. 206 – 7.

37. Maritain, *Reflections on America* (New York, Doubleday, Image Books, 1950), p. 92.

38. Maritain, *Crépuscule de la civilisation*, pp. 76f.

39. Maritain, *Christianisme et démocratie*, p. 36.

40. Maritain expressed again and again during the war years, in the speeches he delivered to various groups in the United States and in

articles he contributed to magazines or in the messages he broadcast in Europe, his profound confidence in and gratitude to the common people of France. Consult *Pour la justice,* "Le Peuple fidèle" (p. 82), "The Plain People of France" (p. 219), "Le Peuple de France" (pp. 319 and 341); *Messages,* "Le Peuple de France" (p. 54), "Les Nouvelles Elites" (p. 58), "L'Inspiration évangelique et l'idéologie bourgeoise" (p. 188), "Les Erreurs politiques de l'idéologie bourgeoise" (p. 192).

41. Maritain, *Christianisme et démocratie,* pp. 33 and 36.

42. Maritain, *Messages,* p. 90.

43. Maritain, *Christianisme et démocratie,* pp. 57–59.

44. Maritain, *Man and the State* (Chicago: Univ. of Chicago Press, 1951), p. 52.

45. Bars, *Maritain en notre temps,* p. 131.

46. Molnar, *Bernanos,* p. 163.

47. Bernanos, *Lettre aux Anglais,* p. 204.

48. Ibid., p. 269.

49. Bernanos, *Le Chemin de la Croix-des-Ames,* p. 368.

50. Journet, *Exigences chrétiennes en politique* (Paris: Egloff, 1946), pp. 27 and 276.

51. Bernanos, *Le Chemin de la Croix-des-Ames,* p. 313.

52. Mauriac, "La Tentation de dégoût," *Figaro,* June 23, 1946.

53. Maritain, *A travers la victoire,* pp. 44–47.

54. Bernanos, *Lettre aux Anglais,* p. 99.

55. Maritain, *Christianisme et démocratie,* p. 32.

56. Bernanos, *Lettre aux Anglais,* p. 251.

57. Maritain, *Messages,* pp. 59–62.

58. Bernanos, *Lettre aux Anglais,* pp. 44–48.

59. Ibid., pp. 228, 251, 285, 312f.; Maritain, *Scholasticism and Politics,* pp. 80f., 94–99.

60. Maritain, *Scholasticism and Politics* (New York: Doubleday, 1960), pp. 95f.

61. Bernanos, *Lettre aux Anglais,* p. 250.

62. Maritain, *Christianisme et démocratie,* p. 39.

63. Bernanos, *Français, si vous saviez* (Paris, Gallimard, 1961), p. 92.

64. Bernanos, *Lettre aux Anglais,* pp. 43f.

65. Ibid., p. 251.

66. Maritain, *Christianisme et démocratie,* pp. 27 and 49.

67. Bernanos, *Le Chemin de la Croix-des-Ames,* p. 438.

68. Maritain, *Christianisme et démocratie,* pp. 59, 69, 85–89; *Scholasticism and Politics,* p. 111; Bernanos, *Lettre aux Anglais,* pp. 181, 252, 311f.

69. Maritain, *Christianisme et démocratie,* pp. 55f.

70. Bernanos, *Lettre aux Anglais,* pp. 73, 180f.

71. Maritain, *A travers le désastre* (New York: Editions de la Maison française, 1941), pp. 66–68.

72. Ibid., p. 132.

73. Maritain, *Pour la justice*, p. 42.

74. Ibid., p. 55.

75. Cohen, *Ceux que j'ai connus* (Montréal: Editions de l'Arbre, 1946), p. 203.

76. See the two letters of Bernanos to the ambassador at Rio de Janeiro in *Le Chemin de la Croix-des-Ames*, pp. 31–36.

77. Maritain, *Pour la justice*, p. 188.

78. Ibid., p. 180.

79. Ibid., p. 184.

80. Ibid., p. 185.

81. Maritain, *Messages*, pp. 100–102.

82. Ibid., pp. 104f.

83. Saintonge, *Lettres françaises* (Sept. 9, 1944).

84. Maritain, *Pour la justice*, p. 299.

85. Cohen, *Ceux que j'ai connus*, p. 204.

86. Ibid., p. 206.

87. Maritain, *Pour la justice*, pp. 79f.

88. Cohen, *Ceux que j'ai connus*, p. 207.

89. Cohen, *Lettre aux Américains* (Montréal: Editions de l'Arbre, 1942), pp. 115–19.

90. Maritain, *Pour la justice*, p. 316.

91. Unpublished letter, Maritain Archives, Kolbsheim.

92. Unpublished letter, in Maritain Archives, Kolbsheim.

93. Green, *Journal*, entries for May 8, 1941, and Feb. 12 and June 30, 1945.

94. Unpublished letter (Jan. 8, 1945) furnished by Anthony O. Simon.

95. Both Maritain and Alexis Léger (St. John Perse) declined. "Réponses différentes mais négatives," wrote de Gaulle in his *Mémoires de guerre* (Paris: Plon, 1954), vol. 1: *Appels*, p. 221.

96. Unpublished letter to Simon of Jan. 8, 1945.

97. Ibid.

98. Ibid.

99. Ibid.

7. *Ambassador to the Vatican and Professor at Princeton*

1. Letter of Jan. 29, 1945. Letters from the Maritain/Simon correspondence were furnished by Anthony O. Simon. Copies of these letters can be found at the Maritain Archives in Kolbsheim, France, and at the Jacques Maritain Center of the University of Notre Dame.

2. Julie Kernan, *Our Friend Jacques Maritain* (New York: Doubleday 1975), pp. 138f.

3. Ibid.

4. D'Ormesson, "Les Propos," *Revue des Deux Mondes* (1975), pp. 651–53.

5. Ibid., passim.

6. Letter from Yves Simon, Feb. 2, 1945.

7. Julio Mienvielle, *Correspondance avec le R. P. Garrigou-Lagrange à propos de Lammenais à Maritain* (Buenos Aires: Ediciones Nuestro Tiempo, 1947).

8. Letters to Yves Simon, Dec. 18, 1946, and Jan. 18, 1947.

9. Mienvielle, *Respuesta a dos cartas de Maritain al R. P. Garrigou-Lagrange* (Buenos Aires: Ediciones Nuestro Tiempo, 1948).

10. Probably the Jesuit periodical *Civiltà Cattolica*, where A. Messineo, S.J., published two articles, "L'Uomo e lo stato" (1954) and "L'Umanesimo integrale" (1956), both attacking Maritain. Charles Journet, Adriano Gallia, Anicetus Tamosaitis and Giancarlo Mura replied in Maritain's defense.

11. D'Ormesson, "Les Propos," p. 652.

12. The most revealing and moving testimony to this deep and lasting friendship was the publication by Jean Piriou in 1979 of the correspondence between Jacques Maritain and Julien Green in *Une Grande Amitié, correspondance 1926 – 1972* (Paris: Plon, 1979). Green's admiration for Maritain was known to all who read his *Journal*, but few realized the depths and intimacy of the friendship between these two great men.

13. *Une Grande Amitié*, letter 88.

14. Ibid., letter 89, pp. 97f.

15. Letter to Yves Simon, Apr. 28, 1947.

16. Letter of Feb. 9, 1948.

17. Letter of Apr. 22, 1948.

18. Letter of Mar. 1, 1948.

19. Letter of Nov. 20, 1948.

20. From the Maritain correspondence at Kolbsheim.

21. *Une Grande Amitié*, letter 110 (Dec. 4, 1960).

8. Peasant of the Garonne and Little Brother of Jesus

1. From the Maritain Archives at Kolbsheim.

2. Mauriac, *Nouveaux Mémoires intérieurs* (Paris: Flammarion, 1965), pp. 226 and 321.

3. Julien Green, *Journal X, 1972 – 1976* (Paris: Plon, 1976), p. 131.

4. *Une Grande Amitié*, letter 122.

5. This is certainly an exaggeration; Mauriac, for example, had been a member of the Académie since 1933 and surely read Maritain. Jean Guitton also was a member at the time.

6. *Une Grande Amitié*, letter 119.

7. Ibid., letter 147.

8. Letter of Mar. 30, 1965, in the Maritain Archives at Kolbsheim.

9. *Une Grande Amitié*, letter 164.

10. Ibid., letter 165.

11. Maritain sent a copy of this letter to his friend Yves R. Simon, who kept it in his papers. The letter was furnished by Anthony O. Simon.

12. Letter from Olivier Lacombe to Jacques Maritain, Sept. 14, 1948, in the Maritain Archives at Kolbsheim. The signers of the manifesto which appeared the following year were Louis Gardet, M. Labourdette, J. H. Nicolas, Th. Philippe, Charles Journet, O. Lacombe, Raïssa Maritain, Jacques Maritain, M. J. Nicolas, C. Rzevuski, J. Kuelin, M. V. Leroy, P. J. de Menasce, and O. Philippe. It appeared in English under the title *Wisdom* (New York: Magi Books, 1965).

13. *Une Grande Amitié*, letter 152.

14. Ibid., letter 154.

15. Letter of Mar. 30, 1965, in the Maritain Archives at Kolbsheim.

16. *Une Grande Amitié*, letter 170.

17. Ibid.

18. From an unpublished manuscript of Henry Bars.

19. From the Maritain Archives at Kolbsheim.

20. This letter, contained in a group of letters from Green to Maritain, was found in the latter's papers after the publication of *Une Grande Amitié*, and was published in *Cahiers Jacques Maritain*, 1 (Sept. 1980): 54.

21. *Courrier Français de Bordeaux*, Nov. 19, 1966.

22. From an unpublished manuscript of Henry Bars.

23. Ibid.

24. Ibid.

25. *Une Grande Amitié*, letter 182.

26. Bruno Ribes, "Jacques Maritain, le grognard de l'Eglise," *Etudes*, Feb. 1967, pp. 189f.

27. James Collins, "Maritain Asks Some Questions," *America*, Jan. 13, 1968, p. 29.

28. Maritain, *Le Paysan de la Garonne* (Paris: Desclée de Brouwer, 1966), p. 130.

29. *Une Grande Amitié*, letter 204.

30. Ibid., letter 205.

31. Ibid., letter 159.

32. The identity of the young girl to whom this letter was addressed is unknown. A copy of the letter, found in Maritain's correspondence, was published in *Cahiers Jacques Maritain*, 2 (Apr. 1981): 71 – 73.

Index of Names

265